INTERVENTIONS: NEW STUDIES IN MEDIEVAL CULTURE
Ethan Knapp, Series Editor

DESIRE
in the
CANTERBURY TALES

Elizabeth Scala

 THE OHIO STATE UNIVERSITY PRESS · COLUMBUS

Copyright © 2015 by The Ohio State University.
All rights reserved.

Library of Congress Cataloging-in-Publication Data
Scala, Elizabeth, 1966–
 Desire in the Canterbury Tales / Elizabeth Scala.
   pages cm. — (Interventions: New Studies in Medieval Culture)
 Includes bibliographical references and index.
 ISBN 978-0-8142-1278-3 (cloth : alk. paper) — ISBN 978-0-8142-9383-6 (cd-rom)
 1. Chaucer, Geoffrey, –1400. Canterbury tales. 2. Desire in literature. I. Title.
 PR1875.D47S33 2015
 821'.1—dc23

                              2014043500

Cover design by Laurence J. Nozik
Text design by Juliet Williams
Type set in Adobe Garamond Pro

∞ The paper used in this publication meets the minimum requirements of the American National Standard for Information Sciences—Permanence of Paper for Printed Library Materials. ANSI Z39.48-1992.

9 8 7 6 5 4 3 2 1

For Doug

contents

Acknowledgments   ix

INTRODUCTION	Mobility and Contestation	1
CHAPTER ONE	"We Witen Nat What Thing We Preyen Heere": Desire, Knowledge, and the Ruse of Satisfaction in the Knight's Tale	43
CHAPTER TWO	Misreading Like the Reeve	85
CHAPTER THREE	Symptoms of Desire in Chaucer's Wives and Clerks	123
CHAPTER FOUR	Disfigurements of Desire in Chaucer's Religious Tales	153
CONCLUSION	Reading and Misreading Chaucer	203

Bibliography   *207*

Index   *219*

acknowledgments

This book has been very long in coming; the debts I have accrued are extensive. My first one is, and will always be, to my husband, Douglas Bruster. He reads everything that I write numerous times and always makes it better: sharper, clearer, and crisper in its articulations. It is no overstatement that I owe my entire career to him.

To the press's two readers I own an incredible debt. Since they both fortunately signed their reader's reports, I can thank them here by name and in very specific ways. They offered two incredibly different responses to the book and made very different demands on it, both of which were important to the way I thought about my project. That they both were positive about the book and "got" what I was trying to do in it was incredibly gratifying and motivational. They diverged from each other in the very best of ways. Karla Taylor kept me philologically honest. Her comments made me articulate the historicist and philological stakes of the psychoanalytic argument concretely and emphatically. Mark Miller was an ideal reader of a different kind. He asked for a more Lacanian account of desire and stopped me from overindulging at the level of pilgrim intent. He always encouraged me to go further with my reading of Chaucer's tales in productive ways.

A number of friends, colleagues, and students discussed this project with me and read various parts of it. Patricia Clare Ingham probably read the entire book in pieces a number of times. She has been the very best of academic friends and has always kept me sane when associate professor life just seemed too difficult. Daniel Birkholz, Coleman Hutchison, Cathy Sanok, Christopher Bradley, Jonathan Lamb, Meghan Andrews, Brooke Hunter, Charlotte Mark, and Noah Guynn read different chapters and offered good advice. All of the students I have taught in my *Canterbury Tales* course over the past ten years have heard this material in some form or another. Their tolerance, enthusiasm, and good-humored questions have been much appreciated.

A version of the third chapter appeared as "Desire in the *Canterbury Tales*: Sovereignty and Mastery Between the Wife and Clerk," in *Studies in the Age of Chaucer* 31 (2009): 81–108. A small portion of the first chapter on the Knight's Tale overlaps with material first published in an essay, "Desire," in Marion Turner's *A Handbook of Middle English Studies* (Malden and Oxford: Wiley-Blackwell, 2013), 49–62. I thank the publishers of these essays for permission to reprint.

I also want to thank the University of Texas and the chair of the English department, Liz Cullingford, for supporting my work with various kinds of leave time and research assistance. Finally, a big thank you to my kids, Madeleine and Claire, who have heard more about desire and the *Canterbury Tales* than any children really want to know.

introduction

MOBILITY AND CONTESTATION

This is a book about the pilgrimage frame of the *Canterbury Tales* and its means of generating stories by gathering disparate figures together. It is thus a study of the relations among tales in the poem. Pilgrimage is situated, of course, within important historical and cultural contexts specific to medieval Christianity and the work of redemption. It is also a literary trope and thus an occasion for exploration, especially self-exploration, of various narrative kinds. Chaucer invokes the pilgrimage frame lightly, as part of an ordinary world of experience in the late fourteenth century. As the surround for his stories and their narrating figures, it does not impose itself as a strict grid of intelligibility that anchors a rigid moral framework. Rather, pilgrimage provides the meeting ground for a diverse group of figures and an occasion for divergence itself, as the group forms a "compaignye" (1.717) to do nothing so emphatically as to depart.[1] And once they get going, leaving the suburb of Southwark for the Canterbury road, they continue to depart, finding ways to diverge from what others have said as each of them tells his tale. The pilgrimage forms a site of continued mobility and a productive metonymy of stories.

---

1. All quotations from the *Canterbury Tales* throughout this book are taken from *The Canterbury Tales, Complete*, ed. Larry D. Benson (Boston: Houghton Mifflin, 2000) and will be noted by fragment and line number parenthetically. Other Chaucer quotations, as well as material from the textual notes, come from its parent text, *The Riverside Chaucer*, gen. ed. Benson (Boston: Houghton Mifflin, 1987).

In calling this a book about the pilgrimage frame, then, I do not mean that it's a book about medieval pilgrimage so much as about what happens when Chaucer conjoins pilgrimage and contest, journey and competition, as a framework for a tale collection. Doing so sets a number of things in motion, not just his pilgrim narrators. He assembles this varied group of speakers; he gives their journey purpose and direction without explanation; he pretends a unity that then gets tested and discomfited; he allows for spontaneous generation, open conflict, and diversion as the stories propel the journey and its narrating figures along. My interests are in the generative entanglements of the stories as competitive fictions, sometimes directly so as in the tales of the first fragment or the so-called marriage group,[2] where certain stories are set in open conflict with a particular narrative or claim, at other times more indirectly as the products of the social contract the Host, later named as Harry Bailly (1.4358), has organized. Of course, they all originate in the agreement he formulates in the General Prologue and to which each of the pilgrims assents. It is only reasonable to tell tales to pass the time, or so the Host claims. Where silence might have enabled or encouraged one to consider one's spiritual condition, no such thing is ever mentioned. For Bailly it makes little sense "to ride by the weye doumb as a stoon" (1.774) because neither "confort ne myrthe" would be at all possible (1.773). The pilgrims are reminded throughout the journey of what they have agreed to do "as forward is" (2.34)—"For whan a man that is entred in a pley, / He nedes moot unto the pley assente" (4.10–11). They are continually threatened with the cost they must bear in breaking their "biheste" (5.698). This initial pact explains why each comes to tell a tale; they agreed to it before they even had an idea what they were agreeing to: "Us thoughte it was noght worth to make it wys, / And graunted hym withouten moore avys" (1.785–86). But it does not explain what happens when those tales are set in their competitive context and within particular fragments or against generic conventions and constraints. Both within and across fragments, Chaucer posits more subtle relations between tellers and their stories and between stories and their situations: as taunts, rebuttals, departures, continuations, or remedies over and against the tales that have been told before. The pilgrimage is not a fixed system that installs meaning but a point of dramatic departure from which different tales and interpretations can proliferate.

As a contest, the *Canterbury Tales* sets the stories against one another, making comparison and contrast inevitable. Chaucer enlivens his literary journey with different tale-tellers in contrast to more static, allegorical invo-

---

2. The heuristic term "marriage group" is the subject of fuller discussion in chapter 3.

cations of pilgrimage. The dissonance produced therein is the very hallmark of Chaucer's poem, invoking various systems of order ("degree" 1.744) its narrator claims he is unable to sustain because his "wit is short, ye may wel understonde" (1.746). There are also those the Host is unable to impose, despite his best efforts. Much of the poem's success lies in these failures, as no one and nothing remains capable of imposing final order. Instead, Chaucer's poem derives its energy from the power of disruption. In fact, with much of the *Canterbury Tales* its various hierarchies or orders appear only belatedly *as they are disrupted* by one who interprets them as such.

The mechanism for this signature variability, dissonance, and disruption is the pilgrims: a fiction of narrating figures with different voices, intents, desires, interests, experiences, and learning that is created by the generic and rhetorical variety of the tales. The friction between and among tales produces a fiction of conflict between and among narrators—though our need to label each tale with its pilgrim speaker's name often makes it sound like the reverse. Thus Chaucer literally writes about the generative power of stories and language. The characters of the pilgrim narrators are not the determining force behind their tales nor the ultimate truth revealed by them. The *Canterbury Tales* does not offer us character psychology dressed in medieval garb. Instead, the language of the tales—as H. Marshall Leicester explained some time ago—produces the pilgrims, the fiction of "character."[3] Or, to put matters in terms of the old debate about "roadside drama" and the potential tyranny of the frame: the stories do not exist for the sake of the pilgrims, the pilgrims are mere focalizers for the sake of the stories. And the stories interrelate far more through their embeddedness in a symbolic system of language than through the fiction of pilgrim intentions or reprisals.

In organizing a group of fictive tale-tellers to generate a collection of stories, Chaucer formulates the *Canterbury Tales* as a discourse of desire. Many of the pilgrims' stories make desire their explicit concern. The Wife of Bath, for example, sets a knight in search of "What thyng is it that wommen moost desiren" (3.905). The Knight's Tale asks: "What is this world? What asketh men to have?" (1.2777). The so-called religious tales—the Man of Law's trial of constancy, the Physician's exemplum, and the Second Nun's hagiography—are also fueled by desire: physical and erotic impulses compel their political and social dramas.[4] The seductions of a self-aggrandizing

---

3. H. Marshall Leicester, *The Disenchanted Self: Representing the Subject in the "Canterbury Tales"* (Berkeley: U of California P, 1990). On the once pervasive "dramatic theory," see esp. 7–9.

4. The very difficulty of defining a "religious" tale has been the subject of a number of critical essays and provokes the collection *Chaucer's Religious Tales,* ed. C. David Benson and Elizabeth

power linked to erotic force in these stories can also be located in the economic dominance of satires found in the Summoner's, the Friar's, and the Pardoner's performances. But desire is more than a thematic concern of the pilgrims' stories or the by-product of their varied social locations and types of expertise. Desire circulates in more structurally significant ways in the *Canterbury Tales,* accounting for the rivalrous nature of the poem's fiction and its intense focus on language in both the tales and the frame narrative negotiating the frictions they contain.

As a discourse of desire, the *Canterbury Tales* is also a drama of misrecognition and misreading. We find the subject and the subject's desire located precisely where the subject misrecognizes himself and misreads his surroundings (and thus the possibility of satisfaction) in some way. At every turn in Chaucer's fiction, the pilgrims he has set in the frame narrative misread one another's tales as provocations for their own stories, sometimes seeing themselves in the discourse of an other. Another word for this misrecognition is sociality, as one fabricates, fantasizes, and hazards a relationship to another and to the big Other: the social world in its entirety that fixes the subject with its laws. But this sociality already inhabits the subject, who is not prior to the social but a product of its rules and regulations. Misrecognition reveals that the subject is always other to itself, other than it knows and, more precisely, what it knows.

This mechanism fuels the tale-telling game and underwrites its rivalrous competition, which readers have long accepted as a mere imitation of nature rather than the nature of social engagement itself, predicated upon rivalries within subjects rather than between them. Exploring the operations of desire inhabiting language through its self-conscious interests in storytelling, the entire poem tracks the circulation of the signifier, as each narrator seeks the recognition of others in his or her appropriation of and attempt at mastery over the language traversing various stories. That does not mean that the narrating pilgrims knowingly quote each other, though sometimes this happens. Language is shared and reshaped by different stories well beyond the narrating figures who present the tales. As such, the *Canterbury Tales* is a product of desire and language, misreading and misrecognition, through its aggressively competitive structure. For those wishing to interpret the poem, this structure is especially compelling because it obviates any master hermeneutic by which the tales ought to be understood. Indeed, the interpretive gestures deployed in the poem—whether the explicitly retaliatory and personalized mode of reading performed by

---

Robertson (Cambridge: Brewer, 1990), especially Derek Pearsall's contribution, "Chaucer's Religious Tales: A Question of Genre," 11–20. I discuss this issue in more detail in chapter 4.

the Reeve or the Clerk's depersonalized and abstract allegorizations, for example—are undone by the poem's competitive and ultimately substitutive structure, leaving Chaucer's readers with no secure interpretive method. In approaching desire by way of misreading, Chaucer incites our critical designs upon his text even as he thwarts our attempts at interpretive mastery.

From the very opening of the General Prologue, Chaucer frames his fiction as a function of desire, rather than just a story about it. The poem's memorable 18-line opening sentence sets the occasion for the tale collection as a response to its main action: "longen." Delineating the forces at work in the natural world, these opening lines are anything but natural. Instead, they artifice nature—its rains, warming winds, and budding stems—in artful and artificial terms, which I here quote in full:

> Whan that Aprill with his shoures soote
> The droughte of March hath perced to the roote,
> And bathed every veyne in swich licour
> Of which vertu engendred is the flour;
> Whan Zephirus eek with his sweete breeth
> Inspired hath in every holt and heeth
> The tendre croppes, and the yonge sonne
> Hath in the Ram his half course yronne,
> And smale foweles maken melodye,
> That slepen al the nyght with open ye
> (So priketh hem nature in hir corages),
> Thanne longen folk to goon on pilgrimages,
> And palmeres for to seken straunge strondes,
> To ferne halwes, kowthe in sondry londes;
> And specially from every shires ende
> Of Engelond to Caunterbury they wende,
> The hooly blisful martir for to seke,
> That hem hath holpen whan that they were seeke.
> (1.1–18)

This first sentence has always stood out among the rest as "artful lines, superbly modulated through an unusual hypotactic syntax that adds to their graceful dignity."[5] Mythology, astrology, natural philosophy, and new science imbue the natural world with a glossy cultural veneer. "Aprill" is

---

5. Robert Jordan, *Chaucer's Poetics and the Modern Reader* (Berkeley: U of California P, 1987), 123.

personfied with "his shoures soote." Birds mime human behavior as they sit up all night "with open ye," singing their lovesickness because Nature has pricked "hem . . . in hir corages." The gentle awakening of the spring comes in a sexualized discourse almost violently erotic and certainly penetrative ("priketh," "perced"). The force of these lines is even more striking when one reflects on the non-nativeness of this English spring. April, the "cruelest month" in T. S. Eliot's memorable formulation, can hardly be remembered for its sweet showers and burgeoning landscape. Instead, Chaucer has transplanted the gentle Mediterranean climate of his poetic sources in English soil in order to align the awakening of spring with the Easter season, natural with spiritual rebirth.[6] In the elaborations of desire in the General Prologue's opening sentence, then, we find the very first misreading that gives the game away.

More than mere description of what makes "[folk] longen," then, this opening actively incites desire, making things happen both inside and outside the poem. Its first eleven lines offer various discourses, both learned and aesthetic, for the classical *raverdie*, enrapturing the audience in its details and with its own syntactical delay and deferral.[7] The main subject and predicate—the folk who long—are withheld, inciting our desire across those first eleven lines. But such matters do not end there, nor do they continue in expected ways. Where the *raverdie* appears consonant with the human desire it inspires, the nature of that longing, "to goon on pilgrimages," disrupts our expectations. Critics have had to explain what comes next, for it is not what other books—even Chaucer's own—have led us to anticipate.[8] Writing for a generation (much like our own) more used to realist genres and expectations of verisimilitude, Donald Howard had to remind readers where to locate their astonishment: not in the ornate open-

---

6. E. T. Donaldson has made the point with regard to this fiction of dryness: "Chaucer's drought is a metaphorical one, taken from a rhetorical tradition that goes back to classical literature, and to the Mediterranean countries where March is a dry month" (*Chaucer's Poetry: An Anthology for the Modern Reader*, 2nd ed. [New York: Harper Collins, 1975], 1036–37). Arthur Hoffman, in "Chaucer's Prologue to Pilgrimage: The Two Voices," *ELH* 21 (1954): 1–16, also writes about the ambiguities of the General Prologue, noting its "phallicism," both an "upthrust" and an "outpouring" of energy and figures (2). Mentioning the same "springtime surge of human energy and longing" (3), Hoffman prioritizes the significance of what he calls "nature to supernature," which is "a move from Aphrodite and *amor* in their secular operation to the sacred embrace of 'the hooly blisful martir' and of *amor dei*" (4).

7. For the concept of *raverdie*, see John A. Rea, "An Old French Analogue to General Prologue 1–18," *PQ* 46 (1967): 128–30, at 129; and, more extensively, Rosemund Tuve, *Seasons and Months: Studies in a Tradition of Middle English Poetry* (Paris: Librairie Universitaire, 1933).

8. Studies connecting the *Canterbury Tales* through this opening to Chaucer's early work in the dream visions include David Lawton, "Chaucer's Two Ways: The Pilgrimage Frame of *The Canterbury Tales*," *SAC* 9 (1987): 3–40 and *Chaucer's Narrators* (Cambridge: Brewer, 1985).

ing sentence but in the uncourtly subjects that follow. "There would have been nothing surprising in the very literary opening lines which describe the spring," Howard explains: "it was the kind of poetry read at court most of the time. The Tabard, Harry Bailly, or the Miller would have been more surprising, but only because they violate our critical expectations and their familiarity in everyday life is what seems out of context."⁹ The effect of this opening is to take us aback, to make us unsure of the conventions and the context in which we are reading.

Though often memorized, this opening sentence has yet to be brought to bear fully on the subjects of Chaucer's poem—its stories *and* its fictional speakers. The opening conjoins erotic, sexualized urges to spiritual movement, positing a shift that has itself provoked critical debate. But what we experience, in fact, is a kind of double alienation—both within the first sentence and between it and what follows. As with Howard's earlier remarks, much of the debate has to do with where our expectations lie, what conventions are recalled or shattered: is the form of the opening, even the Prologue itself, new or old?¹⁰ Should the erotic and penitential be forcibly reconciled or does the contrast, and its abrupt shift in priorities, stand? Is that division and disruption, in fact, the opening's point, as well as a point to which the collection will continually return?

The extent, even purpose, of the contrast between nature and pilgrimage has been debated in the familiar terms of irony and exegesis. On one hand, the spiritual concerns of pilgrimage provide a corrective to the libidinal and reproductive demands of springtime. We are called to consider a different "vertu" than the one that produces flowers, and an alternate means of being "inspired" than that by which Zephirus moves "every holt and heeth." And while not entirely oppositional, as texts like *De Planctu Naturae* would suggest, the difference here begs for some adjustment. A patristic reading of pilgrimage as the "correct" desire produced by nature rescripts the amorous work of spring toward a different kind of love, embarrassing our worldly perspective.¹¹ Yet, on the other hand, no sooner is pilgrimage

---

9. Donald Howard, *The Idea of the "Canterbury Tales"* (Berkeley: U of California P, 1976), 159.

10. It is difficult to relegate these concerns merely to the poem's opening sentence. Discussions of the pilgrims quickly ensues and what one thinks of Chaucer's view of medieval society often influences one's opinion of the opening, which can orient the Prologue as a conventional estates satire or, alternately, a recategorization that emphasizes a new group of merchants and tradesmen. See Loy Martin, "History and Form in the General Prologue to the *Canterbury Tales*," *ELH* 45 (1978): 1–17.

11. There are a number of ways the two discourses are reconciled in critical accounts, including mythographic readings of the classical allusions. See, for instance, Paul B. Taylor, "The Alchemy of Spring in Chaucer's *General Prologue*," *Chaucer Review* 17 (1982): 1–4; and Colin Wilcockson, "The

invoked than it too becomes problematized by those professional pilgrims, "palmeres," who have turned penitence into profit. Traveling to far-off shrines ("ferne halwes") became an objective of its own for some pilgrims who enjoyed the pleasures of travel and were only too glad to undertake it for others who could not.[12] And, as in any form of religious employment, when one was paid to do the spiritual work demanded of another, all manner of corruption followed. Lollards complained about pilgrimage precisely for this reason. Thus even in this scene-setting opening, the orthodoxy of pilgrimage itself has already been called into question.[13]

Pilgrimage is no more certain a kind of activity in late fourteenth-century England than the arrival of spring; neither has absolute meaning. Conjoined in the Easter season, spiritual rebirth and renewal is potentially mirrored in the rebirth and renewal of nature. Of course, pilgrimage was used in the literary tradition before Chaucer. Texts like Dante's *Commedia* and Deguileville's *Le Pèlerinage de la Vie Humaine* (whose apotheosis is perhaps Bunyan's *Pilgrim's Progress*) deploy pilgrimage as a metaphor for the journey of the soul to its heavenly destination and thus man's arduous way through life. But even this standard metaphor is unsettled by Chaucer's poem. The convention typically depicts a one-way journey in which the soul strives toward its final destination and received truth. Chaucer's pilgrims travel decidedly in *this* world; their round-trip voyage will return them to the morally questionable suburb of late medieval Southwark and to Harry Bailly's inn for a different kind of judgment. The attention Chaucer gave to this late, likely expanded, round-trip journey in the General Prologue suggests his undoing of the standard metaphor was intentional, perhaps a more forceful articulation of what he was adumbrating in the pilgrims' approach to but nonarrival at Becket's shrine or even Canterbury

---

Opening of Chaucer's General Prologue to *The Canterbury Tales*: A Diptych," *Review of English Studies* 50 (1999): 345–50.

12. Pilgrimage, closely related to idolatry, was a standard target of Lollard critique. See William Thorpe's famous condemnation of pilgrimage in *Selections from English Wycliffite Writings*, ed. Anne Hudson (Oxford: Oxford UP, 1978) as well as Matti Peikola, "'Whom clepist þou trewe pilgrimes?': Lollard Discourse on Pilgrimages in *The Testimony of William Thorpe*," in *Essayes and Explorations: A "Freundschrift" for Liisa Dahl*, ed. Marita Gustafsson (Turku: Anglicana Turkuensia, 1996), 73–84. On the complexity of Chaucer's relation to pilgrimage and popular religious practices oriented by the "commercial terms of redemption" (86), see Linda Georgianna, "Love So Dearly Bought: The Terms of Redemption in *The Canterbury Tales*," *SAC* 12 (1990): 85–116.

13. Peggy Knapp explores the various rivalries and competitiveness that inhabit the stories the pilgrims tell with an eye to their mode of reflecting social and historical pressures in late fourteenth-century English culture, particularly Wycliffism in *Chaucer and the Social Contest* (New York: Routledge, 1990), esp. 61–76.

itself.[14] The Host addresses the Parson and asks for his tale just as they enter "at a thropes ende" (10.12). The destination may be in sight, but it is also decidedly out of focus.

If the General Prologue's first sentence catches us in a scene of misreading—erotic energy for what should be spiritual redemption; serious penitence for what might really be professional enjoyment or organized corruption—potential misreadings are all over the poem and absolutely central to its operations. Despite an increasingly precise setting, "Engelond," and an orientation "from every shires ende" toward a single destination, "to Caunterbury," we little know this context and how it is meant to signify. Chaucer has instead built a flexible stage for the figures he will introduce, deploying in this opening sentence a variety of languages for understanding the pilgrims and their stories. Even further, Chaucer's opening *repeats* the division of the first sentence as he transitions in the next to the more mundane and quotidian register the entire poem assumes. No longer speaking in the elevated language of his classical precursors or his own early poetry, Chaucer turns to the here and now: "Bifil that . . . on a day / In Southwerk" (1.19–20). Once again he moves from distant sources to what seem local observations. We have gone from the cosmic and calendrical to England and Canterbury, more precisely to Southwark and the Tabard "faste by the Belle" (1.719). The details of local and social context almost entirely overwhelm whatever spiritual and penitential journey had been only just invoked, such that Peter Brown finds "the extent to which Chaucer scrupulously avoids the expected account of pilgrimage . . . quite extraordinary."[15] Howard even calls it an "anti-pilgrimage."[16] What happened in this brief opening? How many interpretive frameworks have been erected and then, just as suddenly, disabled?

At the same time that we find human desire and its perplexities at the very center of the General Prologue's opening, we realize we hardly know what desires move individual figures to take up their pilgrimage. In bringing together scientific, amorous, and natural causes of desire with

---

14. On Chaucer's revisions to and expansion of fragment 1, see Charles Owen, *Pilgrimage and Storytelling: The Dialectic of "Earnest" and "Game"* (Norman, OK: Pilgrim, 1977), 10–47; and Elizabeth Scala, "The Deconstructure of the *Canterbury Tales*," *Journal x* 4 (2000): 171–90, at 172. For Chaucer's biography, see Derek Pearsall, *The Life of Geoffrey Chaucer* (Oxford: Blackwell, 1992). On the textual problems of the Parson's Tale and its problematic position in the poem as a whole, see Lawton, "Chaucer's Two Ways," and James Dean, "Dismantling the Canterbury Book," *PMLA* 100 (1985): 746–62.

15. Peter Brown, *Chaucer at Work: The Making of the "Canterbury Tales"* (London and New York: Longman, 1994), 25.

16. Howard, *Idea*, 162.

the spiritual longing of the Easter season, the rebirth of nature, and the Christian rebirth of the spirit, Chaucer makes possible various reasons for travel, ranging from the solemnities of penitent redemption to the opportunistic pleasures of holiday entertainment. But he never designates one at the expense of the other. Jill Mann's critically influential research into the estates literature providing the model for the pilgrim descriptions articulates the paradox at the heart of this opening in terms of the Prologue's expectations for and failure to produce moral judgment. She writes, "Chaucer has no *systematic* platform for moral values, not even an implicit one, in the *Prologue*."[17] The General Prologue displays the absolute confusion of moral and emotional responses to the pilgrims, amounting to "Chaucer's *consistent removal of the possibility of moral judgment*" (197; emphasis in original). The flux between and the absence left at the center of these structures allow Chaucer to write what feels like an intensely "modern" collection of stories.

Such disruptions of expectation characterize our experience of the General Prologue and, as I will show, the *Canterbury Tales* more generally. Only seemingly burdened by previous genres (like estates satire) and finite meaning (like Christian allegory) do Chaucer's pilgrims set off for Canterbury.[18] Moreover, with the contest outcome nearly assured by the preeminent status granted to the Knight, these travelers immediately diverge from what seem the Host's unspoken but clearly felt priorities. Disrupting the "degree" that the Host would establish, the figures later designated as "cherls" (1.3182) seek recognition via a translation of the "noble" terms of the Knight's story. One way of reading that shift is debasement (though that might be taking the Knight's point of view), as when the Miller describes his heroine Alison in "noble" terms. Using the form of a rhetorical *effictio* such as appears in the Knight's introduction of his heroine, Emily, the Miller rewrites the terms of feminine description in another register. Alison's complexion shines brighter than the "noble yforged newe" (1.3256), a revaluation of the Knight's static feudal ideals in the Miller's cleverly constructed and flexible economic register. These are, of course, terms that a Miller, rather than an aristocrat, would use. But the Miller does more than speak in his own idiom. As many readings of the Miller's Tale have shown, he reveals the Knight's "noble storie" as an ideological construct. The noble is not a guarantee of worth, but a sign, a coin that must be forged and that

---

17. Jill Mann, *Chaucer and Medieval Estates Satire* (Cambridge: Cambridge UP, 1973), 192.
18. Donald Howard would call these times "obsolescent" in his description of the nostalgia marking Chaucer's last work (*Idea* 89–94).

circulates to gain its value. (And his heroine's complexion far exceeds its color, even when just newly minted.)[19]

Beyond mere debasement, the Miller's appropriation of the Knight's "noble" reveals language's inflationary power. More than simply economic terms appropriate to nobles and coins, the inflation noted here is the capacity for words to change and to change things, including the value of what was previously assumed. The Miller's comic narrative contestation posits retroactively the Knight's misunderstanding of the terms of desire in the partly heroic, partly courtly, romance he offered. Given the generic variations and sources of Chaucer's stories, and their relationships to each other as they are set in the poem's larger, competitive, tale-telling framework, such a misunderstanding or partial view of one's own discourse gets belatedly refigured as a misreading in the response of another. In his fabliau parody of the Knight, the Miller reveals this necessary structure of misreading to which his own discourse will be subject the minute he finishes speaking and the Reeve erupts in response, failing to understand what the Miller's brilliant parody had been all about. As I will detail more fully in chapter 2, the Reeve's Tale misreads the Miller's in what is perhaps the most dramatic paradigm of misreading and misrecognition—and the desire in language that fuels them—in fragment 1.

Instead of delineating a set of private motivations lying behind each narrator's speech, desire inhabits the language of the tales in larger and more abstract ways. The conscious means by which speakers pursue various desires and goals with their stories—what happens when anyone begins telling a tale—is underwritten by the structure of unconscious desire assumed with language, which psychoanalysis explains more fully in terms of the subject's position within the complex and socially structured world of symbolization, the Symbolic order. Elaborated as the emergence of the subject in the psychoanalytic theory of Jacques Lacan, desire accounts for what fundamentally *eludes and thus constitutes* the subject as such. It is far more than a "topic" of some romances or bawdy tales. Desire's intimate relation to language accounts for the entire poem as a provocative set of verbal bids for recognition and recompense, and reveals an inherently substitutive structure linking the tales to each other and propelling the poem forward. Such a linguistic and symbolic means of accounting for the poem stands in some contrast to the models formerly imposed upon it (labyrinth,

---

19. Andrew Cowell makes explicit the connections between money and language as unfixed semiotic systems in *At Play in the Tavern: Signs, Coins and Bodies in the Middle Ages* (Ann Arbor: U of Michigan P, 1999), 2–6.

tapestry, interlace, gothic cathedral), offering the benefit of accounting for the generative and restless movement of Chaucer's tale collection.

Important to both the movement of desire and the movement of the *Tales* (and their powerful provocations) is the nature of the signifier, an idea as central to Lacan's psychoanalysis as to the literary criticism attending its form. Taken from Saussure's structural linguistics, the signifier is the "audible image" of a sign, the material collocation of sounds (representing letters) by which beings communicate. For Lacan it is the most important part of the linguistic sign and is separate from the mental concept it invokes (the signified) by a bar, tenuously marking their connection but preventing any one-to-one correspondence, for, of course, different words can suggest the same mental image, which no single word can itself fully express.[20] Lacan prioritizes the equality and mutual interdependence of the two parts of Saussure's sign, resituating the signifier above the signified, under which it slides. We could think, by analogy, of how a sentence takes on its meaning as we slide from word to word along its enchained phrases or, more apt for the lexical process described here, how a dictionary leads from one word to another in search of meaning. The end of each movement is arbitrary and conventional, and the process linking signifiers ultimately has no end. This means that the signified is something produced by the signifier. Indeed, this new priority of the signifier in Lacan's thought makes language not a system of signs but a system of signifiers, which work in a closed system of differences and combine in signifying chains according to metonymic laws that we call syntax.

The imperfectly disguised manner in which desire inheres in the signifier is dramatized repeatedly in the *Canterbury Tales*, and nowhere more so than when someone's exact words are at stake. This situation, for example, confounds the Franklin's Dorigen, whose words "in pley" (5.988) tell her suitor Aurelius in no uncertain terms how impossible it would be for her to return his affections. Following an absolute rejection that she punctuates thus, "Taak this for fynal answere as of me" (5.987), she offers him this consolation: "whan ye han maad the coost so clene / Of rokkes that ther nys no stoon ysene, / Thanne wol I love yow best of any man" (5.995–97). Language is on display in this crucial scene, and it accomplishes almost too many things. Aurelius's response, "Madam . . . this were an inpossible!" (5.1009), only makes clearer her point (the event's impossibility) and her intent (of loving only her husband). By suggesting a task that cannot be

---

20. See Jacques Lacan, "The Insistence of the Letter in the Unconscious, or Reason Since Freud," in *Écrits: The First Complete Edition in English*, ed. and trans Bruce Fink (New York: Norton, 2006), 412–41, esp. 414–16. All quotations from Lacan's essays throughout this book come from this volume.

accomplished, she says in other words that she will never love him, and his lament proves he has understood her perfectly. But these other words are what we might call the Other's words, and they are important: doesn't Dorigen want the stones removed and the coast cleaned? Captivated by the danger that they signify for her seafaring husband, she complains continually of "thise grisly feendly rokkes blake" (5.868), which accounts for why she put her refusal into these terms in the first place. What the Franklin calls "hire derke fantasye" (5.844) amounts to an obsession with a clean coast that sets the tale's plot in motion. It is the reason her friends have taken her to the party at which Aurelius speaks to her and blurts out his affections. Her playful speech with this would-be suitor expresses, then, undivided love for her husband, her intent to remain ever faithful to him, disdain for Aurelius's suit, and, most significantly, her very deepest desire. In her obsession over the rocks and her wish to have them removed, we could say that Dorigen also wants to be able to give Aurelius her love, however paradoxical that may seem. The fact that we debate the cruelty of Dorigen's consolation is itself telling. Some see her challenging words of refusal as cruel and heartless language she need not have used and thus read her ordeal as punishment for this unnecessary speech. Others see her response as just the opposite. Working in a courtly world where a lady's refusal is an incitement to woo more ardently, Dorigen speaks in the only language available to her to put him off.[21] Her efforts here are a form of politeness and necessity. This debate has failed to resolve fully the significance of her words "in pley." But it has also shown the impossibility of a "fynal answere" (5.987), a self-sufficient signifier that closes interpretive possibilities. By no means transparent, the logic of desire grounds the logic of narrative and its signifiers, with all their swerves and surprises. It is spoken in the language that makes up the Symbolic order—here the social codes, politesse, and idioms of courtly refusal—out of which desire arises and is promulgated.

Within the signifier, then, lies the entire structure of the linguistic system, the Symbolic order, and its determining force. To assume the signifier is to enter the Symbolic order, which is what happens to the child who makes a noise in order to get attention or who begins to learn how to talk, or to anyone who makes himself the subject of enunciation—stepping forward to tell his tale. In any of these cases one must take the signifier upon oneself, using it to make oneself heard and potentially understood, but in doing so one must submit to the signifying system, the very possibility of

---

21. On such responses to Dorigen and courtly language as a hindrance to denial, see Susan Crane, *Gender and Romance in Chaucer's "Canterbury Tales"* (Princeton: Princeton UP, 1994), 65.

unintended or misdirected meaning, perhaps even meaninglessness. Language is something wielded by human beings and something vastly larger, imposed on them. Made up of just such language, literature is part of the Symbolic, participates in it and is governed by it, invoking it at every turn. It is where everything, including any understanding of Lacan, must start. "The symbolic order [is] society's unwritten constitution," as Slavoj Žižek shows, the set of codes and standards into which we are born.[22] But even more basically, it is "the grammatical rules that I have to master blindly and spontaneously," both as a baby and throughout adult life (Žižek 9). Even as a child begins to acquire language by the repetition of meaningless sounds—one of my girls' first words was an enthusiastic "Spum!"—the whole system of language was already there for her to struggle to claim, and it continues to claim us as well beyond the point at which we have grasped a complex vocabulary and the laws of grammar.

Much like Lacan's subject, the pilgrims find themselves and their place in the Symbolic order with the assumption of the signifier, not in some prescribed set of professional rivalries that exist for some characters but not for others.[23] Such a pre-existent set of rivalries threatens to rehearse the assumption of pre-existent "selves" dismantled by scholars like Lee Patterson and H. Marshall Leicester, both of whom show that it is not the pilgrims who stand behind and guarantee language; it is instead language, the tales, that creates the pilgrims.[24] The assumption of the signifier governs their status as divided subjects, both speaking and spoken by the institutional and generic codes of the Symbolic, as well as their movement forward and momentarily apart from the group. In the *Tales*, this movement is accomplished by a number of fictional means and is sometimes left unexplained, which is what sets the stories, literally, into their places and organizes our initial ways of considering their thematic relations. While we certainly do have professional rivals on the pilgrimage who are conscious of their aggressions—the combative Friar and Summoner, for example—every one of Chaucer's narrators submits to a competitive and inherently rivalrous structure as he assumes the signifier and seizes, or more gently receives, the audience's attention.

To illustrate this point, one might consider not the most obvious example, the obstreperous Miller who disrupts the Host's ordered plans, but

---

22. Slavoj Žižek, *How to Read Lacan* (New York: Norton, 2006), 8.
23. The classic essay on these rivalries is Frederick Tupper, "The Quarrels of the Canterbury Pilgrims," *JEGP* 14 (1915): 256–70.
24. See Leicester, *The Disenchanted Self*, and Lee Patterson, *Chaucer and the Subject of History* (Madison: U of Wisconsin P, 1991).

the quiet and unobtrusive Prioress, a figure who can hardly be accused of cultivating any such disruptive behavior. This stately nun travels with near fastidious attention to polite and decorous fashion, as well as a group of attendants to serve her. Despite her misplaced conscience, her mannered efforts are to offend no one. Yet in her tale she makes an offhand remark about monks and abbots—men, she says, who are holy "or elles oghte be" (7.643). This comment is in some ways a characteristically Chaucerian one by which we identify the voice of a unique narrator in the act of individuating herself. But it does not show a "secret" animosity between the Prioress and the Monk, a pilgrim described by Chaucer as "a manly man, to ben an abbot able" (1.167), or some deep conflict between gendered branches of the avowed religious that can offer the key to her tale's interpretation. Indeed, the General Prologue suggests just the opposite when it conjoins descriptions of the Prioress and the Monk, whose portraits directly follow upon the Knight and his retinue. Their prominent position at the head of the Prologue posits a similar social status, suggesting they are aristocrats who have joined the ranks of the regular clergy following what are likely financially motivated, familial decisions. Nor should we adduce some personal inferiority complex stemming from her status as second in command to an analogous abbess in her convent. Yet there *is* something rivalrous and even aggressive in her speech arising from the nature of language itself. Where does it come from and at what does it take aim? The delicate lady Prioress's remark has a sharp edge because such is the price of speaking—even speaking devotionally—in the socially structured network that the *Canterbury Tales* imitates in miniature. It is the way anyone makes her claim. We may not know why any of the pilgrims has undertaken this journey, but we know precisely what each of them wants insofar as each has submitted to the contest, a game that mimes the subjection to the Symbolic more generally: recognition. Each of them wants to win. In setting forth his tale, each pilgrim seeks recognition from the others as well as from the Other. In this context, winning need not mean achieving Harry Bailly's prize so much as merely being heard.

Such attention to the signifier resembles on its surface one of the foundational practices of professional literary study, New Critical close reading. Removed from the historical bounds and theoretical claims of the New Critics—that close reading should strive to remove the work from any outwardly focused, historical context and instead isolate it as a self-reflexive and self-contained verbal artifact—close reading supplies a methodology for the analysis of the written or textual object (not only the exclusively verbal). We know from good philology that language carries with it history and genealogy, long-standing debts and connections of which we are often unaware but that no less inhere in our verbal choices, our grasping for words. As scholars we are trained to attend to the signifier—to the particularities of sound, similarity, and quantity by which any poetic sense at all can be derived and from which all meanings are made. Poetry focalizes attention to the signifier in the condensation of words and images, the deployment of conventional (even "filler") phrases that shape the metrical line as well as the metaphors with which we usually associate it. Rhyme, assonance, alliteration, stress, and arrangement: these particular features of Chaucer's narrative couplets, rhyme-royal stanzas, double ballads, and descriptive prose tracts make a spectacle of the signifier throughout the *Canterbury Tales,* not merely where one story quotes or parodies another. And most of our critical industry, in whatever way it deploys close reading and philological skills, bases its claims on specific instances of the signifier's appearance.

These observations about the poetic focus upon the signifier's power and agency are not merely formal concerns, confined to the aesthetic (though they are that too). They are also the only means to any knowledge of a signified: those historical meanings, associations, and resonances we hope to glean from Chaucer's poetry. Decrying the dominance of (and our fetish for) the signified, what gets reified as historical "meaning," Aranye Fradenburg writes, "The signifier's insensible iterability is the source of its remarkable combination of durability and mutability, and hence of its power to persist, not timelessly, but in time. Persistence in history is not the same thing as persistence in a timeless realm of universal values."[25] Her critique aims at a misunderstanding of the power of the signifier, which has been both oversimplified and underestimated in the name of a historical specificity separate from and antecedent to it that it should inscribe.

Desire, of course, has a historical dimension no less important to this study than the ways in which it manifests itself in language. But these will be more difficult to distinguish than this claim might suggest. Desire "differs from other forms of affection like friendship and divine love," according to Robert Edwards, "by its self-interest, intensity, and undercurrent of sexuality."[26] But as Edwards too discovers, writing about desire, like writing about sex and sexuality, is complicated because of the way its historicity is always at issue. We have to mediate between fabricating a theory of medieval concepts and recuperating an historical impasse, in the words of

---

25. See L. O. Aranye Fradenburg, "Simply Marvelous," *SAC* 26 (2004): 1–27, at 12.
26. Robert Edwards, *The Flight from Desire: Augustine and Ovid to Chaucer* (New York: Palgrave Macmillan, 2006), 4.

Pierre Payer, since "claims made about medieval theories of sexuality are, in fact, contemporary theories."[27] No such category governed knowledge, discourse, or the organization of human persons. There are no linguistic counterparts for "sex," "sexual," and "sexuality" in Latin. "The adjective *venereus* ('venereal,' substantive *venerea*) is as close as the language came to a general term referring to sex, but its employment is not frequent and it is never used as an object of study" (Payer 14). Tracing the pervasiveness of sexual concerns expressed in theological and legal writings, medical and biological treatises, Payer compiles the complex (sometimes contradictory) history of ideas about and theory of desire in the Middle Ages. In his historicization of sex and sexual behavior, Payer, following Foucault, reminds us of its late invention. And yet we know sex and sexuality were major concerns for medieval thinkers and were considerations of daily life for medieval people. The human species, even in times of plague, was never in danger of extinction (and despite the sinfulness to which the plague itself was attributed). Aware of academic debates about the status of wives, marriage, and sexual practices, Chaucer is obsessed by the venerean. Much like the Wife of Bath's own description of her body, the mark of Venus appears all over the Chaucerian corpus.

In spite of a lack of naming such a sexual discourse, managing one's desire might be seen as the central difficulty of human life as explicated by Christian theology. Moral discussions of sin and the revolt against reason and natural justice made all desire sexual desire; sin is grounded in the unruliness of the body (Payer 45–60). Lacan himself is well aware of the problem desire has posed for human history, as he considers "the age-old paradoxes desire has created for moralists and the mark of the infinite that theologians find in it, not to mention the precariousness of its status . . . [as] a useless passion."[28] To that very effect, Augustine sermonizes about the obliteration of reason in the midst of physical passion: "in the act and at the time of fornication the mind is not free to think of anything else. The whole man is so absorbed by it in his body that his mind [*animus*] cannot be said to be his own but at once the whole man can be said to be flesh."[29] Aristotle and Aquinas held similar views. Many patristic and scholastic writers have expended considerable energy on what to do with it—but

---

27. Pierre J. Payer, *The Bridling of Desire: Views of Sex in the Later Middle Ages* (Toronto: U of Toronto P, 1993), 14–15. See also Vern L. Bullough, "Sex in History: A Redux," in *Desire and Discipline: Sex and Sexuality in the Premodern West*, ed. Jacqueline Murray and Konrad Eisenbichler (Toronto: U of Toronto P, 1996), 3–22.
28. Lacan, "Subversion of the Subject and the Dialectic of Desire," 687.
29. Augustine, Sermon 162.2, *Patrologia Latina* 38.887. Cited by Payer, *Bridling of Desire*, 82.

deep down they work in a system, like Lacan's, where it can hardly be done without. Remaining with us, desire has to be accounted for in the stories of our origins. Desire is related to the will and, along with reason, forms a component part of what makes a human being, created in the image of God *and* marked by sinfulness and originary disobedience. Such logic placed desire at the very center of creation and made the Fall, the original separation of desire from right reason, the beginning of everything.

Many of the commentaries Payer studies address the condition of man in the state of nature, or, more precisely, its garden. Such writers worked to differentiate current matters with those in Eden, interrogating the dignity of the two genders (as, and if, originally created), the conduct of marriage, and the inheritance of sin. No topic of human status was exempt from the infiltration of sin and desire. What is Eve's function as "helpmate"? What does God's command to increase and multiply say about sex in Eden? But no issue brought forward greater intellectual acrobatics than the moral assessment of sexual pleasure. Did Adam and Eve enjoy sex before the Fall, and, if so, what was that enjoyment like? Was it like the enjoyment of sex "now," and what might that suggest about sexual pleasure itself?

For the then-present state of matters, the conditions in Paradise were crucial. Sex and desire could not be evil in and of themselves if they were part of God's plan and his command. Payer writes, "The concupiscence that is the material component of original sin must not be confused with the natural concupiscence that is simply the desiring, appetitive aspect of the lower sense part of the soul. Adam and Eve would have had the latter before the Fall to the extent that they would have had natural desires for the pleasures associated with sense experience" (48). Under the control of reason these natural desires were legitimate and regulated. By these means thirteenth-century theologians refined the Augustinian definition of original sin as mere concupiscence, such that it became "the basic disorder in the human affective dimensions resulting from the refusal to obey the dictates of right reason" (Payer 47). These writers, particularly Peter Lombard and Albertus Magnus, as well as Aquinas, labored to place procreation within the purview of man in his "pristine" state. But theologians were also left to imagine, by implication, what never got said explicitly in the Bible. What was the purpose of that reproduction if Adam and Eve were immortal creatures? In trying to discern the meanings and implications of Genesis 1:27–29, and its lack of subordinating syntax, theologians were left to invent, for instance, "the idea that the purpose of reproduction was to fill out the number of the elect," those lost when Lucifer rebelled (Payer 26).

The management of desire and its relation to reasonable and justifiable behavior is not only a historical problem, it is also a historicist one. In Chaucer studies specifically we have dealt with this problem for a long time and not always in full awareness of how we were doing so. Endorsing Augustinian models of reading literary texts as the only properly historical means of interpretation, D. W. Robertson famously places desire at the very center of medieval Christian culture as well as our understanding of it. In Steven Justice's terms, Robertsonianism reads all medieval poetry as "allegory, whether it looked that way or not; it was indifferent to worldly and humane engagements and *pursued the single aim of wrenching human desire from its self-deforming attachments* ('cupidity') toward love of God ('charity')."³⁰ But even further, Robertson influentially *reproduced* this pursuit within medieval literary studies itself, by making control over modern interpretive desires the major problem of the discipline. His critical method not only delineated but *performed* the asceticism enjoined by some medieval texts. In reading those texts, we are thus caught up in the structures of their desires even if those desires are to abjure and to control desire itself.

Not just the patristic injunctions examined by Robertson but both history and literature evidence a medieval fascination with desire, leading me to explore what lies under explicit statements, in much the same way medieval academics were obsessed by what was behind or implied by specific biblical utterance. If the narrative and effects of the Fall give this topic its grounds of intelligibility, Chaucer's tales repeatedly return to the story of the Fall in both serious and comic ways. Its apotheosis appears in the Nun's Priest's Tale and its re-enactment of the story of the Fall in a chicken coop. Though he makes specific reference to Thomas Bradwardine and the academic debates on predestination at Oxford, the Nun's Priest takes a more generally comic view of matters. Foxes are predators on the lookout for tasty chicken dinners, and conditional necessity need not be marshaled to account for this fox's actions. Certainly one way to read Chaucer in the guise of the Nun's Priest is as a learned mockery of the very academic discourses that overexplain the operations of nature and its drives (like hunger), matters that are also diffused into what scholars (who are both imitated and mocked by the Nun's Priest) like to call historical context. But this is less a refusal of the historical context I have spent the last few pages examining and more an effort to navigate between one kind of

---

30. Steven Justice, "Who Stole Robertson?" *PMLA* 124 (2009): 609–15, at 609; my emphasis. Justice discusses the long influential reach of the work of D. W. Robertson, especially his *A Preface to Chaucer: Studies in Medieval Perspectives* (Princeton: Princeton UP, 1962).

historical context and another. All these are heavily dependent on the way language works in and on the subject, both beyond the text's own terms and yet manifested precisely within them.

Before proceeding further, we might address the looming historicist objection—that medieval "selves" were radically different from modern ones in terms of external determinations of one's "self." These determinations have been expressed most often in terms of corporate identity, in which medievals primarily expressed and thought of themselves as part of a group rather than as individuals. In literature particularly, the typologies of character also suggest a similar externalization. Literary characters (always dangerous to treat like "real" people no matter the density of the illusion) are far more likely to be based on "abstract types rather than psychologically motivated human beings."[31] These concerns pose a hard opposition, then, between a fully external set of typologies or a wholly internal, autonomously generated selfhood. But I would point out that neither historicists nor poststructuralist critics have been fully satisfied with these definitions on either side of the opposition. The "typology" argument has been dismissed as a facile prescription that ignores the kinds of changes wrought by confessional injunction after 1215 and the wealth of literature produced for and around the self-displaying, self-analyzing practices of confession, as well as changes in the later Middle Ages reflected in university disputes and brought on by economic and social crises in the wake of the Black Death.

A careful reading of Lacan, too, also problematizes some of the assumptions about psychoanalysis that are frequently made in the name of historicism and the all-too-easily presumed binary distinction of psychoanalytic and historicist interests.[32] Returning to the "Mirror Stage," and the structuring conditions of subjectivity developed beyond its terms in Seminar II, we need to read more carefully the work of the Other and the power of the signifier in the determination of the individual—what Lacan prefers to call the "subject" for its multiple senses. The "subject" as we have learned undoes the unity and coherence of the "self" upon which too many Anglo-American scholars presume all psychoanalytic criticism rests. But Lacan

---

31. John Ganim, "Identity and Subjecthood," in *Chaucer: An Oxford Guide*, ed. Steve Ellis (Oxford: Oxford UP, 2005), 224–238, at 224.

32. Psychoanalysis has productively permeated Medieval studies in the exemplary work of L. O. Aranye Fradenburg, H. Marshall Leicester, Gayle Margherita, Carolyn Dinshaw, Sarah Kay, Simon Gaunt, Paul Strohm, Patricia Clare Ingham, Mark Miller, and George Edmondson as well as in places it might be less easily recognized, such as the work of Lee Patterson. On this phenomenon, see my essay "Historicists and Their Discontents: Reading Psychoanalytically in Medieval Studies," *TSLL* 44 (2002): 108–31.

also devotes considerable time to the way the social inhabits the subject before it comes to be an individual, the way language (in all its historical specificity) infiltrates the subject from the very start. Bruce Fink uses, as an example, the idea that a child's name locates him in the Symbolic order before the child itself has any chance to do so.[33] Parents choose a name, often before the child's birth, designating him in the world and making a relation to others who might have had (or rejected) that name. It might also relate him to complete and total strangers as it situates him in society and culture at large. The shaping power of the signifier and the Symbolic order grounding such acts of naming sound like complicated theoretical formulations, but they are very familiar and very common—as the popularity of any baby name book will attest. Though not invoking anything like Lacanian terms, such books articulate this aspect of the signifier in commonsensical and often humorous ways. Being named "Jennifer" or "Jason" (or, more recently, "Ava" or "Aiden") has important implications about which the child who bears the name cannot be aware or control.[34] Not merely inventorying popularity or the uniqueness of one's baby's potential name, such books chronicle both denotations, the linguistic origins or etymology of names, and the connotations they carry: in the cultural or fictional others who have popularized them; in their historicity (as old-fashioned or "classic"—what the authors of *Beyond Jennifer and Jason* call "Volvo names," those that never go out of style) by offering different associative value; and in their currency—both their rate of occurrence in the immediate past and the class conscious value they suggest in the present. We see such matters all over the *Canterbury Tales* as various names are fraught with meaning and dragged into the texts before a particular character speaks. The names Alison and John, for example, that appear in the Miller's Tale attached to the "carpenter and . . . his wyf" (1.3142) are simple verisimilar pronomen from the bourgeois class. So common, in fact, a number of other Alisons and Johns appear in the *Canterbury Tales,* some of whom are related directly (the Reeve's scholar John bears some relation to the Miller's carpenter because the Reeve explicitly tells his tale to revenge himself on the Miller) and some more indirectly (we do not yet know the Wife of Bath and her gossip, Alys, share this name). Chaucer knew other

---

33. Bruce Fink, "The Subject and the Other's Desire," in *Reading Seminars I and II: Lacan's Return to Freud,* ed. Richard Feldstein, Bruce Fink, and Maire Jaanus (Buffalo: State U of New York P, 1996), 76–97, at 80.

34. See Linda Rosenkrantz and Pamela Redmond Satran, *Beyond Jennifer and Jason: The New Enlightened Guide to Naming Your Baby,* 2nd rev. ed. (New York: St. Martin's, 1994) and its later editions, *Beyond Jennifer and Jason, Madison and Montana: What to Name Your Baby Now* (4th ed., 2006) and, most recently, *Beyond Ava and Aiden* (St. Martin's Griffin, 2009).

names with the needed metrical value and social "degree." Something else has to be at work in the signifier.

The signifier one takes up in one's name, a signifier that takes one up, is paradigmatic of the way the signifier designs the subject who speaks. In choosing words we choose from the battery of signifiers beyond us—again, the Symbolic order—that carries meanings which we sometimes intend but some of which we are often unaware, histories that we do not know, but that no less help determine who we are. For example, when Arcite calls himself "Philostrate" when he returns disguised and disfigured to Athens, the Knight has not merely given him a name to hide his identity from Theseus or to acknowledge his condition as one "stricken by love." Arcite has also unwittingly chosen to switch sources and literary affiliations. In Boccaccio's *Teseida,* Arcita restyles himself as Pentheus, a name that posits a specific mythologic inheritance and violent end. Instead, Chaucer's Arcite chooses the name that refers to Troilus in the title of Boccaccio's other romance, *Il Filostrato,* setting Arcite up as an equally but differently tragic figure. One's identity, then, is a social product before and after one speaks oneself. In depicting the work of the signifier, Lacan depicts a process by which the social world in its historical specificity is both internalized and simultaneously expressed.

As both Arcite and Lacan reveal, the neat binary opposition between wholly external types and completely internal fantasy is untenable and rather oversimplified. Working the same problematic from the historical side, John Ganim describes Chaucer's characters as internally conflicted by the institutions (and their types, their group identities) that define them. He writes, "Chaucer's often conflicted characters, lashing out at the very structures which define them, such as the Monk mocking the counterintuitive rules of monastic orders, or the Wife of Bath railing against a patriarchy that has in fact seeped into every crevice of her consciousness, are typical."[35] These are not so much ironic as Symbolic productions and as such have tensions already built in them. One could question where to assign this power of the signifier: in the example outlined above, is it attributable to Arcite, to the Knight, and/or to Chaucer? Ultimately, all such choices fall to Chaucer as reader of Boccaccian texts and author of these fictions. But his story promulgates the power of the signifier, both in the way the Knight selects and abbreviates his tale when he has "drawe[n] cut" (1.835) and the way Arcite obeys the command of Mercury in returning to Athens in his unrecognizable state. Chaucer may be responsible, but he has

---

35. Ganim, "Identity and Subjecthood," 227.

also made the taking of such responsibility for one's words, here the name one assumes, an elaborate part of his fictions as well, not merely something that he does silently behind them.

While the Symbolic order of language is everywhere at all times (as in before one's birth and after one's death), sometimes it's not working. Its breakdown or incompleteness suggests the other orders of reality Lacan theorizes to explain the complexities of human perception and determination: the Imaginary and the Real. Just how the Symbolic provokes our understanding of Imaginary and Real dimensions emerges from Lacan's elaboration of the way language structures human subjects, how it binds them to particular rules and permeates all thought and feeling. The very name Lacan uses, the "subject," for the being in the Symbolic helps get at what is complex about it. The subject is at once the grammatical subject of speech, the one who says "I" and who predicates things. But it is also one who is subjected to rules and laws. As Žižek puts it, "For Lacan, language is a gift as dangerous to humanity as the horse was to the Trojans: it offers itself to our use free of charge, but once we accept it, it colonizes us."[36] We can use language to say what we mean, but we are ultimately subject to its rules and are thus spoken by it in equal measure.

So what happens when the subject speaks? To whom is its speech addressed and what kind of gesture is that? Here we have to introduce the other, an important term in Lacanian thought in both major and minor forms, and the stakes of recognition that are located in relation to the other. Language is our fundamental means of communicating with another, and it always supposes this other in the communicative situation. Someone has to be there to transmit the message. Language is our tether to other people, as well as a barrier. It is proof that the other person is different from us and needs tethering in the first place. And we have to admit that lack of sameness in the other every time we use language as a recognition of and a means of traversing this fundamental distance. Citing Roman Jakobson, Žižek explains that "human speech never merely transmits a message, it always also self-reflectively asserts the basic symbolic pact between the communicating subjects," much like the link between individuals established by a gift (12). But there is another other in this communicative situation, and Lacan calls it the big Other, with a capital letter. The Other is the witness that establishes the pact (God, History, Culture): the Symbolic order itself, and it is more involved in the act of communicative link-making than might at first appear. In one of his delightful examples in which most of

---

36. Žižek, *How to Read*, 11–12.

us can recognize ourselves, Žižek defines this Other as the one for whom we say "oops" aloud when we stumble or make a mistake. Explaining how we come to grasp and internalize this Other as we try to engage with others, Lacan posits (retroactively) the Imaginary, which is the field of our identifications. In such Imaginary scenarios one comes into contact with another and makes a demand to her, a demand that can never be fully met. Demand is always more than need, Lacan tells us, it is always also "a request for love."[37] Desire is the surplus when biological need is subtracted from demand, "desire's irreducibility to demand" ("Subversion of the Subject" 681)—it cannot be fully spoken. Fink glosses the difference: "A young bear is given honey to eat by its mother, gorges itself, and lies down for a nap, sated. We receive the blanket we demand from our mother and then dream about cars and dolls and world domination. For there is always something more to be desired."[38] In what seems a simple and most natural gesture lies a psychic complexity that makes human speech a coterminous component of desire as something only ever partially satisfiable. The response to a demand cannot fully answer for what triggers articulation in the first place. What tale then could fully answer the demand supposedly made by another—or by Harry Bailly, for that matter? There will always be a remainder, an impulse for another story.

Not only have we mistaken other subjects as images of ourselves in our imaginary identifications and gestures of communication, more importantly we have mistaken our "selves" as other, potentially aggressive and demanding beings. His "Mirror Stage" essay and its companion, "Aggressiveness in Psychoanalysis," are foundational here. They work to dramatize—as indeed any well-used "stage" should—the experience of alienation and separation in the subject's acquisition of language over and against a false duality and gestalt self-aggrandizement. Where human development gets narrativized as progress and continually increasing mastery (of motor coordination, of speech, of understanding), as a story of learning, it is experienced, according to Lacan, with more frustration as a series of halting and fitful gestures. The difficulty with this process comes from what Lacan calls the "generic prematurity of birth" and the "specular capture" that it provokes ("Subversion of the Subject" 686). The child's dependence on others for its survival places it in a divided position where it sees something other than it feels. Described in the two essays mentioned above, this division in experience between the specular image of wholeness and the felt dis-coordination of

---

37. Lacan "Subversion of the Subject," 681.
38. Bruce Fink, *Lacan to the Letter: Reading "Écrits" Closely* (Minneapolis: U of Minnesota P, 2004), 118–19.

the body marks humans as split subjects from the beginning, in terms, as here, of being and having, but also between conscious and unconscious knowledge. Lacan writes:

> What the subject finds in this altered image of his body is the paradigm of all the forms of resemblance that will cast a shade of hostility onto the world of objects, by projecting onto them the avatar of his narcissistic image, which, from the jubilation derived from encountering it in the mirror, becomes—in confronting his semblables—the outlet for his most intimate aggressiveness. ("Subversion of the Subject" 685)

The mirroring scenario, with its specular double and perceived self-difference, self-recognition, and alienation, already intimates that there are more figures in play than at first appear. Most importantly, there is no "autonomous ego"—a distinction that forms the main objection psychoanalysis levels at Anglo-American ego psychology. The explanatory force of the Mirror Stage posits an "imaginary" duality (here with the mother) in which one encounters a self-reflection that is misrecognized in both spatial and temporal ways. And this same misrecognized duality will be repeated in all future identifications.

The aggressivity unleashed in this Imaginary dimension particularly warrants discussion for the way it, too, colors all future relations with others. Lacan writes: "It is in this erotic relationship, in which the human individual fixates on an image that alienates him from himself, that we find the energy and the form from which the organization of the passions that he will call his ego originates" ("Aggressiveness" 92). This aggressivity may take the form of a tense and oppositional stance to others, but at root it is an inner conflict, a relation to a misrecognized part of the self. Along with the demand for love, then, we must also include the more violent and aggressive impulses (toward the other, the object, and the self) that are borne along with it.

Once demand is made, desire and language are on the scene, opening upon a world of lack and difference that will never be escaped. That lack proliferates with the others we are dealing with. Demands are not made in the abstract but are addressed to someone, to another, an Other that comes with language and desire. These self-duplicating positions splitting the subject from itself make Lacan's question of desire, "*Chè Vuoi?*," a complicated one. It not only asks the subject, "What do you want?" but turns the question upon the subject, "What does he [the other] want from me?" One of Lacan's most famous formulations is "that man's desire is the Other's desire" ["*le désire de l'homme est le désir de l'Autre*]," ("Subversion of the Subject" 690). We should note the important ambiguity and multiplicity in desiring "*de l'Autre*," of the Other, "in which *de* provides what grammarians call a 'subjective determination'" ("Subversion of the Subject" 690). Lacan means that one must read in both subjective and objective senses, which would translate "*de l'Autre*" thus: "desire for the other, desire to be desired by the other, and, especially, desire for the other's desire."³⁹ In his explication of Lacan's commentary on desiring qua Other, Fink elaborates: "Lacan's first answer to these questions seems to be that what I want, as a subject, is recognition by the Other, and this recognition takes the form of being wanted: *I want to be wanted*. . . . I imagine myself in relation to the Other's desire for me" (119; emphasis in original). This Other is not merely another (the mother or one of her substitutes) but the entirety of the social world that teaches us what and how we should want, a social world, we might emphasize here, that is figured in historically situated ways.

This complex formation makes desire difficult, even counterintuitive. The various positions the subject must occupy and the others to which it must accommodate itself make desire both an impasse and a self-replicating machine. Because desire can be met by the satisfaction of no need precisely because it is excessive of need, desire can never be fully satisfied, can never know an end. It will only ever be temporarily circumvented. Instead of attaining pure satisfaction, we sustain desire by replacing one object of desire with another in an endless chain of substitutions that probes the limit of our importance to the Other. Language traces this circuit of desire, in which we name and rename what we want, a naming that rehearses the advent of desire itself, when the signifier was first assumed in the place of the imaginary object. But we never fully achieve satisfaction, never stop desiring; we merely replace the temporary objects of our desire with new ones, none which can satisfy its "cause," the originary desire to recapture something—originally the body of the mother—we never actually possessed.

Explaining in these early essays the intersubjective dialectic of recognition, Lacan reveals the influence of Hegel, whose ideas about the importance of recognition to one's sense of self-importance (however fragile that turns out to be) helps him formulate what is going on in the Mirror Stage, which is increasingly in Lacan's thought not a "phase" one passes through but a dimensionality to one's perception.⁴⁰ Like Hegel, Lacan here empha-

---

39. Žižek, *How to Read*, 36.
40. Judith Butler outlines the importance of Kojève's lectures to the way Lacan understands Hegel in *Subjects of Desire: Hegelian Reflections in Twentieth-Century France* (New York: Columbia

sizes the importance of the other to the "I," and it will help us particularly as we think about what Chaucer's Canterbury pilgrims do when they speak before each other, when they take up the signifier, a gesture that always implicitly asks for recognition no matter the ways one may work to deny or escape it. The recognition configured by social relations appears overtly in Chaucer's General Prologue description of the Wife of Bath, the figure on the pilgrimage we have always most securely associated with desire, if not at this particular juncture. Not only does her performance make clear her desires for serial monogamy and marital sexuality, as well as her interest in the question of "what thyng is it that wommen moost desiren" (3.905), she first appears as a figure deeply invested in the recognition she gets from others. Besides her ostentatious garb (red hose and large hat), the Wife is identified by her behavior in church at the offertory:

> In al the parisshe wif ne was ther noon
> That to the offrynge bifore hire sholde goon;
> And if ther dide, certeyn, so wrooth was she
> That she was out of alle charitee.
> (1.449–52)

These lines are memorable for their intimation of the Wife's speech in the free indirect discourse detected through some of the details that the narrator must have learned just recently from speaking "with hem everichon" at the Tabard (1.31). How could he otherwise know her customary behavior had she not mentioned it herself? Even further, in these lines we hear the Wife's tone and her idiom ("out of alle charitee"), in her assumptions of social priority and her impatience with what she perceives as others' impertinence. Her portrait might seem like a varied and sometimes random assortment of details, but their implicit connections and juxtapositions are often illuminating, revealing an order to their disorder that characterizes the General Prologue as a whole.

The Wife is a figure characterized by movement, here a mere walk up to the altar, that always means more than it literally says. Movement carries an even greater significance for her. An experienced pilgrim, she knows

---

UP, 1987; rpt. 1999), 63–79. It is important to understand Lacan's heavily philosophical grounding, the way thinkers like Hegel (via Kojève), Heidegger, and Sartre affected his work. While he departs from each of them at some point, he has important debts to their dialecticism, phenomenology, and existentialism, respectively. For a good introduction to these philosophic influences on Lacan, see Jacques-Alain Miller's introductions to Seminars I and II in Feldstein, Fink, and Jaanus, 3–35; as well as the more general introduction to Lacan by Sean Homer, *Jacques Lacan* (London: Routledge, 2005).

much of "wandrynge by the weye" (1.467). This simple description implies far more than habitual travel, which is itself relevant to the journey she's currently undertaken and her freedom to leave home. Such "wandrynge" and indirection also suggest the stereotypical behavior of women who frequent pilgrimages for illicit purposes, as Mann adduces from estates satires.[41] Her physical and geographical wandering carries a suggestion of moral wandering and "daliance" (3.565) that her autobiographical prologue partially confirms when it links the "visitaciouns," "vigilies," and "processiouns" (3.555–56) with her negotiation with "Jankyn, oure clerk" (3.595)—now her fifth husband—if ever she were to be a "wydwe" (3.568). Yet even more, the significance of her mobility is articulated in her behavior at home, and in circumstances in which she would appear to be rooted. Her position in her parish as premiere cloth maker and veteran wife is transmitted by the foremost position she takes processing "to the offrynge" each Sunday (1.450). The Wife is defined by movement both practically and in more abstract ways that express her agility within and manipulation of the traditional confines of the domestic sphere. Moreover, the metaphorical priority she holds in her town "biside Bathe" (1.445) is taken rather literally by the Wife herself, and it determines her attitude and, Chaucer implies, her generosity.

Movement and mobility are thus both literally and figuratively important to understanding the Wife. And in this description, paradoxically, the metaphorical precedes the literal. "Out of charitee" could be rendered in a modern idiom as "put out" or "out of sorts," certainly what the line means at its surface. The Wife is "deeply upset," according to the editorial gloss. But under that colloquial surface lies a more literal truth, in which the Wife's self-possession affects her distribution of possessions, her charitableness, not simply her mood, and thus may produce a stingy offering. Of course, the material status of the Wife conditions her signifying function. Not just her dress but her wealth, her ability to offer charity in monetary terms, configure her in a specific historical context and gendered register. But her material means do not explain everything. Who she is in terms of her "charitee" depends on the others "in al the parisshe" and the recognition they confer. She can always afford to be generous, but she is not always so inclined without proper acknowledgment.

This exaggerated demonstration of the importance of recognition in the Wife's portrait is central to the self-expression or "character" of Chaucer's pilgrims more generally and their distinctive stories. Different pilgrims are

---

41. Mann, *Chaucer and Medieval Estates Satire*, 123.

looking for recognition from various others and by different verbal means: the Wife from her fellow parishioners; the Miller from the Knight; the Pardoner from anyone who might buy his relics. That attempt at recognition is related to self-recognition and realization, and it comes with an antagonism, a view of that Other (both individuals and the more abstract pressure of the social world) as obstruction, which is why it appears in those stories wholly unconnected to others or in the more retiring pilgrims who do not seem to be seeking attention. Because of the way this third term, this other, competes with the subject over some object, and potentially finds the subject lacking as a potential object of desire itself, "envy and resentment," in Žižek's words, "are a constitutive component of human desire."[42] It forms the nagging wonder whether what one wants is, in fact, what one should want after all. The aggressivity in desire and the aggressions in which desire is represented also make language a mediating as well as expressive force: "The main function of the symbolic order with its laws and obligations is to render our co-existence with others minimally bearable: a Third has to step in between me and my neighbors so that our relations do not explode in murderous violence" (Žižek 45–46). With its doubled hero and violent spectacle, the Knight's story practically outlines the regulating structure of the Symbolic, its prolific language managing the forces of chaos.

The recognition each figure seeks is not always apparent at the level of each teller's address; it is not fully consistent with what appear as the motives of the tales. The Wife may want recognition from other wives at home or from the pilgrims when she travels, but that does not mean she fully understands the nature of the recognition her tale seeks. Such a lack of understanding might be detected in her infamous digression on Midas, an attempt to explain how women love to tell secrets, which has certainly drawn critical attention to her. Not only does the Midas story completely arrest and disrupt her Arthurian romance, the need for such an example to illustrate the way women behave seems to undercut her larger purpose. The Wife's rhetorical power rests upon what she knows about marriage and women, and this knowledge shows up in various forms in her Prologue as well as her Tale. But there certainly seems to be more going on in the Wife's Tale than any consistent presentation of feminine wisdom. There are more ways in which we feel we recognize her and in which she seems to demand recognition than appears merely at the tale's surface. It may also explain the way she addresses "ye wise wyves" (3.225) on a pilgrimage at which she

---

42. Žižek, *How to Read Lacan*, 36.

is the only secular woman: it forms her address to the big Other. So too we might wonder at the recognition sought by the Reeve, who hides at the back of the pilgrimage and whose admission of old age appears to keep him out of desire's competitive circuits. Or the Merchant, who spontaneously reacts to the "wepyng and waylyng, care and oother sorwe" (4.1213) that he recognizes in the Clerk's epilogue but refuses to discuss from personal experience because it might be too painful. The subject's bid for recognition is not always an extroverted performance; it may actually look like a retreat from the limelight other figures actively seek.

Already in this quick sketch of the Lacanian terrain, I have tread on the Real, the realm beyond signification. The Real is the unbearable aloneness of the human being in the world and the felt chaos from which it comes. Beyond imaginary identifications, aggressive misrecognitions, or the substitutive reparations of language, the Real presses upon these other dimensions, both threatening them and holding them in place. With the concept of the Real, which is anything but reality, Lacan rewrites the order of human beings out of the state of nature: man is no *tabula rasa* gradually acquiring impressions of the world but a being bombarded with the world around him from birth, from which he must separate and order himself. Both material and psychical reality in its disordered state, the Real is "extimate," a neologism of Lacan's that combines ideas of intimacy with exteriority.[43] It is a place beyond the subject intimate to him that he also calls the Thing, another word poised between what is human and inhuman in us.[44] Whatever is unbearable or beyond putting into words, like orgasm, occurs in the Real. But we should also here stress the interconnection of Imaginary, Symbolic, and Real. These are not phases one passes through but dimensions in and between which one lives. Human existence may be characterized as series of imaginary identifications (and their attendant aggressions) that must be navigated through the often-sublimating substitutions of the Symbolic, efforts that ultimately keep the Real at bay.

I have lingered over Lacanian terms and concepts because they will be used throughout this book to explain the stakes and complexities of Chaucer's discourse of desire—the place from which each of the Canterbury tales issues, as well as their substitutive relation to each other in the poem's still

---

43. The discussion of extimacy is found in *Seminar VII: The Ethics of Psychoanalysis 1959–60*, ed. Jacques-Alain Miller and trans. Dennis Porter (New York: Norton, 1992), 139–54.

44. Dylan Evans defines the Thing in the context of *jouissance* as the object of desire, "the lost object which must be continually refound, . . . it is the prehistoric, unforgettable Other" (*An Introductory Dictionary of Lacanian Psychoanalysis* [London and New York: Routledge, 1996], 205; *s.v.* "Thing [*chose*]").

forming structure. Further, Lacan's focus on sociality, and the recognition at stake in social systems, helps to make some sense of the conjunction of pilgrimage frame and storytelling contest, two aspects of Chaucer's poem that have been taken in transparently naturalistic terms when they have been considered at all.[45] The frame narrative has been long admired as one of Chaucer's great achievements, but it has not been easily assimilated to literary models or historical sources. Instead, we have taken the storytelling contest as an imitation of "real" life, at the same time that we have rejected mere realism as the basis of almost everything else in the General Prologue, including the pilgrims themselves.[46] This seems a perennial feature of Chaucer criticism: what cannot be found in his literary sources must be an observation from life, in the words of J. V. Cunningham, "the triumph of originality over convention and of realism over artifice . . . [whereby] the defect of literary history becomes the glory of literary criticism."[47] But that glory is short-lived. Where pilgrimage has been examined for the contexts it provides the tales (even if it is a context the reader must actively provide because its spiritual aims are largely unspoken), competition has stimulated surprisingly little investigation. Furthermore, Lacan will help us to analyze the rivalrous aggressivities of competition precisely at the point we imagine—in what has to be a misrecognition, of course—we see such a glimpse of real life.

Lacan offers us a subtle language to trace the various things that happen when Chaucer's pilgrims speak out and tell their stories, when they take up their position in the Symbolic order arranged by the Host, "under [his] yerde" (4.22), as he reminds them of their "biheeste" (2.37). Not every speaker has to be corralled or antagonized in this way, though the Host clearly enjoys it. He is much more polite to the "lady Prioresse":

> by youre leve,
> So that I wiste I sholde yow nat greve,
> I wolde demen that ye tellen sholde
> A tale next, if so were that ye wolde.

---

45. Such "naturalistic" terms have been called into question by Mark Miller, with whose work I share a number of concerns. See his *Philosophical Chaucer: Love, Sex, and Agency in the "Canterbury Tales"* (Cambridge: Cambridge UP, 2004).

46. This is, in fact, the very point of Mann's book, which was to deny the "historical" reading of various pilgrims as images of real people from Chaucer's social acquaintance promulgated largely by John M. Manly's lectures in *Some New Light on Chaucer* (New York: Holt, 1926). The vagaries of the signifier "historical" in medieval scholarship is both acknowledged and repressed.

47. J. V. Cunningham, "The Literary Form of the Prologue to the *Canterbury Tales*," *Modern Philology* 49 (1952): 172–81, at 172.

> Now wol ye vouche sauf, my lady deere?
> (7.447–51)

It is not simply a legal or economic or political or ethical or associational relation between subjects that the Host calls up in his address to each pilgrim, but all of them at once. He chooses different terms, according to their station, to demand participation from each pilgrim (and sometimes he simply endures the mode of participation they foist upon him), affirming the role he has given himself in the process: "governour, / And of our tales juge and reportour" (1.813–14), by reminding himself as he reminds them that they stand at his judgment. But the Host's authority is merely temporary and often sporadic. The tight drama of interruption and imitation in fragment 1 is not sustained. There is often little or no dramatized connection between tales. Indeed the fragments are not in any sense fully stitched together. Instead, substitution serves to pull the tales into relation with each other, its metonymic force propelling both pilgrims and pilgrimage journey forward.

Substitution governs the *Canterbury Tales* in large and small ways. At its very surface the fiction of narrative exchange is just such a substitutive structure linking stories in a forward progress from London to Canterbury (and, ostensibly, back again). One of the exciting and underexplored areas of the *Canterbury Tales* are the links, those points at which the poem moves between tales by Harry Bailly's ministrations or by more dramatically generated means. But they are also some of the least secure points of contact we have in the poem. At times there are no links, no introductions, forming what scholars have labeled "headless" fragments. Alternately, there are "cancelled" links, which display an excess of linking material—the same lines appearing in two different places—that has suggested the movement of material from one position to another. Despite an editorial language of deprivation, "headless" fragments, "cancelled" links, what we have is often too much. There is wide revision still going on. While we can see some kind of order being formed in Chaucer's mind—as, for example, when he moves an idea for the Wife of Bath's story to the Shipman, writing a new Prologue and Tale for her or as he expands the General Prologue and weaves fragment 1 together as dramatic versions of repetition—we know what we have is incomplete. Chaucer is still experimenting, changing his mind, and moving things around. The process of substitution in terms of tale placement and maybe even assigned narrator has clearly not yet ended.

Substitution offers a sense of playfulness-in-incompleteness, as with a logic or jigsaw puzzle. The tales following the Wife of Bath's performance are instructive here. Though clearly participating in an open debate on marriage and challenging clerks (who never have anything good to say about wives), the Wife is not followed directly by the pilgrim she most provokes. Instead, Chaucer's Clerk, whose tale of patient Griselda rises to her challenge, speaks after what appears a slight digression in the Friar–Summoner debate. Despite the fact that they have been trying to interrupt her from the beginning, these figures do not supply the detour they seem to promise. Using her sermon as an excuse to put each other down, these tales also seem to fit into proper position after the Wife's.[48] Both responses to the Wife, the Clerk's and the Friar–Summoner's, are fitting, suggesting that Chaucer is well aware that more is going on in the stories than any one other (including the narrator itself) might understand. Not only does substitution help us see how we move from one tale to the next, substitution governs the very idea of order, which is inherently flexible even as it is in the process of being formulated.

If we have imagined the storytelling competition to be a natural thing to do in Chaucer's England, we might explore more fully the models he rejected in the structure he created within his elaborate opening to the tale collection. Turning away from the pilgrim portraits to just this structure, David Wallace has helpfully focused on the establishment of the fellowship at the Tabard Inn, showing a strong tie between the *Canterbury Tales* and the *Decameron,* the organization of the General Prologue and the formation of the brigata in Boccaccio's Introduction.[49] His inventive means of pairing the two texts reveals the debts Chaucer may owe to Boccaccio, as well as showcasing what remains uniquely Chaucer's own. Too often we neglect competition, as I have claimed, naturalizing it as an effect of the Host's commercialism or Chaucer's own postplague economic conditions. Yet neither of these explanations is simple or merely self-evident. The economic changes in late medieval England were the source of many anxieties about the ways society might be reshaped or destroyed by them.[50] Similar anxi-

---

48. For a compelling argument about the Friar's Tale as a direct response to and replaying of the Wife's, see Penn R. Szittya, "The Green Yeoman as Loathly Lady: The Friar's Parody of the *Wife of Bath's Tale,*" *PMLA* 90 (1975): 386–94.

49. David Wallace, *Chaucerian Polity: Absolutist Lineages and Associational Forms in England and Italy* (Stanford: Stanford UP, 1997), esp. 65ff.

50. Dealing explicitly with France, Cowell adduces the late twelfth and early thirteenth centuries as the period of economic growth and the decline of famine leading to the rise of a mercantile economy. See *At Play in the Tavern,* 41–53. On the economic changes in late medieval England, see

eties are elaborately wrought throughout Boccaccio's Introduction to the *Decameron,* not merely in its description of the plague of 1348. His concerns about the pestilence that his fictional figures seek to flee are interwoven with, and inseparable from, anxieties about social propriety, the regulation of servants, self-governance, and polite language, concerns which he articulates in terms of his plans for organizing his tale collection.

With the plague as such a source, Boccaccio arranges his stories rigidly and considers competitiveness a problem, working explicitly to neutralize its effects. Each member of his group of ten aristocrats tells a story a day, with one member acting as king or queen to select the day's topic.[51] In fact, the brigata chooses tales rather than plays games because in games there can be only one winner but with tales, everyone enjoys. Pampinea organizes the group with this cooperative logic in mind: "I suggest we spend this hot part of the day not playing games (a pastime which of necessity disturbs the player who loses without providing much pleasure either for his opponents or for those who watch)" ["Ma se in questo il mio parer si seguisse, non giucando, nel quale l'animo dell'una delle parti convien che si turbi senza troppo piacere dell'altra o di chi sta a vedere, ma novellando (il che può porgere, dicendo uno, a tutta la compagnia che ascolta diletto] questa calda parte del giorno trapasseremo)"].[52] Invoking pleasure and equality, Boccaccio's tale-telling plan thereby seeks to replicate and thus produce an ideally functioning society.

Deeply concerned with order and rule at every point of the *Decameron*'s Introduction, Boccaccio explicitly avoids competition in order to avoid social impropriety with his group of aristocrats. As Paul Strohm notes, the brigata is "an ideal body of tellers and listeners who are uniformly gentle and who differ only in modest respects."[53] Around this group of travelers, Boccaccio describes the breakdown of social rules and laws generally, as magistrates and property owners flee areas of disease. He simi-

---

Patterson, *Subject of History,* 247–53 and especially his detailed notes. For some of the social effects of and the reactions to these new merchants, see Roger Ladd, *Antimercantilism in Late Medieval English Literature* (New York: Palgrave Macmillan, 2010).

51. Dioneo's consistent location as each day's final speaker does not position his tale as a winner so much as complicator and ironizer, a stance Chaucer distributed differently throughout his collection.

52. Giovanni Boccaccio, *Decameron,* ed. Vittore Branca, 6th ed. (Torino: Einaudi, 1991), Int.110. English translation in *The Decameron,* trans. Mark Musa and Peter Bondanella (Harmondsworth: Penguin, 1982), 20.

53. Paul Strohm, *Social Chaucer* (Cambridge, MA: Harvard UP, 1989), 68. N. S. Thompson also notes that the brigata shows restraint in the way "potentially disruptive material" is handled; "they are chastely removed from the passions and desires they narrate," in *Chaucer, Boccaccio, and the Debate of Love* (Oxford: Clarendon, 1996), 268.

larly worries about the situation of the ten young nobles in his fiction. He protects supposedly real identities out of the "wish [that] any of them [not] be embarrassed in the future because of what they said and what they listened to—all of which [he] . . . recount[s]." He offers a historicizing explanation as well: "Today the laws relating to pleasure are rather strict, more so than at that time, when they were very lax" (12; "io non voglio che per le raccontate cose da loro, che seguono, e per l'ascoltate, nel tempo avvenire alcuna di loro possa prender vergogna, essendo oggi alquanto ristrette le leggi al piacere," Int.50). The author's concerns about his fiction are not limited to the way he organizes the group and keeps the social order intact. They are also the concerns of the brigata itself, seen in deflected form in their conversation with each other.

In confabulating plans to escape plague-ridden Florence for the countryside, Boccaccio's ladies voice analogous concerns, worrying just as much about traveling without male companionship and rule as about their safety away from the city. Filomena, "who was the most discerning" ("la quale descretissima era") articulates these anxieties: "Remember that we are all women, and any young girl can tell you that women do not know how to reason in a group when they are without the guidance of some man who knows how to control them. We are fickle, quarrelsome, suspicious, timid, and fearful, because of which I suspect that this company will soon break up without honor to any of us if we do not take a guide other than ourselves" (15–16; "Ricordivi che noi siam tutte femine, e non ce n'ha niuna sì fanciulla, che non possa ben conoscere come le femine sieno ragionate insieme e senza la provedenza d'alcuno uomo si sapiano regolare. Noi siamo mobili, ritrose, sospettose, pusillanime e paurose: per le quali cose io dubito forte, se noi alcuna altra guida non prendiamo che la nostra, che questa compagnia non si dissolva troppo più tosto e con meno onor di noi che non ci bisognerebbe," Int.74–75). None of Boccaccio's ladies exhibit the traits Filomena mentions, causing us to read these concerns as the expression of general cultural anxieties—about women living on their own outside of the city as well as traveling with young men to whom they are too tenuously attached. The Introduction thereby witnesses multiple anxieties about the decay and disorder precipitated by the plague. Leaving the polluted and dangerous confines of Florence for the countryside, one also leaves the security of its laws and regulations, its conventions and customs. Authorial concerns about tale-telling and topic are not separate from social concerns about status, propriety, and order; they are versions of each other. Even Boccaccio's description of the spreading of "gavocciole" ("bubboni," or "buboes," as the English would have it), marking the bodies of its victims and a sign of unavoidable death, participates in larger concerns for the ways the social fabric was similarly blotched and then ripped apart by fear of the pestilence, spread by even the slightest contact with an infected person's belongings, and the cruel attitudes toward the sick and dead that it inspired.

In this historical environment, competition is clearly something to be avoided as it further decays a social world already under threat. Each day in the countryside is ruled by a different member of the brigata so that power will be shared equally. Moreover, Boccaccio separates classes, keeping servants (and thus anyone outside the noble class) largely inaudible.[54] Not only is conflict within the aristocratic circle thereby forestalled from the very start, but, as Wallace notes, "The possibility of lower-order rebellion that might disturb the prescribed order of storytelling in the *Decameron* is entertained only by way of dramatizing its containment."[55] The comparison with Boccaccio's brigata and the organization of the *Decameron*'s tales, which, as Wallace argues, surely must have affected Chaucer's conception of the *Canterbury Tales*, is illuminating. If competition is a result of post-plague conditions (because of a shortage of labor), it was by no means an unproblematic one.

By contrast with Boccaccio, Chaucer actually cultivates the dissonance the Italian writer avoids: a multiplicity of voices, opinions, and perspectives without clear hierarchy. Indeed this description fits the depictions of the General Prologue's pilgrims, as much as it does the stories they tell.[56] Chaucer's narrator asks "to foryeve it me, / Al have I nat set folk in hir degree" (1.743–44), focusing his audience upon ideas of rank and order he supposedly neglected in his introduction of these figures. His loosely descending social order conflicts with other ways of accounting for "degree"—moral worth and material success, for example—that throws into some relief "the order of the disorder" Chaucer has theatrically produced.[57]

---

54. Of course, these voices can be heard from within Boccaccio's fictions, but they are contained, as it were, at that level of utterance. Similar to the way fabliaux were often contained in the very same aristocratic manuscripts that held courtly romances, Boccaccio's vision of the lower classes are circumscribed by the articulations of the aristocrats. Thus does Chaucer's invention of "a miller's tale"—that is, the naturalism of a working-class comedy in the mouth of a working-class figure—appear all the more striking.

55. Wallace, *Chaucerian Polity*, 30.

56. While Chaucer pretends to a lack of order in the General Prologue, many readers have pondered the shape he gives that disordered group and the different ways of organizing the pilgrims within and beyond estates categorizations. See, for instance, Harold Brooks, *Chaucer's Pilgrims: The Artistic Order of the Portraits in the Prologue* (New York: Barnes and Noble, 1962) and remarks by Wallace, *Chaucerian Polity*, 66–72.

57. This formulation is from Jacques Derrida, "Différance," in *The Margins of Philosophy*, trans. Alan Bass (Chicago: U of Chicago P, 1984), 1–28, at 4.

Some of this friction has been explained in terms of professional animosity, while others have looked to the ways the General Prologue allows the poet's methods of individuation and perspective to develop from the static gallery of portraits in moralizing genres like estates satire. Whether to be found in historical reality, personal experience, or satirical literary forms, Chaucer's poem rests on a productive sense of social conflict that other writers, including Langland and Gower, instinctively tried to quell.

As we have seen, Jill Mann's now classic study of the General Prologue reveals Chaucer's divergence from the "absolute standpoint" of the moral genre of estates satire.[58] Her work explores the techniques by which "Chaucer calls forth contradictory responses—a positive emotional or sensuous response, conflicting with an expectation that moral disapproval is called for—in order to make us feel the complexity of his characters. . . . Chaucer forces us to feel that we are dealing with real people because we cannot apply to them the absolute responses appropriate to the abstractions of moralistic satire" (189). Where an earlier generation saw these techniques as part of Chaucer's "genial" nature, more recent readers understand them in terms of Chaucer's astute political awareness.[59] On the one hand, such techniques soften whatever criticism his use of satiric types levels; on the other, such softening saves his own political skin—not only by blunting the point of such criticism and showing vice from its own point of view, but also by creating intermediary figures like the Host and the naïve narrating persona to deflect judgmental blows.

Comparing Chaucer's use of estates satire with both Gower's (in *Vox Clamantis* and the *Mirour de l'Homme*) and Langland's, Mann shows not only was it likely he knew and consulted the works of both poets as he was writing the *Canterbury Tales* but also the extent to which he diverges from their didacticism. Ultimately, she intimates that Chaucer shares more with Langland than had been at that time recognized and urges more attention in that direction. Mann looks to Langland, in fact, for the genesis of Chaucer's idea of a literary pilgrimage. Following the imagery in the Prologue to *Piers Plowman*, in which "Pilgrymes and palmeres · pliȝted hem togidere / . . . Thei went forth in here weye · with many wise tales" (*PPl Prol.* 46–48), she asks, "Is it not likely that although pilgrimages, both literal and allegorical, had been put to literary use elsewhere, it is Langland's picture of the roads of England thronged with minstrels, beggars, hermits and pilgrims travelling to Walsingham or London, Spain or Italy,

---

58. Mann, *Chaucer and Medieval Estates Satire*, 190.

59. Stephanie Trigg, *Congenial Souls: Reading Chaucer Medieval to Postmodern* (Minneapolis: U of Minnesota P, 2002); Patterson, *Subject of History.*

and enjoying the journey more than the arrival, that stimulated the ride to Canterbury?"[60] The image of Chaucer sitting with his friends' books before him and making a new work out of their material answers our desire for both a textual source to the fiction in the General Prologue and the spark of originality—what Stephen Greenblatt has elsewhere called "the touch of the real"—we sense there.[61] It answers our need, that is, with both historical conviction and personal investment, which is a version of what we see in the competition of the General Prologue itself. Tales on the road to Canterbury are familiar history, and the competition seems a representation of a personal investment, on Chaucer's part as much as Harry Bailly's. Ensuring a potential profit for the Tabard Host, the competition has also amounted to one for the London poet, the success of which possibly accounts for the illusion of authenticity in the first place.

With these considerations about the Canterbury frame, its relation to other textual models and genres, I have raised the issue of the origin of the competition in order to denaturalize its form. The success of Chaucer's fiction makes such denaturalization necessary. Issued in the General Prologue from a London innkeeper, the contest is certainly meant to look like a natural thing to do.[62] Offering "confort," "myrthe," "ese" without expense, "and it shal coste noght" (1.767–73), Bailly's gesture appears part of the "rekenynge" atmosphere of the Southwark inn (1.760). Readers have certainly commented on the lively way the Host gathers the pilgrims together, joins their company, and organizes the game as their "governour, / And of oure tales juge and reportour" (1.813–14).[63] His motivations (to escape work, his nagging wife, or to secure another large group of customers upon their return) have been the subject of some speculation. But Chaucer's motivations, less so; we tend not to want to think in these terms.[64] We are skittish about Chaucer, unsure of his biography, and absolutely terrified to put the two together in other than purely institutional ways. Where

---

60. Mann, *Chaucer and Medieval Estates Satire*, 211. Mann cites the Prologue to *Piers Plowman* from the edition of W.W. Skeat, *Piers Plowman*, 2 vols. (Oxford: Clarendon P, 1886) rpt. 1961.

61. Stephen Greenblatt, "The Touch of the Real," *Representations* 59 (1997): 14–29.

62. But that naturalism perhaps only makes this fiction all the more rife for our investigation. See, in an analogous context, Miller's account of the "naturalist" logic of the Miller and his tale in "Naturalism and Its Discontents," chapter 1 of *Philosophical Chaucer*, 36–81.

63. On the Host, see Cynthia Richardson, "The Function of the Host in *The Canterbury Tales*," *TSLL* 12 (1970): 325–44; and Barbara Page, "Concerning the Host," *Chaucer Review* 4 (1970): 1–13.

64. Some earlier critics argue for continuity between the *Canterbury Tales* and French dream poems, seeing the dream form as a precursor to the indeterminacy of tellers' stories—both have similar relations to authority. See Howard, *Idea*, 155 and Jordan, *Chaucer's Poetics*, 188ff. For the ways Chaucer may be motivated to take his distant stance by his precarious court position, see David Carlson, *Chaucer's Jobs* (New York: Palgrave Macmillan, 2004).

competition is surely a part of court politics and procedure as well as a basis for economic activity in the late fourteenth century, which Chaucer would have known intimately from his youth (as a prosperous vintner's son who gained a lifetime position proximate to the royal households and city bureaucracies of London), we have failed to consider the terms of competition for Chaucer the poet, not to mention the ways in which competition and aggression underwrite human subjectivity and its social investment in and through language more generally.[65] I advance the issue in terms of Chaucer himself because of his two most strikingly original decisions: to use different narrators to take responsibility for the tales in the collection and to conjoin journey to tale-telling contest. Whether he does so to cover himself politically and doctrinally or because he is enthralled by the deconstructive play of the voiced text, *avant la lettre*, the contest and competition among pilgrims appear to be Chaucer's alone.[66]

Bailly's competition gives form and purpose to the tales' relation to each other, leaving the poem as anything but a mundane miscellany or mere collection, like the *Gesta Romanorum*. Is this, in fact, one of the poem's silent claims to the modernity many have attributed to it? Far from the "quiet hierarchies" we once assumed the Middle Ages to embrace, we find a social contest (perhaps like the pilgrimage route it follows) with variously profit-driven ends.[67] But to situate the tales in some kind of protocapitalist or salvationist structure does not explain or explain away the deformations that come with its powerful competitiveness. Restricting competition to economic context threatens to oversimplify the range of questions I mean to raise with this kind of historical contextualization.

Substitution, I have argued, organizes the stories and accounts for their relation in Chaucer's poem. It is how one tale comes to take the

---

65. Writing from the position of an independent scholar and professional performer of the *Canterbury Tales*, Baba Brinkman provides one of the few considerations of the importance of competition in the fame of the poem. See "Wrestling for the Ram: Competition and Feedback in *Sir Thopas* and *The Canterbury Tales*," *LATCH* 3 (2010): 107–33. Brinkman compares it to the competitive work of jongleurs and the professional scene of performance in the courts described by Richard Firth Green in *Poets and Princepleasers: Literature and the English Court in the Late Middle Ages* (Toronto: U of Toronto P, 1980).

66. Paradigmatic here is the groundbreaking work of Leicester in the introduction to *Disenchanted Self* in dealing with an array of issues long affecting Chaucer studies, including the relation of Chaucer to his narrating figures, as well as the relation of poststructuralist theory to historicism, especially pp. 16–18. In further defense of Leicester's pursuit of the text beyond the terms available to it, we might turn to historicist Paul Strohm, *Theory and the Premodern Text* (Minneapolis: U of Minnesota P, 2000) and the much more playful George Edmondson, "Naked Chaucer," in *The Post-Historical Middle Ages*, ed. Elizabeth Scala and Sylvia Federico (New York: Palgrave Macmillan, 2009), 139–60.

67. This term is Robertson's; see *Preface to Chaucer*, 51.

foregrounded position of another, and it is what articulates their aggressive, displacing force without ever asserting any necessary development or progress—we are not building up to something per se. We could again make recourse to Derrida's order of the disorder found in this substitutive structure. Desire governs the process of substitution (one tale in place of the last; one signifier in place of another) fueled by misrecognition (an image in the place of something else). Insofar as the subject (as a split being) emerges from desire and its linguistic substitutions, that scene of misrecognition is also a scene of misreading and misinterpretation, which are, not surprisingly, the particular concerns (and effects) of many of Chaucer's stories. It thus might be fully expected that the pilgrims most explicitly concerned and thus critically associated with desire, Chaucer's Wife and Pardoner, would also be the most notorious misreaders of texts.[68] For instance, symptomatic of the desires propelling her movements are the misreadings the Wife of Bath offers to account for her thoughts and opinions. Far from characterizing her particularly (as they have often been read), these misreadings provide an origin for the literary and critical misreadings that continue to dominate her. Those that follow in the marriage group are only the most localized of these. As far as the Canterbury pilgrims go, Alison may be the most notorious of Chaucer's misreaders: "Witnesse on Myda—wol ye heere the tale?" (3.951). But there is no narrator on the pilgrimage who is not a misreader of another story, either one that has been told on the journey or a familiar source that underwrites a pilgrim's particular version. The difference between the ways one tells a story and its source has always been important to our investigation of Chaucer's purpose and design. Setting those textual transformations within the fiction of the storytelling voyage, however, restages such derivation as deviation, misreading, and misrecognition. Thus the Wife's misreading does not make her idiosyncratic; it makes her an archetypal narrator of the *Tales*.

Even more importantly, misreading is a trope deployed by the *Canterbury Tales* itself in both global and local terms. If the critical industry operating for and around Chaucer avoids misreading as its primary goal—arguing for the validity or superiority of its readings as a *raison d'être*—the individual Canterbury tales themselves use misreading in extraordinarily

---

68. Robertson's condemnation of the Wife's interpretive skills as a carnal misreader of texts is well known, but various critics have looked at her textual expertise, including Mary Carruthers, "The Wife of Bath and the Painting of Lions," *PMLA* 94 (1979): 209–22; Judith Ferster, *Chaucer on Interpretation* (Cambridge: Cambridge UP, 1985); and Alastair Minnis, *Fallible Authors: Chaucer's Pardoner and the Wife of Bath* (Philadelphia: U of Pennsylvania P, 2008).

productive ways. From Chaunticleer's misreading of the Bible, "*Mulier est hominis confusio*," in the Nun's Priest's Tale (7.3164) to the awkward, misplaced, and misused examples in the Manciple's Tale, to the ill-fitting morals concluding the Physician's and Friar's Tales, a certain kind of willful misreading drives the stories in the collection. It is the poem's basic gesture as well as its method of self-generation. Even as it is thematized within the tales, misreading, like misrecognition, is the mark of desire behind and beyond each narrative. In a deep sense, then, the *Canterbury Tales* cannot be read so much as misread. The *Tales* function (and have historically functioned) as a place to locate desire, whether that be for a Protestant Chaucer, who could be exonerated from Henry VIII's ban on popish books or a Chaucer-the-nature-poet immortalized in the pages of William Morris's *Kelmscott Chaucer*. Much like the Canterbury pilgrims, then, scholars have been productively misreading tales in the form of what they write in response to them all along.

Like misreading, desire is a function of the signifier. Insofar as the signifier is the primary unit of language, the signifier brings desire into being and makes misreading possible. Each an effect of the other, desire and misreading share an intimate relation. We misread according to our desire; the mark of our desire appears as a misreading. Such remarks are typically devoted to modern subjects of analysis, but Chaucer's medieval text indexes the relevance of these ideas in an exceptionally telling way. Precisely because of its historical distance and linguistic difference, as well as its more precarious variability in a manuscript culture, the medieval text is always acutely in danger of being misread and thus subject to our desires upon it.[69] And far from a historical anomaly, the Middle Ages resonates with desire in forceful and far-reaching ways. We have long claimed the Middle Ages as the source of our forms of erotic desire via the discourse of courtly love. And as a number of recent critical readers have shown, our interest in the Middle Ages is caught up in the traces of desire we have been dreaming since our earliest childhood, and much of our fantasy is still caught up in its narratives and scenarios.[70] This play of fantasy and historical form has been a source of embarrassment, out of which our historical rigor has partially been created.[71] We divide work from play, ethics

---

69. See my chapter on "Desire" in *A Handbook of Middle English Studies*, ed. Marion Turner (Malden and Oxford: Wiley-Blackwell, 2013), 49–62.

70. Fradenburg, "Simply Marvelous"; on the power of our medievalist fantasies, see Marilynn Desmond's introduction to *Ovid's Art and The Wife of Bath: The Ethics of Erotic Violence* (Ithaca: Cornell UP, 2006).

71. On this paradox, see Stephanie Trigg and Thomas Prendergast, "The Negative Erotics of Medievalism," in Scala and Federico, 117–37.

from enjoyment. The harder it is to do Medieval studies, the more seriously we can take its literary productions (however naïvely enjoyable they once were) and ourselves. But such division and resistance merely betray the centrality of a desire otherwise denied.

Discussions of desire appear everywhere dispersed in the critical tradition about the *Canterbury Tales*. And yet, desire has not been read literally as the subject of the General Prologue, has not been invoked in the large-scale, productively structural sense I have articulated here for the entire poem. Both the pilgrimage and the professional capacities of the pilgrims have trumped desire as organizing rubrics and interpretive frames, particularly because of the historical specificity with which they imbue Chaucer's stories. Yet that prioritization makes for a kind of opposition between religious and worldly concerns we have already seen problematized by the General Prologue's opening. Often conflated with the pilgrims' individual personalities, and thus with treating them somewhat unfairly as "real" people, desire gets misunderstood as merely the object each of these narrators (or their fictional counterparts) would possess. In this way desire is held at the level of content and treated as a theme of particular tales. Desire must instead also be understood structurally as the relation to lack around which subjects and tales are constellated. Desire is the subject of the *Canterbury Tales* in a number of ways, and this book seeks to delineate that subject through the diverse generic forms Chaucer's storytelling contest deploys. In chapters primarily devoted to the Knight's romance, the Reeve's fabliau, the Wife's magical tale, the Clerk's exemplary rejoinder, and the moral offerings of the Physician and Second Nun, as well as by numerous references to other stories in the collection, I show the ways desire—and the signifiers by which it circulates—pervades and constitutes the discourse of the *Canterbury Tales*. Yet, far from suggesting that desire, both critical and textual, operates over the *Canterbury Tales* as some new and startling discovery, I would emphasize the way our readings—or, better, our misreadings—have paid witness to desire all along.

one

"WE WITEN NAT WHAT THING WE PREYEN HEERE"

Desire, Knowledge, and the Ruse of Satisfaction in the Knight's Tale

Writing about the *Canterbury Tales*, it is difficult not to begin with the Knight, whose long, ornate story both calls out for and has received so much critical attention. And it is perhaps Chaucer who has engineered it that way. The General Prologue narrator makes his own selection of the Knight as the first pilgrim to be described sound like an accident, a random choice, but we know it is part of a design, much like the Knight's Tale itself, a design that imitates chance. The Knight is the first to be described, the first to be called forth to "draweth cut" (1.838), and, as the winner of that competition, the first to tell his tale. For the highest-ranking secular pilgrim in the company, this triplet of "firsts" can be no accident. Made to look like "aventure, or sort, or cas" (1.844) by both the narrator and Tabard host Harry Bailly, the Knight is deliberately granted priority in fictional Prologue and tale-telling game alike.[1] Put this way, it is difficult to read the position of the Knight as anything but deliberate. It is almost certain that matters would have concluded with the Knight's Tale too, if the pilgrims had returned from Canterbury and the contest were settled. Given Bailly's priorities and social awareness, it is hard to imagine his judgment (like the drawing of straws) going any other way.

---

1. Harry Bailly's machinations to fix the straw-drawing contest in the Knight's favor have been recognized since E. T. Donaldson's Commentary on the tale in *Chaucer's Poetry: An Anthology for the Modern Reader, Second edition* (New York: Harper Collins, 1975), 1061.

This first tale has always been important to understandings of the *Canterbury Tales,* in terms of both its organization and its thematic interests. Whether one sees the Knight's Tale as a font of imagery, ideas, and motifs from which the other tales draw or as the institutional and ideological origin from which the other tales recede, revolt, and turn away, there is hardly a reading of the *Canterbury Tales* that can avoid the story altogether.[2] This is perhaps what it means to hold primary status, to set the contest in motion, even if the tale competes with no other, since no one has spoken before. It's what the Host calls "unbokel[ing] . . . the male" (1.3115), opening the pouch or purse, at the end of the Knight's performance to indicate that "the game is wel bigonne" (1.3117). But the tale clearly means more than what it articulates at its surface. In the context developed by the General Prologue, the Knight's fiction of desire is also implicated at a structural level in another desiring discourse the *Canterbury Tales* proffers.

Few of Chaucer's tales are as explicit about desire's centrality and significance. "Desire" (and its alternate forms) appears fourteen times in the Knight's narrative, more than any other fiction in the *Canterbury Tales.* Only the Parson uses the word twice more than the Knight, and this we might expect from a teller that refuses the pleasures of fiction and fable, and instead produces a redaction of a confessional manual.[3] As a prose translation of Raymund de Pennaforte's *Summa de poenitentiae,* the Parson's Tale offers a means to expose a sinner's struggle with desire to his confessor. Not wholly unlike such an aid to confession, the courtly romance itself is a form of exploring the contours of and inner struggles with desire, and this is what the Knight's Tale offers in much of its stylized language and classical "guise." Taken in toto, the Knight's Tale operates as an elegant meditation on erotic and worldly desire, managing it through various forms of sublimation, which appear as the tale's courtly love romance *and* the Boethian "prime mover" speech at its close—a philosophy that would assimilate the romance narrative's outcome to its metaphysical goals.

This description of the story makes the romance sound far less difficult than has been critically registered. Readers often express a lingering "discomfort" with the Knight's Tale, some even refusing to read it as romance.[4] While abbreviating his Italian source, Boccaccio's *Teseida,* Chaucer mangles,

---

2. For the Knight as thematic origin of many of the tales, see Helen Cooper, *The Structure of the Canterbury Tales* (London: Duckworth, 1984).

3. On the ways the Parson's Tale indulges in that which it disavows, see Nicole Smith, "The Parson's Predilection for Pleasure," *SAC* 28 (2006): 117–40.

4. See J. A. Burrow, "The *Canterbury Tales* I: Romance," in *The Cambridge Companion to Chaucer,* ed. Piero Boitani and Jill Mann, 2nd ed. (1986; Cambridge: Cambridge UP, 2003), 143–59, at 155.

some have argued, any clear sense of genre.⁵ And this problem may be grounded in the *Teseida*'s origin in book 12 of Statius's *Thebiad*—itself echoed in the Knight's Tale's Statian epigraph—where the claims of epic muddle the expectations of romance. A principal complaint against the Knight's story concerns Chaucer's flat characterization, seen in contradistinction to the more rounded figures in *Troilus and Criseyde,* another classical romance based on a Boccaccian source that Chaucer was simultaneously reworking. Yet that very flatness in characterization makes other matters more distinct. The Knight's Tale practically diagrams the workings of desire through its often awkward means of dispensing with the distractions of human attraction, the play-acting and the gossiping that constitutes the representation of falling in love that *Troilus and Criseyde* anatomizes in dramatic detail. Almost all of that poem's second book is devoted to representing an unrepresentable change in feeling and self-awareness, first in Troilus, and then in Criseyde, through their individual conversations with Pandarus, who encourages and reveals to each of them the fine qualities of the other. But desire hits the knights Palamon and Arcite instantaneously and with complete force. They do not need to "know" Emily, the object of their desire, in any specific way. Neither do they need to be coaxed into relation with her, as Troilus must through Pandarus's excessive orchestrations. There is no back and forth, for instance, between Theseus and Emily to introduce her to masculine subjects inside and outside the poem, as if her particular attractions were necessary to ground her position in fantasy.⁶

Romances chronicle a pursuit of desire and proliferate in cycles and continuations, as well as in the parody of courtly conventions offered by the fabliaux. Such pursuits occur at the level of plot but also within actions and behaviors that would otherwise seem to derail it. In Ruth Parkin-Gounelas's words, "In lacking the satisfying object, desire endlessly pursues a phantom satisfaction," what appears in the Knight's Tale as the arguing, posturing, praying, fighting that supplants any kind of possession of the love object, "deriving *jouissance* only from the pursuit."⁷ Her claim makes

---

5. John Finlayson, "The *Knight's Tale*: The Dialogue of Romance, Epic, and Philosophy," *Chaucer Review* 27 (1992): 126–49, at 142. Admitting that Chaucer's omissions from and compressions of Boccaccio's *Teseida* result in the tale's "concentra[tion] on the rivalry of Arcite and Palamon for Emily," Finlayson argues that epic also rivals romance within the Knight's Tale. For him the clash of genres "mirrors the basic conflict in the poem between the social responsibilities and existence of the knights and their individual, internal desires" (129).

6. On Criseyde's position in critical masculine fantasy, see Carolyn Dinshaw's reading of the Donaldson–Robertson debate about *Troilus and Criseyde* in *Chaucer's Sexual Poetics* (Madison: U of Wisconsin P, 1991), 28–39.

7. Ruth Parkin-Gounelas, *Literature and Psychoanalysis: Intertextual Readings* (New York: Palgrave, 2001), 83.

sense of the particular enjoyments of romance—which come from the implicated and intricate middle—enjoyments of desiring itself in a genre that nearly defines the Middle Ages in the popular imagination. These pursuits, the detours of adventure rather than their ends, make for what Patricia Parker has called "inescapable romance," and it has been inescapably captivating for medieval and modern audiences alike.[8] In this genre, conclusions are awkward, abrupt, and far less satisfying or memorable than the detoured, delayed, and painfully enjoyable middle parts. More interested in these extended middles, romances tend to end swiftly once their objective is reached or their detour can no longer be sustained, as at the close of the Wife of Bath's Tale. Her ending, "And thus they lyve unto hir lyves ende / In parfit joye" (3.1257–58), offers only a slightly more elaborate "happily ever after" than the Knight's own conclusion: "Thus endeth Palamon and Emelye" (1.3107). Further examples could be multiplied, since this abrupt close to the Knight's Tale is as awkwardly conventional as everything else in the story, where enjoyment is clearly in the middle rather than its end(s).

Chaucer's changes to Boccaccio make the Knight's Tale more clearly about desire too, which is precisely what we find so disturbing. Interested in something other than character, Chaucer scripts Emily differently from her Italian counterpart Emilia, who plays a much larger part in Boccaccio's poem, where her name appears in its subtitle, *Teseida delle nozze di Emilia*. Vacant and undeveloped, Chaucer's Emily has been widely disappointing to the Knight's readers, and her absence from the romance a subject of critical vexation.[9] Making matters unpalatable for modern readers, the knights' immediate and all-consuming passion for this barely glimpsed lady seems too far-fetched to be believed and too remote from our interests.[10]

---

8. Patricia Parker, *Inescapable Romance* (Princeton: Princeton UP, 1979). On narrative's fetishistic methods of delay, see Peter Brooks, *Reading For the Plot: Design and Intention in Narrative* (New York: Vintage, 1983). Brooks focuses on nineteenth-century realist fiction where the fabrications by which desire's gratification is frustrated appear fantastically coincidental. But such fabrications appear almost natural to medieval stories, which are unrestricted by such realist expectations. See especially 32–35.

9. John Ganim calls Emily "too undeveloped to even be enigmatic." See "Chaucerian Ritual and Patriarchal Performance," *Chaucer Yearbook* 1 (1992): 65–86, at 66. Critical interest in the structural role her absence plays in the Knight's story can be easily related to the patriarchal assumptions underwriting the heroic conquest and repression of Amazons. See my *Absent Narratives: Manuscript Textuality and Literary Structure in Late Medieval England* (New York: Palgrave Macmillan, 2002), chap. 3; Elaine Tuttle Hansen, "Women-as-the-Same in the A-Fragment," in *Chaucer and the Fictions of Gender* (Berkeley: U of California P, 1992), 209–44; and Mark Sherman, "The Politics of Discourse in Chaucer's Knight's Tale," *Exemplaria* 6 (1994): 87–114.

10. Mark Miller helpfully styles this aspect of the tale "the aestheticizing voyeurism of masculine desire [that] here seems flat and clichéd, so familiar in the Middle Ages and today that it is hardly

And yet, with such starkly presented conventions the Knight's Tale thereby distills the workings of desire to a bare form that makes its operations that much easier to see as a force pressuring the figures in the tale. In other words, by minimizing the attention of these chivalric subjects to the particularity of the object (hence Emily's minimal characterization and almost complete lack of speech), Chaucer's awkwardly literal adherence to the dictates of courtly love readily display the operations of desire beyond its various and changeable objects.[11] But if the tale is thus explicitly about *desire*, naming "desir" as its subject in various places, it is also *about* desire, skirting its terrain and transformations, in ways less easy to recognize. The Knight's Tale is a story that articulates desire in ways that drive the poem's larger competitive structure.

Emily's noncharacterization is not the only swerve Chaucer makes from Boccaccio. The rigorous leveling of Palamon and Arcite works as another strategy to make the hero of his romance, like its heroine, nearly impossible to recognize. Where *Teseida* clearly marks Arcita as the nobler knight throughout, not merely in the tournament, the Knight's Tale works incredibly hard to equalize its figures.[12] One of Chaucer's major changes to the *Teseida*'s plot has Palamon spying Emily first, which he uses (and some readers would concur) as a means of arguing his prior claim to the lady. But rather than grant Palamon the priority he would himself urge, Chaucer here looks to rebalance the scales in his version of the story by tipping matters away from Arcite's elevated status in this source. Unlike Boccaccio who clearly prefers his Arcita, Chaucer means for us to conflate the knights, and his strategies for doing so often make their relationship to each other the center of attention. But the rebalancing act has not been easy. Their separation out of the Theban "taas of bodyes" (1.1005) occurs in somewhat conflating (and thus confusing) terms. In one and the same scene we have two nearly identical cousins, individuated by the sight of Emily but also continually equated with each other, pulling us forward and backward in the romance's supposed progress.

---

even recognizable." See his *Philosophical Chaucer: Love, Sex, and Agency in the "Canterbury Tales"* (Cambridge: Cambridge UP, 2004), 6.

11. Finlayson characterizes Chaucer's refinement of the genre of epic into romance by these terms: "The depersonalization of the characters moves us away from the epic concern with the collision between character and circumstance and turns us to the romance preoccupation with the emotion itself, or the nature of the predicament rather than the protagonists" ("Dialogue" 130).

12. On Arcite's more clearly heroic depiction in *Teseida*, see Boitani, "Style, Iconography and Narrative: The Lesson of the *Teseida*," in *Chaucer and the Italian Trecento*, ed. Boitani (Cambridge: Cambridge UP, 1983), 185–99. Images of Arcita in the manuscripts of Boccaccio's poem show a distinct resemblance to the portrait of the author presenting his book to Fiammetta.

Palamon's sigh, "A!," from the prison window as he first alights his gaze on Emily roaming in the garden, announces the shaping force of the image he sees before him. Her position in the garden a-Maying, gathering flowers "party white and rede" (1.1053) that are the mixed signs of virginity, sexual maturity, and the kind of eroticized seasonality with which the General Prologue opened, arrests Palamon's attention and breaks in upon what had formerly been a state of nearly undifferentiated union with Arcite. But that selfsame gesture, "A!," turns Arcite's attention to the source of his cousin's pain and visits Palamon's injury upon him as well "as muche as he, or moore" (1.1116). What individuates the two cousins also equalizes them.[13] Before Emily wounds Arcite, he responds verbally to Palamon's cry:

> And *with that cry* Arcite anon up sterte
> And seyde, "Cosyn myn, what eyleth thee,
> That art so pale and deedly on to see?
> Why cridestow? Who hath thee doon offence?
> For Goddes love, taak al in pacience
> Oure prisoun, for it may noon oother be.
> Fortune hath yeven us this adversitee.
> Som wikke aspect or disposicioun
> Of Saturne, by some constellacioun,
> Hath yeven us this, although we hadde it sworn;
> So stood the hevene whan that we were born.
> We moste endure it; this is the short and playn."
> (1.1080–91; my emphasis)

Their joint imprisonment and shared "adversitee," which also happens to be a conjoined fate, is broken in the space of a few sighs. In fact, it is broken "with that cry," Palamon's "A!"—a single letter. The power of the signifier has never been so dramatically demonstrated. Each knight is "wounded soore" by the sight of Emily, sure that this will be his end, in Palamon's words, this "wol my bane be" (1.1097). What began as a joint fate that they "moste endure" (1.1091) together ends as the same individually experienced pain. Palamon answers Arcite's question as to what ails him by describing the lady in the garden and offering prayer to Venus. But his words also turn Arcite's attention to her:

---

13. On the (non) individuation of Palamon and Arcite, see Elizabeth Edwards, "The *Knight's Tale* and the Work of Mourning," *Exemplaria* 20 (2008): 361–84. She describes the poem as "not about *individuality* but about *singularity*. It is about what is irreplaceable, that for which there can be no substitute" (366; emphasis in original).

> And with that word Arcite gan espye
> Wher as this lady romed to and fro,
> And with that sighte hir beautee hurte hym so,
> That, if that Palamon was wounded sore,
> Arcite is hurt as muche as he, or moore.
> (1.1112–16)

Palamon's "word," like his earlier "cry," shifts Arcite's gaze to Emily in a gesture triangulating their functions as cause and effect. Chaucer's syntax establishes the conflating, equalizing function of love upon both knights, acknowledging the conditionality of Palamon's "wound" in terms of Arcite's "as muche as he, or moore." In both differentiating and equating the two knights, Chaucer's deviation from *Teseida* allows the tale to anatomize the desire inspired in the General Prologue, "by nature," more closely, but it also perplexes us as to what to do with a romance with two heroes and no villain.

For some this leveling of romance protagonists has been taken as part of the Boethian philosophizing of the Knight's story. In confusing us as to which deserves happiness, the story can focus its attention on Theseus as a better example of noble maturity, thus making the romance a story of judgment, wisdom, and interpretation rather than heroic action, almost all of which is disappointingly thwarted. No one's actions can decide much of anything. For others, however, the imperative to judge "Who hath the worse, Arcite or Palamoun?" (1.1348) is central. And while some have turned to historicized categories, heroic and moral, to judge them, little has been firmly decided.[14] Underlying such efforts is not so much the problem of defining the hero (Boccaccio did that), but what to do with the other? Lacan's philosophical orientation in his writing helps us read the complexity of desire as Chaucer presents it here, precisely, in terms of the others(s) located in its structure.[15] So, too, Chaucer's story violates our expectations of romance by engaging this other in the story rather than getting rid of

---

14. The attempt to distinguish the two with philosophical and theological terms begins early in the critical tradition; see, for instance, Hoxie Fairchild, "Active Arcite, Contemplative Palamon," *JEGP* 26 (1927): 285–93. And, though more evenly weighted by most critics, the desire to judge persists; see Catherine Rock, "Forsworn and Fordone: Arcite as Oath-Breaker in the *Knight's Tale*," *Chaucer Review* 40 (2006): 416–32.

15. On phenomenological orientation of the importance of otherness in Lacan's theory, see Judith Butler, *Subjects of Desire: Hegelian Reflections in Twentieth-Century France* (New York: Columbia UP, 1987; rpt.1999); and the introductions to Seminar II by Jacques-Alain Miller in *Reading Seminars I and II: Lacan's Return to Freud*, ed. Richard Feldstein, Bruce Fink, and Maire Jaanus (Buffalo: State U of New York P, 1996), 3–35.

him. It forms Chaucer's principal means of pursuing desire rather than character in the tale.

Desire appears to relate a subject and an object, here a knight and his beloved, yet this situation is *imaginary* in the Knight's Tale, even a bit delusional, in more ways than one. Palamon fundamentally misrecognizes the object upon which he gazes (even before he mistakes her for Venus) and is struck in the heart by "the fairnesse of that lady that [he] see[s] / Yond in the gardyn romen to and fro" (1.1098–99). In the reflective surface that she offers is each knight's own ideal-image (as one worthy to be loved by her) and a rival, who is greater (because more whole, deserving, and attractive) than the unarmed, imprisoned Theban himself can possibly feel. These ambivalences apply to both Palamon and Arcite. Recalling the primary identification of the Mirror Stage, such a moment repeats its proliferation of images and affects. The scene's Imaginary dimension is especially palpable since (as so many of its readers have noted) Chaucer's Emily is completely unaware of either of them, and as such plays the part of the courtly *domna*—cold, cruel, and indifferent—without ever knowing it.

Because we know that both knights are fundamentally mistaken, enraptured by what they think they see as they gaze out the window, any simple relation of two (Palamon–Emily; Arcite–Emily; Palamon–Arcite) is mediated by a third term. Such mediation occurs here on a number of levels, multiplying the other(s) on the scene. Of course, at the story's surface the familial and martial unity of Palamon and Arcite is broken upon Emily's arrival. So too any connection (no matter how one-sided) between Palamon and Emily is already disrupted by Arcite's presence even before his repetition of Palamon's desiring look and wounding "as muche as he, or moore." But the tale's articulation of complex feelings and associations, projections and imitations, in the different ways Arcite and Palamon see matters goes beyond this surface (hence why matters explode into violence instantaneously). Operating in what Lacan calls the Imaginary, an imaginary and even delusional dimension, Palamon has already begun to see himself as someone different after his gaze alights on Emily.

Much more is going on in their heads and in their hearts, as their set speeches to each other (and to themselves) mean to suggest and as they have been traditionally understood. The machinery of an overpowering bodily change, wounding the heart with an arrow from Love's bow as described in the detailed allegorical representation in Guillaume's section of the *Romance of the Rose* (a text Chaucer translated), is invoked by the Knight as both men are irremediably affected by Emily.[16] Chaucer's language for this imagi-

---

16. The God of Love castigates Chaucer for this translation in the Prologue to the *Legend of Good Women* (F.327–32).

nary dimension is as visual as Lacan's, dominated by the eye (1.1096ff.) through which these men are hurt. Where Lacan already situates the rival in this imaginary dimension as a misrecognized projection of the ego itself, Chaucer will explore the relation of this ego, each knight's self-image, to the rival throughout the story—its imaginary aspect persists even as his characters attempt to negotiate matters of their imagined rights (to Emily) or bonds (to each other as "brother") through language, the realm of the Symbolic. The knights do not merely look and feel, pinioned by Cupid's dart ("hurt right now thurghout myn ye / Into myn herte," 1.1096–97); they speak out, owning their desire through the signifier—"A!"—that they use to name it.

We have always read these speeches as importantly distinguishing these two knightly figures. The particular ways Palamon and Arcite assume the signifier here—the terms they choose to express their condition, their worth, their abjection, their confusion, essentially their claim to be the hero and protagonist of the story, as well as the terms that wind up designating their position (intended or not) in the larger social order—have always been important to Chaucer's readers if not articulated in the Lacanian terms I invoke. The words Palamon and Arcite choose are, of course, their own, and they have served to distinguish Palamon's dreamy-eyed goddess worship from Arcite's pragmatic calculations for some time. But they do not fully own them, nor can they. Language precedes and is far more capacious than any individual speaker's (or writer's, for that matter) range, which is why it works within and beyond mere intention. The other(s) at play in this scene are not merely other people, or the others we see in our self-image (the ideal, the rival) in our moments of identification, but also the Other, the big Other out there that inhabits us: the world of language, rules, and law into which we are born. Palamon and Arcite articulate their desire in terms of this Other (indeed there are no other terms). Not only using language to express what they feel and want, they are also colonized by this system of words, which has taught them what to desire and how to desire it. In Lacan's famous formulation, "man's desire is the Other's desire [*le désir de l'homme est le désir de l'Autre*]."[17] The fundamental impasse of human desire appears "de l'Autre," "of the Other" (Lacan 689) and, specifically, "of the Other as the locus of the signifier" (688) in a multiplicity of linguistic positions, as we have seen earlier, that any explanation of this phrase entails. This verbal multiplicity articulates the mode in which desire (the recognition of the subject's own lack)

---

17. Jacques Lacan, "The Subversion of the Subject and the Dialectic of Desire in the Freudian Unconscious," in *Écrits: The First Complete Edition in English*, trans. Bruce Fink (New York: Norton, 2006), 671–702, at 690. All of Lacan's essays are cited from this translation.

comes into being by installing a third term that multiplies and triangulates the experience of wanting. This third term reveals the desirability of the object and the rivalrous, even violent, nature of desire itself. Because of the way this third and other term competes with the subject over the object and potentially finds the subject itself lacking *as* an object, "envy and resentment," in Slavoj Žižek's words, "are a constitutive component of human desire."[18]

Lacan's description of desire and its concomitant aggressivity makes sense of why attention in the Knight's romance is so much more focused on Palamon and Arcite's interactions with each other rather than on Emily herself, even while the tale strives to position her as the sublime object of courtly desire. What makes the Knight's Tale strange, then, are the estranging and alienating operations of desire upon the subject via the intrusion of a third term—one that figures the entirety of the social world to which the subject thereby lays claim. In this social world we see the political upshot of such love, the social position that being in some kind of love will permit. In the Knight's Tale, we see the centrality of this Symbolic order in the overdetermination of the issue of Theban obedience: why Theseus doubly secures the fealty of Thebes to Athens. The marriage of Palamon and Emily is overdetermined and redundant, as the Theban princes have already sworn the obedience to him *before* the tournament in which he offered Emily as prize. Palamon has thus been subdued by treaty and oath, a far more elaborate set of social contracts, before the marriage takes place or Theseus imagines its explicitly political function at the tale's end.

In the Knight's narrative of courtly desire, Palamon and Arcite provide this other desire and third term for one another, since their interest in the feminine object is sustained largely through a fantasy of what the other wants, perhaps even envy of what the other might attain. Since it is "qua Other that [the subject] desires," the subject learns to desire from the viewpoint of another: friends and rivals that he knows; the mentor that he imitates; the social world that forms his taste and prejudices.[19] In struggling through and against their desire, Palamon and Arcite thus spend far more time arguing (and eventually fighting) than they do in the presence or contemplation of the lady. Indeed, the two knights complain about their

---

18. Slavoj Žižek, *How to Read Lacan* (New York: Norton, 2006), 36.

19. Lacan, "Subversion of the Subject," 690. This is where the Knight's Tale begins to resemble René Girard's mimetic triangle, a synchronic snapshot of the envy and imitation at the heart of desiring. Derived from but ultimately very different from Lacan, Girard's formulation of "mimetic desire" has been useful for critics to complicate the positions involved in desire's structures. For a discussion of the tale using Girard as an interpretive lens, see Laurel Amtower, "Mimetic Desire and the Misappropriation of the Ideal in the *Knight's Tale*," *Exemplaria* 8 (1996): 125–44.

lack in terms of what the other knight supposedly enjoys. In this way we can see beyond the "love" we regularly characterize as the emotion evoked by desire, the more violent and aggressive impulses that make Palamon and Arcite appear far more interested in each other.

The Knight's Tale's own particular version of this courtly fantasy further specifies the lady's rejection and historicizes its origin (she wants to remain an Amazon maiden) and the others to whom the subject must come into relation (Theseus–Palamon–Arcite) in order to experience desire. But if the Knight's Tale distills for us the triangulation of self, other, and object in the desires of its two knights in love with Emily, it also shows us how the relation of subject and object reduces to one—how, in Lacan's words, "the sexual relation . . . does not exist."[20] For there is no objective other with which the subject relates, only a displacement of itself, an alienating self-difference. In this way, as Mark Miller has argued, "the longing the Thebans feel for Emily is [contained in] the way she bodies forth for them the perfected form of their own being."[21] Courtly love thus becomes a means of managing the absence of a sexual relation elegantly. The lady, the *objet petit a*, "is the strange object that is nothing but the inscription of the subject itself in the field of objects."[22] This means that the object of desire is a fantasy; it bears little relation to objects in the real world and is far more closely related to the subject that is doing the desiring in the first place. Yet again Chaucer gets romance right by making desire look so wrong. The tale's alienated and distant heroine who wants nothing to do with either of her suitors, and who seeks an entirely different historical and cultural existence with the maidens of Diana, might more simply be saying "there is no sexual relation," even as she is forced to participate in its social inscription as she later watches their tournament conflict from a tower window, replicating their initial view of her.

That Emily is wed in the end to the one who never imagines *her* desire perhaps testifies in Chaucer's ironic terms to this lack of sexual relation

---

20. Jacques Lacan, *On Feminine Sexuality, the Limits of Love and Knowledge: The Seminar of Jacques Lacan XX, Encore*, ed. Jacques-Alain Miller, trans. Bruce Fink (New York: Norton, 1999), 63. Barbara Johnson discusses the imaginary duality where "2 is an extremely odd number" in "The Frame of Reference: Poe, Lacan, Derrida," in *The Critical Difference*. (Baltimore: Johns Hopkins UP, 1980), 110–46, at 119.

21. Miller, *Philosophical Chaucer*, 11. Emily's appearance here is thus much like the ideal imago glimpsed in the Mirror Stage. She is the image of wholeness and completeness, what Miller calls "autonomy" (89) and what [Aranye] Louise Fradenburg calls "a captivating image of freedom" that the Thebans (mis)recognize and through which they form their desire-as-lack. See Fradenburg, "Sacrificial Desire in the *Knight's Tale*," *Journal of Medieval and Early Modern Studies* 27 (1997): 47–75, at 59.

22. Žižek, *How to Read*, 69.

Lacan proffers. Where the Knight's Tale could judge between the two knights in terms of such imagining (which would be incredibly comforting to modern readers looking to settle the difference between Palamon and Arcite for good) and offer Emily to the one who most considers her will, who voices a realization of the (im)possibility of either suitor "to stonden in hir grace" (1.1173), it patently refuses to do so. Instead, the tale insists on her "inhuman" aversion to them and thereby on her vacant status as erotic object. If psychoanalysis posits a lack of sexual relation, the Knight's Tale displays it further by settling Emily upon the one who *fails* in his relation to her most forcefully. In the end, the tale works precisely against its critical readers, who seek to rationalize the tale's outcome, finding for Palamon a greater claim to Emily (either by priority or by devotion to Venus). The Knight's Tale instead, like the *Teseida* before it, lobbies for the one who suffers the greater loss even as the tale refuses to decide matters in such terms.

One of the striking differences between Arcite's worldly and practical point of view and Palamon's dreamy-eyed one centers on Arcite's acknowledgment of Emily's desire, their need for "hir grace" (1.1173). We see it when Arcite equivocates on Palamon's claim of falsity and his own priority, imagining a logic by which both can love: "Love, if thee list, for I love and ay shal" (1.1183). A reader no less subtle than Shakespeare makes this point explicit in his rendering of the conversation in *The Two Noble Kinsmen*: "I will not as you do, to worship her / As she is heavenly and a blessed goddess. / I love her as a woman, to enjoy her: / So both may love."[23] Where Palamon places the two knights in a zero-sum game, in which only one of them can truly love the lady and call her his own, Arcite finds that their different ways of loving—one as a goddess and one "as to a creature" (1.1159)—allows both to love. What is more, Arcite knows how utterly unattainable she is in reality, so the fantasy that both may enjoy her in their differing ways is even more apt.[24] But at the tale's end, Arcite makes the most pointed acknowledgment of Emily's decisive power when he asks "if that evere ye shul ben a wyf, / Foryet nat Palamon, the gentil man" (1.2796–97). Far from "giving" Emily to Palamon (as Boccaccio's Arcita

---

23. John Fletcher and William Shakespeare, *The Two Noble Kinsmen*, 3rd ed., ed. Lois Potter (Surrey: Arden Shakespeare, 1997), 2.2.163–66.

24. Arcite's knowledge is of the order of the Symbolic. She is unavailable to them because she is the enemy's sister-in-law, and therefore subject to his power in a way that emphasizes their own subjected status as well. This realm of the law conjoins the "likeliness" of standing "in hir grace" with their imprisonment (1.1172–74). But it is not the only one alive in Arcite's knowledge. His sense that both may love her (that both can't help but love her) in different ways is dependent on her real unattainability, the fact that in the Real we are separate from and unknowable to anyone, particularly anyone with whom we may hope to have a sexual relation.

more clearly does when he distributes his possessions on his deathbed), here Arcite relinquishes his claim to her through his victory by recommending the gentility of the vanquished Palamon's years of devotion and service.[25] Importantly, Arcite accords Emily the power to desire ("if that evere ye shul ben"), something never considered by anyone in the story other than Emily herself. That these terms should *fail* to decide the matter in Arcite's favor only points more savagely to the lack of sexual relation. We are teased with the idea that such terms can offer a thoughtful resolution, an ethical answer to a question that the tale has generated. But the story almost vindictively turns away from this response; desire will not be answered in any such logical terms.

If the fictions of courtly love are a sublimation of the pain and rejection produced by the lack of (the possibility of) the sexual relation, as well as the logic of sacrifice to which medieval knights are asked to submit, then the sublimation of love in the Knight's Tale masks the emptiness of the subject in the poem's fiction of multiplicity.[26] The elaborate plot of the Knight's Tale and the philosophic exaltations of Theseus, particularly his "prime mover" speech, stand to obfuscate *and* to express the fact that despite Arcite's heroic victory and Palamon's possession of Emily, desire remains inherently unsatisfied and unsatisfiable. Theseus's philosophic wisdom substitutes for and supplants a different kind of knowledge. The romance proceeds and ends as if its goals have been accomplished, but the Knight's narration offers a decidedly *linguistic* satisfaction where in the Real there can be none. Marked by those readers impressed with the length, rhetoric, and grand scale of the story, the Knight's Tale offers a surfeit of words as a substitute for, and marker of, this failed relation. In what follows, I will detail this sublime if delusional accomplishment, what we might call the Knight's fundamentally compensatory fiction and its importance as a structure for the *Canterbury Tales* as a whole.

It is little surprise that Chaucer begins the *Canterbury Tales,* a narrative of longing folk, with the conventional elaborations of amorous longing in

---

25. See Boccaccio, *Teseida* 10.16–30: "let him [Palemone] receive as the reward of his love the lady that I should have had as my own" (10.28). *The Book of Theseus,* trans. Bernadette McCoy (New York: Medieval Text Association, 1974), 266. Among a string of sure commands that Arcita issues to the living in the stanzas of book 10, Chaucer chooses to include only one: "Be pleased to take comfort for love of me, if ever you decide to do in the future what I am about to say" (10.60; 272).

26. On sacrifice see L. O. Aranye Fradenburg, *Sacrifice Your Love: Psychoanalysis, Historicism, Chaucer* (Minnesota: U of Minnesota P, 2002), 155.

the Knight's romance. But as in the General Prologue, the articulation of erotic convention is almost immediately disrupted; a different mood follows its "natural" order. There is a stain in the midst of this tableau. The specter of death looms large, and it has dominated readings of the tale since Robert Hanning's landmark essay reread the terms of Charles Muscatine's idealization of "the struggle between noble designs and chaos," both of which articulate what we have found disturbing.[27] The tale proffers too much death and not enough "romance"; the inhuman outrages of Creon disrupt Theseus's wedding journey, an opening scene of joy's delay and deferral that works paradigmatically for the story as a whole. What looks like a mistake in execution, an unfitting irregularity in the *mise en scéne*, the stain's significance becomes clear only at a distance and "awry."[28] As in the well-known Holbein painting Lacan uses as his example, the deformation takes on its full and absolute meaning with a backward glance. So too the Knight's Tale makes a similar backward glance that exposes its own narrative's relation to death. In the supposedly consoling words of Egeus: "Deeth is an ende of every worldly soore" (1.2849). His comment seeks to install this meaning retroactively over the entire tale, making death the end of desire and putting into perspective the story's otherwise disfiguring accident. Even further, Theseus's speech gives Egeus's recognition of death a more exalted meaning by elongating the perspective on our "worldly soore" in the "faire cheyne of love" (1.2988). So too the critical obsession with death in the Knight's Tale—Arcite's tragic end that both disturbs and resolves the romance plot.

This backward glance that makes virtue of necessity has not produced the easiest of resolutions. As a romance the tale has offered only partial and distinctly complicated satisfactions. Because of the split protagonist created in the frustratingly balanced equivalence of Palamon and Arcite, we have looked to Theseus as the real hero of the story, whose romancing days are already finished and who presides over and "amend[s]" (1.3074) the tragic events to which desire leads his subjects.[29] As such, the Knight's Tale teaches us, through the figure of Theseus, about renunciation. In such readings, and they are rife, Theseus is exalted as a stoic figure of resolution and consola-

---

27. Robert Hanning, "'The Struggle between Noble Designs and Chaos': The Literary Tradition of Chaucer's *Knight's Tale*," *The Literary Review* 23 (1980): 519–41; Charles Muscatine, "Form, Texture, and Meaning in Chaucer's *Knight's Tale*," *PMLA* 65 (1950): 911–29.

28. Lacan reads the anamorphosis of Holbein's *The Embassadors* as a preface to "Courtly Love as Anamorphosis" in *The Seminar of Jacques Lacan: Book VII, The Ethics of Psychoanalysis*, ed. Jacques-Alain Miller, trans. Dennis Porter (New York: Norton, 1992).

29. Such a view of Theseus must deny some of what Chaucer's readers certainly "know" because, of course, Theseus's romancing days do not end with Hippolyta, as Phaedra's tragedy shows.

tion who gestures beyond the devastating forces of the material world.[30] He allows readers to sacrifice their desires for a romance hero for one of superior knowledge. But as Aranye Fradenburg so eloquently explains about such sacrifices, these gestures do not renounce so much as they allow us to keep that which we appear to give up.[31] The way out of the toils of desire that Theseus provides simultaneously helps sustain the knights' state of wanting: their equivalence and undecidable status. Where we would install Theseus in a position beyond the desires of the young knights, that position is always already inside desire's bounds. What appears, then, as an aversion of desire is, in fact, its promulgation by other means.

And what a story of its promulgation the Knight's attention to Theseus offers. His labor to resolve matters via the construction of the amphitheater takes a considerable part of the Knight's narrative energy, encompassing almost all of the tale's *tercia pars*. By giving Palamon and Arcite a civic stage and legal judge, Theseus's law supervenes their private battle, forestalling conflict for an entire year during which time they must gather the means to fight. More than three hundred lines describe the amphitheater itself and the elaborate temples built within, as well as the army of heroes each knight so admirably assembles to his cause (1.1881–2208). But of course these preparations do not suspend desire so much as they provide the form in which it is experienced, allowing desire's duration and continuance by other means: "Who kouthe telle, or who kouthe it endite, / The joye that is maked in the place / Whan Theseus hath doon so fair a grace?" (1.1872–74). These terms describe Palamon and Arcite after Theseus ordains the competition, and they cover the preparations for it as well. It is thus unsurprising that this third part ends with the formal prayers of the tale's triangulated lovers. Even at the level of the signifier, the delay and aversion *produces* a linguistic articulation of desire three times over.

Similarly, Theseus controls and contains their dispute in the grove not by ending matters in a speedy execution but by elaborating them. Theseus helps extend their desire by prolonging their condition of wanting, expanding its limit (now 200 knights will fight to the death) and by making its object ostensibly attainable. Theseus's actions pretend to arrest the lawless working of desire seen in the grove, but in reality his actions propel it even further, elevating private desire to a matter of state and public attention.

---

30. An overview of various readings of Theseus as the heroic or flawed subject of the Knight's Tale can be found in Lee Patterson, *Chaucer and the Subject of History* (Madison: U of Wisconsin P, 1991), especially 166–69. The most sophisticated rereading of the possibility of mastery Theseus represents can be found in Miller, *Philosophical Chaucer*, 91–101.

31. Fradenburg, "Sacrificial Desire," 55.

In this way, Theseus turns their small affair and personal conflict to his own political ends, deriving his power from the spectacle of their conflict and their willingness to suffer.[32] Such elaborations not only apply to the knights' desires in the tale, they potentially multiply the heroic subject sitting at its core. For at this very moment the Knight introduces Emetrius and Lycurge, the leaders of the assembled armies that fight for the love of Palamon and Arcite. These two named figures stand before and in the descriptive place of a multiplicity of warriors, a hundred knights on each side, who take the field for this noble, amorous cause, and this very number calculates its worthiness. What is in one sense a sharp movement away from private conflict to the larger field of historical forces and a greater socially inflected world turns out to be mere detour. Emetrius and Lycurge are not simply figurations of a bygone mythic panoply or an impressive set of classical references the Knight can marshal to his performance, they are figures produced under the substitutive logic of desire driving the Knight's story. They do not forestall or redirect the forces animating the conflict so much as repeat them anew.

The heroic bodies thus literally multiply in the form of two armies even as Emetrius and Lycurge take the place of Palamon and Arcite in the tale's descriptive economy. In this way we see the principle of substitution in the romance writ large. If desire operates by the continual substitution of differing objects in place of ultimate cause, we see here the way courtly culture functions according to a similar design, replacing Palamon with Emetrius, individual with army, in a substitutive logic extending the work of desire across and *into* social forms. But even more globally in the tale, Theseus's noble actions here compete with Palamon's and Arcite's split heroic subjectivity in the critical arena, thus the turn to Theseus as a figure of wholeness and sovereignty who can more securely ground the story. Looking for a higher principle, something above and beyond the merely individual wants driving a particular figure in the tale, we turn not to the abandonment of desire that we presume to seek but to a subtle mechanism by which it is instead elaborated and maintained. We convince ourselves that desire (the wanting of Palamon and Arcite) serves a higher power—the political order in Athens, the aims of medieval knighthood or statecraft—but it is such political, social, and cultural powers that serve desire instead. In this way we can thus understand why desire is everywhere and nowhere in the

---

32. On the tale's spectacles of the willingness to suffer, see Patricia Clare Ingham, "Homosociality and Creative Masculinity in the *Knight's Tale*," in *Masculinities in Chaucer: Approaches to Maleness in the Canterbury Tales and Troilus and Criseyde*, ed. Peter Beidler (Cambridge: Brewer, 1998), 23–35; and Fradenburg, "Sacrificial Desire," esp. 54–55.

critical terrain. Its power lies hidden and diminutized behind the historical forms that it would explain and even sustain.

From the tale's beginning, the multiplications of the heroic subject have meant that it lacks the kind of romance villain (Lancelot's Malegeant, Tristan's Irish giant) normally conquered by the hero in order to prove his value to other men and thus his worthiness to and for the lady.[33] The lack of a villain at the level of Emily's suitors and Theseus's overdetermined role as conquering hero have been read as part of Chaucer's philosophic elaborations on and thus changes to the genre of romance. These changes have (1) aligned the Knight's noble vision with Theseus's as more mature and sophisticated perspectives on the vagaries of love, (2) moved the central concern of the tale—despite its language of desire and its main plot—to the more philosophic reparations of Boethianism, and (3) contributed to an overall critical assumption of Chaucer's disdain for "mere" romance.[34] This third point puts Chaucer in collusion with the Knight and Theseus, as more mature philosopher-lovers. But what of the villain otherwise missing from the tale? Of course this role is played temporarily by Creon, whose "despit . . . and tirannye" (1.941) must be corrected by Theseus's law. The lack of a villain, however, marks the tale's desire as much as what it has refused, and it elaborately tries to produce that desire as Palamon and Arcite play the villain in the tale, at least according to each other, even as they compete for the right to be its hero—the one who can claim Emily's love.

These conditions have contributed to making the Knight's Tale into a metaromance, a meditation on the genre itself. But in seeking this refinement of genre as a means of thinking through its operations, such readings have also whitewashed the Knight's story. The emotional transactions in the romance have been traded for its staged ideals. Such philosophizing readers insist on a resolution that the tale does not and cannot deliver. Instead, the lack of a clear villain in the tale provokes a villainous projection and externalization by the two knights themselves, who are looking to cast each other in this antagonistic role. We hear them do so as early as when Arcite and Palamon debate their right to love Emily through a characterization of the other as "fals" (1.1129–61). With "knytte[d] . . . browes tweye," Palamon

---

33. Ruth Mazo Karras, *From Boys to Men: Formations of Masculinity in Late Medieval Europe* (Philadelphia: U of Pennsylvania P, 2003).

34. For (1) see Muscatine, "Form, Texture and Meaning," and Hanning, "'Noble Designs and Chaos'"; and for (3) see Fradenburg, "The Wife of Bath's Passing Fancy" *SAC* 8 (1986): 31–58; and A. C. Spearing, *Medieval to Renaissance in English Poetry* (Cambridge: Cambridge UP, 1985). One might also read Boethius as a text about desire and its substitutions; see Miller, *Philosophical Chaucer*, chap. 3, 111–51.

situates Arcite in the villainous role of false brother who has broken his sworn oath: "Neither of us in love to hyndre oother, / Ne in noon oother cas" (1.1128; 1135–36). He claims Arcite has "falsly been aboute / To love my lady, whom I love and serve," labeling him "false Arcite" (1.1142–43; 1145). Moving away from Palamon's ethically charged, idealizing language, Arcite replies by showing Palamon how linguistically and logically untrue his accusations are: "thou art false, I telle thee outrely, / For paramour I loved hire first er thow. / What wiltow seyen? Thou woost nat yet now / Wheither she be a womman or goddesse!" (1.1154–57). Characterizing Palamon's state as an "affeccioun of hoolynesse," Arcite lays claim to his own "love as to a creature" (1.1158–59). By a turn of rhetoric, Arcite shifts the signifier in this accusation from a moral or ethical register to a logical one that evacuates the truth content of Palamon's proposition. He also thereby empties Palamon's rhetorical address to Emily as Venus herself of its metaphoric flourish by reading it as (self-)deception. In turning each other into the "fals" villain, Palamon and Arcite can thereby take up the role of heroic subject. But the tale as a whole has greater transformations in store for them as it dramatically turns Palamon and Arcite *into each other.*

We have earlier examined the ways these two knights are, alternately, conflated and distinguished by their love for Emily. As part and parcel of a desire for the poem to render judgment, readers are often driven to judge between them, even though, from the poem's opening, their individual status has been as unclear as the precise nature of their "bond." This does not mean we know nothing about them. They are "of the blood roial / Of Thebes" and cousins, "of sustren two yborn" (1.1018–19). Moreover, these royal cousins address each other as "brother" (1.1136) out of their familial relation as well as a knightly bond of fraternity. But, as we have seen, individuating Palamon and Arcite has been no easy task. Found in a heap of bodies following Theseus's conquest of Thebes, "liggynge by and by . . . in oon armes," the two young men hardly exist apart from each other, "Nat fully quyke, ne fully dede" (1.1011–12; 1015). A number of commentators have indicated their indistinguishability before the sight of Emily begins to separate them from each other in a painful process of heroic, masculine individuation.[35]

---

35. Where Muscatine finds "the equalization of Palamon and Arcite" a "crowning modification" of his source (918), others have less faith in the kind of balance and symmetry he values. Ingham writes: "Poised on death's edge, these two knights seem uncannily alike, bereft of individualization, the particular differences that grant them separate identities. In fact, the confluences between Palamon and Arcite are so deeply woven here that this description [of the way they are found together in a heap in the beginning of the story] has prompted a number of critics to wonder if these two characters are really different from each other at all" ("Homosociality," 26–27).

As the story progresses we might expect the problem of heroic indistinguishability to begin to be alleviated, but the effects of desire exacerbate these difficulties of identification. Just when we start to separate Palamon from Arcite by the form of their verbal responses to the sight of Emily— the metaphors by which they express themselves—the more they begin to resemble one another. That is, where the speeches of part 1 serve to disentangle Palamon from Arcite, these very same terms of distinction return immediately in part 2 to transform the knights back into each other. Far from exhibiting any political or narrative purpose, this transformation emerges as the effect of desire.[36] Once they submit to the Symbolic order, Palamon and Arcite come to desire from the position of the other: Palamon for Arcite and Arcite for Palamon. Indeed, the ultimate act of desiring from the position of the other emerges at the poem's end, where Arcite's death marries the three of them.

Upon their initial sight of Emily, the two knights' set speeches have worked as a means of differentiation. Palamon sees a lady in garden and rhapsodizes "I noot wher she be womman or goddesse, / But Venus is it soothly, as I gesse" (1.1101–2), where Arcite gets right to the "short and playn" (1.1091). These spiritualizing and practical discourses, respectively, describe their differing approaches to the object of desire, and they have been read in more global terms for the philosophic worldview that each one represents, contemplative versus active, ideal versus real, in the tale as a whole, taken, for the most part, as consistent differentiations. Complicating these set speeches and the terms of characterization they offer are the ways the knights' further complaints are wrapped in the fantasies they have of each other. Arcite laments his exile by imagining that a shift in Fortune will eventually make Palamon's proximity to Emily pay off:

For possible is, syn thou hast hire presence,
And art a knyght, a worthy and an able,
That by som cas, syn Fortune is chaungeable,
Thow maist to thy desir somtyme atteyne.
(1.1240–43)

Analogously, Palamon fantasizes about the banished Arcite's ability to raise an army and win Emily by conquest or compact:

---

36. John Bowers has helpfully remarked on the way that Hansen notes, though unwittingly, these effects by asking about "the story's most telling non sequitur. When Arcite returns in disguise to Athens, he makes no attempt to woo Emily," citing *Fictions of Gender* 212. See Bowers, "Three Readings of the Knight's Tale: Sir John Clanvowe, Geoffrey Chaucer, and James I of Scotland," *Journal of Medieval and Early Modern Studies* 34 (2004): 279–307, at 286.

> Thou mayst, syn thou hast wisdom and man-hede,
> Assemblen alle the folk of oure kynrede,
> And make a werre so sharp on this citee
> That by som aventure or some tretee
> Thow mayst have hire to lady and to wyf.
> (1.1285–89)

When in prison together, they each sought the other's obliteration. Palamon wants Arcite to stop loving Emily and so to disappear as a rival suitor. Arcite wishes Palamon to realize they are inconsequential to each other so long as they love in entirely different terms. However, once separated, they desire from the other's point of view and begin to act in accordance with it. Where some might be tempted to read the tale in terms of error (Did Arcite ask for the wrong thing? Did Palamon "win" because he had his eye firmly on Emily herself?), we might instead read these figures in terms of what they know and, particularly, what they don't know that they know—what their language knows about them.

Part 2 of the tale begins after a seven-year lapse. Palamon remains in prison while Arcite languishes in exile. Disfigured by his lovesickness, Arcite becomes unrecognizable to his friends and thus capable of returning to Athens. But his actions also make him unrecognizable to us in a specific way. Unlike his former self, the active, practical figure arguing in prison with Palamon, we now see a *passive* Arcite—a figure who has been and is acted upon. His new name, "Philostrate," indicates this passive condition, marking him as "one stricken by love." As when lying in bed almost lifeless only to be revived by divine injunction from Mercury, Arcite's passivity extends to his position in Theseus's household. Following the gods' instructions—"To Atthenes shaltou wende, / Ther is thee shapen of thy wo an ende" (1.1391–92)—he returns to Athens and labors with his hands for the sake of being near Emily. The Knight is careful to represent these actions as obedience rather than effrontery, keeping Arcite in our good graces. But we ought to notice too how forcefully Arcite has thereby turned into Palamon. Indeed, it would seem that Arcite "knows" Palamon's passive means to possession, which he imitates in his obedience to the gods' command to return from banishment and in his disguised laboring, "to drugge and drawe" (1.1416) in Theseus's household. Like Palamon's initial vision of Emily *cum* Venus, this twist in the plot also imagines for Arcite a divine solution to his situation—as Mercury has promised "an ende" in which he "hast hir presence" and waits for a change in fortune, just what Arcite earlier imagined Palamon could do. Presciently, Arcite called this Palamon's "victorie of this aventure" (1.1235).

Likewise, Palamon "knows" the success of Arcite's active role, which he concomitantly usurps in the act of breaking prison and escaping to Thebes to raise an army. Imagining just the kind of practical solution characteristic of his cousin, Palamon escapes to become an imaginary Arcite, hiding in the grove until he can "take his way / To Thebes-ward, his freendes for to preye / On Theseus to helpe him to werreye" (1.1482–84). Palamon is here determined "outher he wolde lese his lif / Or wynnen Emelye unto his wif" (1.1485–86). The knights' actions in part 2 uncannily follow their imagined plans for each other from part 1. In these ways Chaucer represents the Theban cousins as literally inhabiting the other's desire, to be the thing that they imagine the Other desires and thereby to gain its recognition. Of course they make no such verbal claims. This knowledge comes in the form of a literally uncharacteristic action rather than cognition (they repeat and act out what they cannot remember of their own words). But by the middle of part 2 of the Knight's Tale, Arcite has put himself back into prison (as the disguised Philostrate, who must carry and haul as Theseus's servant), while Palamon effectively exiles himself by breaking jail. If Arcite had been exiled upon pain of death never to be seen in Athens again, Palamon hides in the grove similarly "soore afered of deeth" (1.1518) lest he be found. The way in which these two principals play in the guise of the other is doubly signaled in the text by the curious addition of an "other" for each of them: the sudden appearance of an other figure helping both knights. Where the disfigured Arcite returns to Athens with a squire who knows his secret and keeps "his privetee and al his cas" (1.1411), Palamon breaks prison "by helpyng of a freend" (1.1468). While each knight would clearly have welcomed the assistance of another at various points in the story, the quiet (and parallel) way in which this other appears for each of them at these crucial moments seems more than coincidental. It is a telling intrusion of the social world that their fantasies of each other do not recognize.

Another form of criticism would explain these inversions as irony (from the Greek "eironeia," a "dissimulation" and thus a turning of terms), in which the intended meaning is turned to the opposite of what it appears. By calling the actions of these two characters "ironic," however, we tend to use the term in its more figurative sense, in which the "condition of affairs or events of a character [is] opposite to what was, or might naturally be, expected; a contradictory outcome of events as if in mockery of the promise and fitness of things" (*OED*, s.v. "irony," def. 2b). Here Palamon and Arcite act ironically (in a more literal sense) by turning away from their own "character" and dissimulating in imitation of the other. Of course, these moments are ironic to the reader as s/he watches Arcite act like Palamon and Palamon imitate Arcite, and even more so at the end of the story with its final turn of events. But irony is more than the mockery of the fitness of things in the Knight's Tale, where the promise of such fitness is not at all given. These ironies are themselves an unconscious form of knowledge in which the action of the characters speak a significance the actors in the story do not yet know. In analyzing these parts of the tale, psychoanalysis does not merely offer another descriptive vocabulary for the literariness of its figures but accesses and makes plain the significances left implicit or merely figural and decorative. Where a discovery of irony would be the end of one such reading, this one instead begins its investigation of meaning, particularly the *ways* meanings are produced, at this turn.

The knowledge of desire such psychoanalytic reading offers goes beyond the splitting of romance hero into Palamon and Arcite, into a primordially divided subject. As figures in the romance, the Knight's Tale's characters speak openly about their desires and articulate what they want at every juncture. Yet, as Lacan would maintain, desire is *in* language beyond this surface signification; the structure of desire exceeds the function of the courtly romance plot and its obvious amorous concerns. The Knight's Tale shows, repeatedly, how little the subject knows what he or she desires. The prayers in the temples of the gods showcase readily the operations of desire within and beyond the subject, and proffer a scene of misreading that identifies desire within this language and its discontinuities.

Each of the three young lovers heads to a newly constructed temple within the amphitheater where their fates are to be determined in search of a god that "woost what [s/he] desire[s]" (1.2301). Each asks for something s/he desperately wants and gets it—only to find that once it is received, it produces an undesired end. Once again, desire circumvents its own satisfaction. Even before these prayers, however, Arcite has already theorized the nature of desire and its linguistic bounds early in part 2 when he laments:

> Allas, why pleynen folk so in commune
> On purveiaunce of God, or of Fortune,
> That yeveth hem ful ofte in many a gyse
> Wel bettre than they kan hemself devyse?
> Som man desireth for to han richesse,
> That cause is of his mordre or greet siknesse;
> And som man wolde out of his prisoun fayn,
> That in his hous is of his meynee slayn.
> Infinite harmes been in this mateere.
> We witen nat what thing we preyen heere;
> (1.1251–60)

These lines are typically read as a commentary upon the classical theologic apparatus and its determinations depicted in the tale, which offer a strong contrast to the securities of Christianity in the Knight's world. The oblique invocation of God's providence here (and elsewhere) has far overshadowed the changeable, mobile nature of human desire, its irreducibility to mere utterance *and* its location in speech. Focused on the place from which desire should originate (or return), we have missed the ways in which the Knight's Tale traces the shape of desire, its movements and shaping permutations—the ways in which desire inheres in the signifier. Comforted by what such an oblique reference to Christianity might offer, we neglect what the passage says as well as its relation to the rest of the Knight's story, which is all about the language of one's prayers and the opacity of one's request. Language fails to represent desire adequately, as Arcite's words so eloquently show, yet language is the only form in which desire appears. Desire inheres in and exceeds the signifier, even as the signifier emerges in the subject precisely as a substitute for a lost object and its only means of expression.

The violence retailed by these depictions of desire in Arcite's language and the unwitting danger in which they place individuals, moreover, is telling. Some men are murdered or hurt by the desire for "richesse," while another is slain by his own household upon his release from prison. These examples reveal the ends our desire cannot foresee, the results it "causes." But in detailing these "infinite harmes" Chaucer suggests more than violent accident or mere irony; he reveals the aggressivity and dangerous violence at the heart of desire. Lacan understands aggressiveness as more than mere aggression, though it may express itself as such. Aggressivity describes the fundamental relation underlying loving acts as well as violent ones—an aggressivity underwriting all acts of identification that constitute one's identity in the first place. Lacan writes: "the notion of an aggressiveness [is] linked to the narcissistic relationship and to the structures of systematic misrecognition and objectification that characterize ego formation."[37] Thus, where some have looked to the Knight's Tale as an attempt to ask (and answer) the question of which is more important to chivalry: martial success or romantic attachment, we might note the impossibility of the initial opposition, as if these were fully separable terms. Even looking to Palamon

---

37. Lacan, "Aggressiveness in Psychoanalysis," 94. In Dylan Evans's words, Lacan here "simply restate[s] Freud's concept of ambivalence (the interdependence of love and hate), which Lacan regards as one of the fundamental discoveries of psychoanalysis" (6; *s.v.* aggressivity). See *An Introductory Dictionary of Lacanian Psychoanalysis* (London and New York: Routledge, 1996). "Aggressivity" in previous translations of Lacan is rendered as "aggressiveness" in Fink's more recent complete *Écrits*.

and Arcite as figures of such a division may, in fact, be the problem with such readings. For Palamon is everywhere as ready to fight, just as much as Arcite. Likewise, Arcite, we are told explicitly, is in love with Emily "as muche as he, or moore" (1.1116). Palamon and Arcite are not so much opposed as each other's counterpart. The oppositions they seem to offer are always merely temporary and local to particular situations and their narrative needs.

As has been more fully discussed in the introduction, "the nature of aggressiveness in man and its relation to the formalism of his ego and objects," Lacan writes, "crystallizes in the subject's inner conflictual tension" to produce "the triad of other people, ego, and object" ("Aggressiveness" 92). With the identification and misrecognitions of the ego and others arises both desire and simultaneous aggression for the self conceived as an other, as well as the others desired as the self. In this seemingly simple arrangement the entirety of the sociality of the subject—its relation to and against others—is at stake. The "ego . . . [is] marked, right from the outset, by this aggressive relativity" (92), and it is one reason why "man's ego is never reducible to his lived identity" (93), which is, incidentally, what makes Lacan so alien to the ego psychology dominating Anglo-American thought. In the Imaginary scene of identification, Lacan identifies as indistinguishable two different moments: "when the subject negates himself and when he accuses the other" ("Aggressiveness" 93). Dramatizing that very confusion, the knights must identify themselves to Theseus who has found them fighting "withouten juge" in the grove (1.1712). Palamon stands before Theseus at once negating himself and accusing Arcite—"I axe deeth and my juwise; / But sle my felawe in the same wise" (1.1739–40). Both confessing and condemning the other in the selfsame gesture, Palamon expresses "the very delusion of the misanthropic beautiful soul, casting out onto the world the disorder that constitutes his being" ("Aggressiveness" 93). We cannot be sure whether Palamon's gesture is primarily confessional and self-sacrificing or accusational and aggressive. His open admission to Theseus is both brave and heroic as well as ambivalently childish and marked by fear. He claims his punishment as Theseus's "mortal foo" (1.1736) but first accuses and identifies Arcite as one who has "japed thee ful many a yer" (1.1729). His aggressiveness erupts precisely at the moment of self-identification.

Readings of the Knight's Tale expect a clear separation of love and violence, which is perhaps why we are so disappointed with the images on Venus's temple discomfiting traditional ideas of love. The desirous intent of the knights' amorous pursuit should oppose the violent conflict erupting everywhere in the Tale. But we ought to look more closely at its historical collocation of love and aggressive conflict, which is what draws Lacan to the paradigmatic status of courtly love as the cultural inscription of desire *par excellence*. The subject only desires where it also aggresses. Or in more Lacanian terms, aggression is produced within the arrangement through which the subject of desire emerges. As in the performance of the pilgrim narrators most openly hostile to one another (Summoner and Friar, Miller and Reeve, Wife and Clerk), we see in the Knight's Tale a display of desire in variant social and historical guises. Chaucer here shows the relation of desire and its necessary (dis)guises, precisely at the point desire so explicitly produces the aggressivity at the heart of the story. Once Palamon and Arcite recognize what they lack—"hire that rometh in the yonder place" (1.1119)—they turn the threat she poses to their self-sufficiency upon each other. Formerly indistinguishable, Arcite and Palamon are differentiated only after seeing Emily, and only within the antagonism that symptomatizes desire as such. These comments do not suggest that desire and aggressivity, love and violence, are situated in opposition in the tale and in romance generally. Instead, the Knight's Tale shows the more intimate relation of these states, their mutually constitutive function—much like Palamon and Arcite themselves.

There is no desire without aggressivity, no love without violence, and Venus's temple paints this intimacy in broad strokes. H. Marshall Leicester's extensive reading of the Knight and his tale, and particularly the violent masculine desire "unmasked" in Venus's temple, emphasizes this point.[38] That description "begins with a catalogue of the [masculine] courtly lover's pains and never drifts far from them" (269). As any reader of this portion of the Knight's Tale knows, the temples are so much more than mere descriptions of places or even collocations of the metaphysical forces driving the story, for these would be too easy to historicize as alien to the Knight's own medieval world, part of the "guise" of old pagan stories. They are instead the mythologized formulations of the very ideals of courtly love that showcase its inherent ambivalences. In this way, then, love appears as a violent and destructive power (Cupid's "arwes brighte and kene" [1.1966]) as well as an attractive, erotic one (Venus "naked, fletynge in the large see" [1.1956]) for the male subject imagining her. Holding a cuckoo, Venus thus appears "as a female figure who mocks the dream of possession with the symbol of cuckoldry she holds in her hand, pointing to the male fear and distrust of female independence that underlies the idealization" (Leicester

---

38. H. Marshall Leicester, *The Disenchanted Self: Representing the Subject in the "Canterbury Tales"* (Berkeley: U of California P, 1990), 267–73.

270). Yoking the classical image of the goddess to the Knight's own socially driven concerns are the languages of lordship and mastery in the temple's description: "servage," "champartie," "strengthe," and "hardynesse," which Leicester reads as a revelation of "how selective, how self-deceiving, and ultimately how anxiously distrustful" (273) desire can be. But to return to the concerns voiced throughout this chapter, we could also observe how closely tied the languages of desire and aggressive politics are, as if the sociality of subjects were on display in this seemingly intimate, interior description of the lover internally at war with Venus. War is not opposed to the works of Venus, located securely and separately in the temple of Mars—the erotic is yet another form of war and conflict, and vice versa.[39]

Looking to the intimate connection between classical imagery and the Knight's social concerns in this ambivalent figure of the apotheosis of amorous love, we might also note the *enabling* fiction the conjunction produces. Far from getting in the way of enjoying Emily, then, the aggression of Palamon and Arcite actually *permits* their enjoyment since the knights have no access to her. Chaucer's handling of the narrative yet again shows us that aggression, of which knighthood and chivalry are elaborate and stylized historical forms, works as a means of desiring, another form that desire takes and can be experienced. It is also a particularly effective mode of desire because it makes its own frustration part of its self-perpetuating apparatus. Particularly apparent to the audiences of romance, aggression (like frustration) allows desire to continue and to be experienced in alternate and varying forms of nonsatisfaction. What is the prolonged and irrational rivalry between sworn brothers Palamon and Arcite if not a manner of enjoying their impossible relation to Emily?[40] Because "She woot namore of al this hoote fare, / By God, than woot a cokkow or an hare!" (1.1809–10), they translate impossibility (because she is Theseus's to dispense) into prohibition (she is desired by the other). Sublimating the lady, they also sublimate desire into the desire to desire—which is what, Chaucer's readers have long recognized, Palamon and Arcite childishly argue over in their initial con-

---

39. Anne Middleton remarks on the analogies between military performance, artistic production, and marriage that would allow us to read chivalry in metaphoric terms in "War by Other Means: Marriage and Chivalry in Chaucer," *SAC, Proceedings* 1 (1984): 119–33. Fradenburg takes matters one step further: "The fantasy of chivalry is a sublime economy that powerfully recuperates the *jouissance* of aggressivity by rewriting it as incalculable, inscrutable love" ("Sacrificial Desire" 54).

40. On the ways the obstacles of romance provide "antagonistic complicity," see Slavoj Žižek, "From Courtly Love to *The Crying Game*," *New Left Review* 202 (1993): 1–9, at 7. He offers a complex and refined definition of sublimation, not merely the exaltation of an object but a means for "the impossible [to] change into the prohibited" (4) that is useful for reading the transactions in the Knight's Tale.

frontation. They fight not over Emily herself (whom they do not know) but the right to desire Emily (1.1142–43). Before Theseus installs the tournament and offers them the possibility of self-determination, desire in the Knight's Tale functions at a distinct remove.

Related to this aggressivity, the tale's violence and destructivity—its "derke ymaginyng" or what I earlier discussed as its stain or blotch—has been the focus of our recent interest in the Knight's Tale (1.1995). This interest provides the through-line from Muscatine's now classic formalist treatment, identifying the central thematic of the tale as "the struggle between noble designs and chaos," to its latest feminist, historicist, and explicitly psychoanalytic readings.[41] Whether in terms of the social constraint placed on Emily by feudal romance convention (Hansen), the conscious and unconscious critiques of the institution of knighthood by the chivalric subject constructed from within it (Leicester, Patterson), or the workings of the logic of sacrifice grounding the knightly ethos (Fradenburg, Ingham), modern studies of the Knight's Tale commit themselves to understanding its complex articulation of aristocratic ideals through its representation of violence and death. Celebrated or shamed by superior ethical knowledge, the *destructive* powers of knighthood sit at the center of modern critical attention to this tale.[42]

---

41. Robert Hanning explicitly takes up Muscatine's essay, even citing it in the title of his own, "Struggle between Noble Designs and Chaos." Where Muscatine sees the chaos of the world merely as the material that the Knight's noble designs work to contain, few readers after Hanning have been able to see the Knight's Tale in unproblematically idealized terms.

42. Two important books published nearly simultaneously focus on this violence by explaining Chaucer's characterization of the Knight and the failures of chivalry in the late fourteenth century that are displayed through his tale. Patterson's *Chaucer and the Subject of History* and Leicester's *Disenchanted Self* both take up the historical figure of the knight and the culturally critical discourse offered in the Knight's Tale. Both read the tale's admixture of classical and medieval temporalities and their heroisms skeptically, yet as meaningful. Leicester presents the tale as "stylized" (221), with its "continual exaggeration of hieratic stiffness of an antique epic style" (231). The complexities of amorousness and ferocity in the tale leave us with an "unresolved ambivalence about [the Knight's] own aggressive impulses" (381). So too do we find "institutional contradiction" in his portrayal of knighthood (381). In seemingly sharp distinction from earlier studies celebrating the order Theseus makes from chaos within the tale and which the Knight makes of his disordered literary materials beyond his story, both critics find evidence in the tale for "a culture whose cover is blown" (Leicester, 28). Similarly, Patterson shows readers the way "destructive forces" come from within the institution of knighthood that the Knight's Tale supposedly endorses, as "the dark shape of [its] own drive for order" (207). These studies depend upon an oppositionality at work in the tale and medieval romance more generally, which they read from the underside of idealizing heroism (militant, philosophic, or narrative) both to reveal and to critique that which undergirds the overt values of such stories. These readings might be characterized as variously skeptical of the ideals that genres such as romance and institutions such as knighthood and chivalry supposedly endorse, and they are more and less deconstructive in their readings of the binary logic by which romances such as the Knight's Tale stake their claims.

Violence has always been understood as the intimate partner of chivalric codes in the construction of romance's aristocratic subject. Richard Kaeuper looks to romance for this elaboration specifically in his history of chivalry and violence. Tracing "the priviledged practice of violence," he notes: "The frequent praise of *mesure*, restraint, balance, and reason in all forms of chivalric literature can surely be read as countering a tendency that was real and dangerous. At a minimum, we know that knights in historical combat frequently found it hard to restrain themselves and sought release in impetuous charges, disregarding some commander's plan and strict orders."[43] Where the violence of medieval war was once lionized as the necessary action of premodern masculinity and little calculated in human costs, it is now devalued as chivalry's repressed loss of humanity. The blind eye turned to the more savage actions of medieval military culture has been since transformed into a critical and knowing gaze, entirely skeptical of what it presents as human superiority. Such can be seen on the raw and dehumanized Thracian temple of Mars depicted *en abyme* in the temple to Mars that Theseus's artisans construct in his amphitheater. The images upon this temple are rife with animalistic destruction, wolves, bears, and beasts, epitomized by the "sowe freten the child right in the cradel" (1.2019). The effect of this image, a baby feasted on by a pig in what should be the safety of its bed, is hardly ever lost on Chaucer's readers. The distance between the seemingly inappropriate domestic realm ("the cooke yscalded, for al his longe ladel," 1.2020) and the "infortune of Marte" (1.2021) that should properly concern activity on the battlefield is everywhere on display at this site. Beyond the fact that the gruesomeness of war already displaces the nobility of heroic action we expect from this tale's exaltation of knighthood, the catastrophic misfortune of Mars's planetary influence is calculated for us, and imaged vividly, in familiar and domestic forms: "the barbour, and the bocher, and the smyth" (1.2025) laid low like "the cartere overryden with his carte" (1.2022). These images in the temple of Mars have little to do with the battlefield and instead express the madness of war in distinctly homely terms. It is yet another form of expressing the ambivalences of aggressivity, its appearance within unexpected discourses.

These descriptions of the temples highlight the difficulty of untangling the languages of love and aggression in the Knight's Tale as well as the logic of substitution governing individuation, desire, and the Knight's narrative, even the larger storytelling game that this tale inaugurates and grounds.

---

43. Richard Kaeuper, *Chivalry and Violence in Medieval Europe* (Oxford: Oxford UP, 1999), 145.

From the very opening account of Theseus's and Hippolyta's war, love is an assault, literally, in a courtly universe. Later in the story, Theseus will admit to himself that he was once conquered by "The god of love, a benedictite! / How myghty and how greet a lord is he!" (1.1785–86). But the tale opens with his martial and marital conquest of Hippolyta, indeed a conflation of the two. The Knight abbreviates how Theseus "conquered al the regne of Femenye . . . and wedded the queene Ypolita" (1.866–68), claiming he cannot detail "the grete bataille . . . / Bitwixen Atthenes and Amazones; / And how asseged was Ypolita" (1.879–81). Though rhetorically truncated to mere summary, the Knight's narrative gives the impression of the dual nature, both "feste" and "tempest," characterizing this prelude (1.883–84) and heard in the echo connecting these two terms. Hippolyta is "asseged"—besieged—and won in both martial and emotional senses; the two are not fully distinguishable. The Knight's prelude works then as both literal, historical narrative *and* romance metaphor. Indeed, it is unclear in which sense these words function literally and in which they are metaphorical. Does he romance the language of conquest or martialize the language of love?

Likewise, the terms of marriage appear in the tale thus transposed to other, distinctly combative, relations. Insofar as marriage is a pledge, the language of marriage figures various pledges and promises in the tale's political and conflictual narrative. Most spectacularly, it figures in the relation of Palamon to Arcite via the recollection of the vows of knighthood purportedly broken when Arcite presumes to love Emily. Palamon explains Arcite's betrayal of a bond,

> Ysworn ful depe, . . . ech of us til oother
> That nevere, for to dyen in the peyne,
> Til that the deeth departe shal us tweyne,
> Neither of us in love to hyndre oother,
> Ne in noon oother cas.
> (1.1132–36)

The language of this oath, sworn "ful depe" each to the other and lasting until "deeth departe shal us tweyne" echoes quite openly the Church's ceremony of sacramental marriage.[44] Of course, such ceremonies are not part of the tale's pagan universe but resound only for the Knight's belated, Christian audience. So again, we might ask, which is the literal language and which the metaphor? Do we read forward from the literal to the Knight's

---

44. For these terms of the marital oath, see Barbara Hanawalt, *The Ties That Bound: Peasant Families in Medieval England* (New York: Oxford UP, 1986), 203.

metaphorical understanding or backward from it? Which historical context is primary?

The implicit pledges made by each knight to Theseus also deploy similarly ambivalent terms. Given his judgment of official banishment, Arcite must lay his life on the line by pledging it in return for his freedom. Once released from Theseus's prison, "homward he him spedde. / Lat hym be war! His nekke lith to wedde" (1.1217–18). Of course, "wedde" acts as a synonym for promising and pledging, as it does in the sacramental ceremony, which makes his aggressive relation to Theseus (activated at the moment he is freed by his "enemy") here an erotic and loving one as well. Inasmuch as "his nekke lith to wedde," we might say that Arcite "marries" Theseus's law when he accepts his exile. Such linguistic features, itineraries traced by the signifier, show us that where we have been attuned to the violence of love in epic romances, we have also witnessed a concomitant erotics of violence and aggression in the story.[45] This may explain why, as some readers have found, we see a latent homoerotics in the mutual dressing of Palamon and Arcite in the grove before their private duel. John Bowers writes:

> When Palamon and Arcite meet by accident in the grove outside the city, a location more appropriate as a trysting-place, they experience a "chaungyng of hir hewe" just like two bashful lovers. Then they proceed to help each other dress for battle in the most affectionate, physically familiar manner.[46]

At once noble and sublimating, their actions are also implicitly eroticized and certainly emotive as they prepare to fight each other to the death.

Desire names the ambivalences of love and aggression in the Knight's Tale, the way they substitute for each other in the economy by which desire is maintained and continued. As a narrative of desire, the Knight's Tale is pervaded by a logic of substitution. The Knight's narration is, in fact, driven by this logic from the very start as he substitutes the story of Palamon and Arcite for the one about Theseus and Hippolyta he refuses to tell. But even within the tale's fictional confines, exile substitutes for imprisonment, tournament substitutes for private conflict, blunted weapons substitute for a fight to the death, Arcite's funeral rites substitute for his wedding

---

45. That conflation of violence and erotics comes even earlier in the Theseus–Pirithous allusion, which is how Arcite gains freedom in the first place.

46. Bowers, "Three Readings," 286. For a more emphatic homoerotic reading of the tale, see Andrew James Johnston, "Wrestling with Ganymede: Chaucer's *Knight's Tale* and the Homoerotics of Epic History," *Germanisch-Romanische Monatsschrift* 50 (2000): 21–43.

celebrations. The Knight's Tale uses the logic of substitution as a means of temporarily settling and thereby continuing its conflicts in altered forms. As such, the romance compensates for and qualifies its losses, even its narrative ones—the stories it implies but won't tell.[47]

One of the reasons substitution is so pervasive in the Knight's Tale is that its genre is so invested in the contours of desire and the individuating acculturation of the heroic subjects arising from it. Indeed, if romances are about individuation, that process is, in fact, one of substitution, its sociality founded on an economics of exchangeability and compensation. For the assumption of desire is fundamentally an acceptance of substitution: of objects for cause and signifiers for objects. We might more positively express the situation in terms of profit and production: the process of individuation, which entails the "loss" of the originary cause of desire, comes with a linguistic gain, in which one compensates and is compensated for what is lost with language, the signifiers by which a lack is named and circumscribed. But the compensation is never adequate and its satisfactions only partial. The very content of the Knight's Tale as well as its elaborate linguistic form replay the compensatory structure of these foundational substitutions. In terms of both the Knight's participation in the storytelling contest and the larger profit reaped from Theseus's reparative orchestrations (by Palamon and by us), the tale everywhere enacts the same drama that it records in its fiction.[48]

The narrative of desire the Knight's Tale sets in motion is one that relates to the other stories—as well as to the rivalrous, aggressive, substitutive process by which they are arranged in Chaucer's unfinished collection—and to the nature of storytelling as a functional, productive social form in fundamental ways. In fact, we might say this process *relates,* in both senses, the stories themselves. The tales are, of course, rivalrous narratives of desire connected by their shared content, but they are also narrated products of desire. If the pagan characters in the Knight's Tale speak a significance that they do not themselves know—"we witen nat what thyng we preyen heere"—so too does the tale, as part of a larger fiction,

---

47. For the way in which Chaucer's narratives are structured by missing stories, see my *Absent Narratives, Manuscript Textuality, and Literary Structure in Late Medieval England* (New York: Palgrave Macmillan, 2002), esp. 99–133 on the Knight's Tale.

48. The tale's narration (whether we call it the Knight's, knighthood's, or Chaucer's), so careful about what must be omitted or abbreviated, must imitate Theseus, its avatar, by turning loss into social productivity. Ingham forcefully shows how the tale's use of the discourses of excessively feminine mourning are in danger of blindly reproducing its ideological assumptions in our critical appreciation of its order and its form. She warns, "The image of an inevitably lethal mourning of women, moreover, disciplines the rest of us: we will, like Theseus, order our responses to loss more moderately" ("Homosociality" 35).

speak in terms it cannot by definition comprehend. Readers have noted such significances in the ways in which various other stories, like the Miller's Tale or the Merchant's Tale, respond to and rework formal features of the Knight's. But this relationship has only been read unidirectionally, positioning the fabliaux quotations of the Knight's "pitee renneth soone in gentil herte" (1.1761) as ironic deployments. They have not been examined as moments that reveal something particularly important about the Knight's story itself.

Arcite's contemplative language regarding fate and free will encountered earlier (1.1251–60) takes up the question of desire in terms important to our understanding of mastery and control, as well as the knowledge that undergirds them. These terms are central to a number of fictions, comic as well as serious, and to their role as interpretations of Chaucer's *Tales*. When Arcite asserts "We witen nat what thing we preyen heere" (1.1260), he raises the object of desire (the "thing") in terms of both language ("preyen") and knowledge ("witen"). While articulated in language, in the prayers or requests that register our desires—We do not know what we ask for; We do not understand what it is that we want—desire itself is not fully speakable and cannot be completely understood. In Lacan's terms, the cause of desire is encountered in the realm of the Real, lying beyond what can be consciously formulated. As real, and thus more than irony or any kind of poetic reversal, desire is what *knows us*. Just think of the ends to which the tale moves: Palamon's possession of Emily and Arcite's victorious death. These ends are and are not the thing these characters wanted; yet, they are *precisely* what they asked for. Arcite's case is, of course, the more provocative in terms of his own responsibility for the end he receives from Mars: "Yif me [victorie]; I aske thee namoore" (1.2420). As far as his end goes, Arcite has clearly asked for it in no uncertain terms.

And yet, the instability of the object of Arcite's desire is never more apparent than at this point in the tale, when he names what he wants in Mars's temple. The *Riverside* text places his desire, "[victorie]," in square brackets to mark its curious status as editorial insertion and critical formulation. The majority of manuscripts otherwise used to produce Chaucer's text, Ellesmere and Hengwrt principal among them, do not contain this exact reading. Replacing the more prevalent "the victorie" with merely "victorie," this editorial mark traces an absence that cannot otherwise be expressed. The wish to remove the definite article before "victorie" neatly coincides with the critical search for a definite means of reconciling the story's end to the questions the tale poses, making the more general concept of "victorie" into a critique of Arcite's limited fixations. Where "the victorie" could more easily be identified with the singular goal of Arcite's upcoming battle, "victorie" on its own registers an abstract care about winning for which Arcite has been faulted.

These brackets do not provoke us to ask for another word in this place, some addition to the line that more reliably establishes matters. On the contrary, the editorial mark calls attention to the precarious material articulation of a question the poem has been asking all along: What really belongs in this space? What is it that Arcite (or anyone else, for that matter) desires? What should he have said? Focusing on the bracketed signifier here, at a point where every signifier's interchangeability with other signifiers (in the form of other manuscript readings) is most apparent in the text's editorial production, we are reminded of the ways the signifier stands in for what Arcite wants, the ways "victorie" is equivalent to yet different from "Emelye." Not only metrical equivalent in the way the terms can complete the poetic line, "Emelye" even end-rhymes with "victorie," making more audible the connection between them.[49]

For Arcite, the noble warrior par excellence who operates under the chivalric code, victory in the amphitheater *means* Emily, being worthy of her as tournament prize. Working with confidence in the chivalric system, he here seeks to replay Theseus's martial victory over the Amazons that earned him a wife. And this understanding of Arcite's actions is entirely central to the way we typically read these figures in the tale. He does not, as some readers have tried to argue, make a mistake when he places victory before the lady herself: "Yif me [victorie]; I aske thee namoore" (1.2420).[50] Arcite instead knows that before he can receive any mercy from her, he must "wynne hire in the place" (1.2399). We are called in this instance (much like the opening scene in which Palamon is struck by the sight of Emily and speaks to her as the embodiment of Venus) to understand figural equivalences and all that such figuration entails. In placing "victorie" in the signifying chain that articulates his desire for Emily, Arcite does not err. This is not some kind of individuating or psychologizing gesture by which his limitation as a true lover is revealed. Instead, he places his actions in the tournament in culturally and historically specific terms. In a world of armed combat in

---

49. On the textual issues generated at the point at which Arcite makes his prayer for "victorie" and the variability of the signifier here, particularly its relation to "Emelye," see the material previously published in "Desire," in *A Handbook of Middle English Studies*, ed. Marion Turner (Malden and Oxford; Wiley-Blackwell, 2013), 49–62, esp. 58–61.

50. Judith Perryman, for example, blames his death on such mistaken and condemnable speech acts; his oath breaking seals his fate in Chaucer's tale. Faulting him as an "opportunist and pragmatist rather than a premeditated deceiver," she finds his death a reward for his false behavior in "The 'False Arcite' of Chaucer's *Knight's Tale*," *Neophilologus* 68 (1984): 121–33, at 131.

which knights must battle for and earn their rewards, Arcite seeks a decision as to his superior worth and desert—as if in a judicial combat. Only if we dehistoricize his actions here can we say that Arcite puts his own renown and reputation above Emily "herself," whatever the Knight's Tale imagines that might be.

Instead, Arcite's request for "victorie" speaks a desire to be *worthy* of the lady in heroic terms. Indeed, the term "worthy" has been an important one both to the rest of the Knight's Tale and to the Knight himself, as he is described in his General Prologue portrait, where Chaucer uses the word ("worthy," "worthynesse") no fewer than four times in the Knight's thirty-line description.[51] According to this logic, Arcite asks for Emily when he asks for victory. But, of course, the signified slides under and away from the signifier, separating the two in the most unexpected of ways. He is awarded Emily as soon as Theseus calls for the end of the competition: "Hoo! namoore, for it is doon! . . . Arcite of Thebes shal have Emelie, / That by his fortune hath hire faire ywonne" (1.2656–59). But, of course, Arcite never "shal have" Emily in the way that Theseus (or his own prayer) meant. Despite Theseus's words (and perhaps *only* within them), Arcite's prayer has been granted; Emily is "ywonne." He obtains "victorie," possesses Emily for a brief moment *within* Theseus's speech, and "namoore."

The variability of signifiers allows these turns of events to emerge out of the language in which they are uttered. Because there is no absolute meaning to these terms, we can imagine the various ways in which these prayers could work, none of which have to meet any particular narrative ends but all of which must be true.[52] We might feel as if we were back at the beginning of the poem, equivocating on the sense of "fals" to be deployed—whose words in the prayer will end up being "true"—and what will that truth look like? Equally ambiguous, Palamon's request for "possessioun" is similarly subject to this linguistic slippage, no more fixed to the necessity of the tale's final events, as the Miller's and Reeve's revisions of the Knight's

---

51. For more discussion of the worthiness of the Knight and how his worth is maintained, see my "Yeoman Services: Chaucer's Knight, His Yeoman, and the Pleasures of Historicism," *Chaucer Review* 45 (2010): 194–221.

52. Hence we find a multiplicity of critical arguments, especially over the nature of these determinations. Such is what makes the ending of the tale so provocative, prompting its readers to look for ways that the tale (or the temperaments of Palamon and Arcite, or their prayers, or the gods they worship, or their champions, etc.) determines this end. But there is, in fact, no point at which the tale firmly determines this end because there is no way to determine what the signifiers constituting the prayers or laments (and thus articulating desire) firmly and absolutely mean. The Miller will stake much of his comedy on the play of these signifiers of desire (cf. "melodye") as well. In his elaborate (and sometimes mundane) quotations of the Knight's Tale, he turns the signifier to spectacular uses.

Tale will show. Where Arcite's request for "victorie" has received some scrutiny, little attention has been paid to Palamon's request to Venus: to "have fully possessioun / Of Emelye, and dye in thy servyse" (1.2242–43). We have always already read these lines in romantically metaphorical terms, as the Knight's Tale demands, where "possessioun" is neither legal nor sexual, despite what the "service" of Venus might elsewhere imply, not to mention "dying" in it. Yet legal and sexual possession *are* everywhere at stake in Palamon's prayer, which the tale's fabliaux responses suggest in belated fashion. Not until we compare this wish of Palamon's to Nicholas's rhetorical death wish in the service of Venus in the Miller's Tale do we notice the particularly sexual potential in the literal terms of Palamon's vow. Declaring to Alison "for deerne love of thee, lemman, I spille" (1.3278), Nicholas's linguistic play on the signifier ("spille") abruptly desublimates the language of Palamon's amorous pursuit, as it more fully acknowledges in retrospect the latent erotics of Palamon's prayer. These meanings are harbored within the language of the Knight's Tale, even if they are not initially heard there, inhering in the signifier in almost palpable ways.

Far from showing that Arcite did not understand what he asked for in Mars's temple, this episode suggests that Arcite's language knows him better than he knows himself and his own desire (and for that matter, so does Palamon's). By giving him *exactly* what he asked for, the Knight's Tale draws a distinction between desire and one's articulation of it—the putting into words that is always already a substitution for an object from which one is, by definition, barred. As soon as Arcite receives what he asked for, "victorie," we realize that articulation is an inadequate formulation of desire *and* its only means of promulgation. This is and is not what he sought. Palamon, by contrast, attains Emily arbitrarily, because that is the way language works, because his language (like Arcite's too) remains open to the unpredictable movements of the signifier. Presciently, he admits to what he cannot know: "I ne have no langage to telle . . . I am so confus that I kan noght seye" (1.2227–30). Confused almost to the point of silence, he leaves it up to Venus:

> I kepe noght of armes for to yelpe,
> Ne I ne axe nat tomorwe to have victorie,
> Ne renoun in this cas, ne veyne glorie
> Of pris of armes blowen up and doun;
> But I wolde have fully possessioun
> Of Emelye, and dye in thy servyse.
> (1.2238–43)

Having "noght [to] seye," Palamon's words express the inherently linguistic and substitutive laws of desire. The number of terms relating to language and its effects in this short speech are striking. Palamon wishes to avoid speech, the "yelp[ing]" and "blow[ing]" that makes up the fame coming from such "renoun" in "pris of armes" and in the form of "veyne glorie." Indeed, what he most wishes to avoid is becoming the subject of someone else's envious speech. What does it mean, then, that Palamon ends the tale married to Emily by Theseus's verbal decree? What power does the recognition of (and subjection to) the power of language hold in the Knight's Tale, and how might that allow us to reread Theseus's conclusive "prime mover" speech?

The language by which we attempt to describe this end is literally decisive, threatening to decide the matter between the two knights in ways the tale's own language patently refuses to do so. To say, for instance, that Palamon is more successful than Arcite would place his "possessioun" of Emily above Arcite's "victorie," when, in fact, they are equivalent articulations, denoting at once success and failure. Each knight has spoken a desire in terms that are technically satisfied, which thus makes each of them the one "that moost desireth" Emily (1.2325). Similarly, to say that Palamon "wins" Emily is patently false. Palamon did not win at all, and winning has been entirely unimportant to him all along, as we see from his speech to Venus above.[53] Palamon's advantage, could he be seen to have one, is to articulate a difference between "victorie" and "possessioun," being and having, as the nature of his desire. But as openly confused as he is, it is one he cannot claim consciously to know. And yet this *un*knowing perhaps permits the end he receives. Remember that Emily, wanting to remain a maiden all her life, resigns herself to the gods' will by asking Diana "if my destinee be shapen so / That I shal nedes have oon of hem two, / As sende me hym that moost desireth me" (1.2323–25). Palamon does not ask for the right "thing," so much as Palamon leaves himself open (and not in the way he intends) to the vagaries of substitution and therefore desires, stands in relation to lack, more nakedly. Admitting his confusion, he does not arrest the sliding of the signifier of desire. He also acknowledges the signifier's power in the very language he uses. Palamon fears the signifier itself: leery "for to yelpe" and refusing to ask ("ne I ne axe nat") he eschews all kinds of words: "renoun," "veyne glorie," and the news of his arms "blowen up and down." His language is principally *about language* he wishes to avoid. In this way

---

53. As Fradenburg writes, "win" and its cognates are terms that one can only use about Theseus, "that sovereign subject from whom one must receive and to whom one must yield in order to be recognized as subject" ("Sacrificial Desire" 60).

we can say, perhaps, that Palamon speaks the language of desire fluently, if reticently, for desire *is* language.

Despite her request to be sent "hym that moost disereth me," both cousins are "sent" to Emily in the end—a circumstance that decides nothing. Arcite comes to her directly as the result of Theseus's plans for judgment and decision (though in conflict, precisely, with the rules he appoints to decide them). Palamon marries her in the tale's conclusion. The one who desires her "moost" is both undecidable and fully decided by the tale's close. The Knight's Tale ends with desire's and language's rigorous undecidability.[54] Which one deserves Emily? "Who hath the worse"? The problems set in motion by the tale are gone, but none of its many questions has been answered for good.

One of the major effects of the Knight's Tale is the kind of narrative satisfaction it ostensibly offers with this ending, despite the fact that its consolations may not be complete. The Canterbury pilgrims feel it too: "And namely the gentils everichon" (1.3113). We are used to parsing this last detail, its specificity of the "gentils" who find the tale "worthy," in light of the Miller's interruption and act of "quiting" the Knight. But Bailly also finds the tale satisfying in some way: "This gooth aright; unbokeled is the male" (1.3115), at least for his social and economic purposes. We also find the tale somewhat satisfying, particularly on a first reading, when we are less likely to foresee the means by which its triangulated conflict gets resolved.

One way in which we might understand these satisfactions, which are, of course, merely temporary and partial, resides in Freud's pleasure principle (what Lacan more aptly renamed the unpleasure principle) as well as its "beyond." The pleasure principle is not what it sounds like, a principle of enjoyment, but instead a principle of stasis in which the excitation or anxiety of displeasure is reduced or eliminated. The pleasure principle is a fundamentally regulatory mechanism.[55] If we see the Knight's Tale as operating at various stages of excitation, personal and romantic, political and cosmic, we can see its ending as more clearly an outcome regulated in

---

54. Barbara Johnson, "Rigorous Undecidability," in *A World of Difference* (Baltimore: Johns Hopkins UP, 1987), 17–24.

55. Discussion of the pleasure principle and its regulatory operations is found in "Beyond the Pleasure Principle," *The Standard Edition of the Complete Pscyhological Works of Sigmund Freud*, 24 volumes, ed. and trans. James Strachey et al. (London: Hogarth P, 1958), 18:1–64. Lacan's discussion of the concepts of pleasure, unpleasure, and the Real occur throughout his writing. For his rereading of the pleasure principle as the unpleasure principle, see *The Seminar of Jacques Lacan, Book II: The Ego in Freud's Theory and in the Technique of Psychoanalysis, 1954–1955*, ed. Jacques-Alain Miller, trans. Sylvana Tomaselli (New York: Norton, 1991), 79ff.

accordance with Freud's law. Much in line with its critical reception, the story produces for its characters less pleasure than a regulation of anxiety. This perhaps explains why the description of the wedding of Palamon to Emily is so measured and even restrained (1.3094–106). As the conclusion to a romance, we could expect for Emily's wedding to be elaborately narrated, especially seeing how it stands in the place of Theseus's own wedding at the beginning of the story. Instead Emily and Palamon are brought together as a remediation for Arcite's loss: "looketh now, wher moost sorwe is herinne, / Ther wol we first amenden and bigynne" (1.3073–74). There, where we find most sorrow and suffering, Theseus presumes to make "O parfit joye" (1.3072). But rather than convincing us of their pleasure and happiness ("alle blisse and melodye," 1.3097), the union compensates for something else. We look to the end of romance for perfect joy, an ultimate ecstatic pleasure we presume the story to be pursuing, but that *jouissance* is actually opposed to the pleasure principle and to pleasure itself. Such "joy" could not be a conclusion, a state to which one arrives at the end of frenzied action; it is frenzied action. We *think* we are going to be repaid with the scene of enjoyment at the end of such tales, as the reward for the kind of long suffering and "greet adversitee" (1.3087) in which romances embroil their protagonists and their audiences, only to have such a scene displaced or deferred. Like the story of the "feste . . . at [Theseus's] weddynge" (1.853) that the Knight never narrates at the opening of the tale, we find that we never hear such stories. The best the Knight can offer is silence: "all [the] welle" in which Palamon resides "in blisse, in richesse, and in heele" (1.3101–2) is a pleasure that can be summed up as quiet.[56] The tale's final bliss, then, could be better defined as the reduction of anxiety Freud described: "never was ther no word hem bitwene / Of jealousie or any oother teene" (1.3105–6). Such is not the stuff of romance, particularly one in which the hero and heroine have had no such jealousy or anger between them previously.

But if this ending appears abruptly tacked on, we are satisfied by the disposition of the plot—the Knight has tied all his loose ends together: all prayers have analogously been answered; the gods have all had their decrees passed; the lovers have gotten what they have asked for. These satisfactions are decidedly linguistic and literal, like Arcite's equivocation on the word "fals," dependent upon the point at which the signifier is installed, not on what it "means" in any absolute sense. Through this use

---

56. We might briefly note here the way the marriage group tales return to this idea—especially the Franklin's Tale, where initial oaths are made "to lede the moore in blisse hir lyves" (5.744).

of language, the tale offers the form of satisfaction, what Jean Laplanche calls "the appeasement linked to a reduction of tension," without any specific content.[57] If our anxieties in reading the story have analogously been diminished and our energies withdrawn in accordance with the pleasure principle, our *jouissance* remains alive, postponed for the future and, in the specific context depicted here, for yet another tale. Though poised in opposition to it, the pleasure principle allows for the continuance of our *jouissance* by relieving us of the acknowledgment of its foundational and irreparable loss. It is still somewhere else, yet to be had. We experience a compensatory pleasure through the promise of later enjoyment—the future happiness remediates the less pleasurable past. By this economic action, our access to enjoyment is maintained; we live in our fiction of the future and sustain its continuation, as we await the next story.

The climax of the Knight's Tale is thus no climax at all, but a compensatory fiction that tries to manage our suffering and our uncertainty, which have been provoked throughout. In the end, the Knight's Tale offers us a brilliant means of leaving all its questions unanswered ("who hath the worse," 1.1348), even those that are rhetorical ("Who looketh lightly now but Palamoun? / Who spryngeth up for joye but Arcite? / Who kouthe telle, or who kouthe it endite[?]," 1.1870–72) and those that go unasked (Which one deserves Emily? What is worse, death or defeat?). Yet its narrative problems are resolved: "thus with alle blisse and melodye / Hath Palamon ywedded Emelye" (1.3097–98). The marriage of two figures concludes the poem (just as one also began it), but this fact in no way relieves us from the burden of meaning, from our attempt to understand the rough justice of all that has occurred. Theseus's fabricated "parfit joye" at the end of the Knight's Tale doesn't quite satisfy us in the way we expected but offers the ruse of satisfaction, an ultimate substitution and end to his discourse. It puts an end to the spectacular substitutions that have moved the tale along. Thus, what the recent discussions of death in the Knight's Tale tell us is that Arcite's funeral does some powerful work in the story, fundamentally exposing and acknowledging (and at the same time obfuscating) the loss upon which desire is founded by continually dramatizing a fresh one.

In her discussion of the tale's sacrificial logic, Fradenburg asks us to see how the inscrutability of the law governs our *jouissance*. But to turn to the more familiar terms I have been using to invoke our satisfaction and pleasure at the end of the story, we might note how this tale keeps asking us

---

57. Jean Laplanche, *Life and Death in Psychoanalysis*, trans. Jeffrey Mehlman (1970; Baltimore: Johns Hopkins UP, 1976), 105.

questions, both explicitly (at the ends of parts 1 and 2) and implicitly—asking us to decide between Palamon and Arcite—only to prevent us from ever having or being able to do so. When we enjoy the orderliness of the tale, its means of satisfying the linguistic claims any of its characters presumed to utter, we enjoy never having to render our judgment—which might itself be a more important gesture for the entire poem rather than just for this opening story. The transformation of the signifier, wherein "victorie" slides from a signification of "Emelye" to meaning (and becoming the means to) "death," offers the ruse of satisfaction in its place. It literally lets us have it both ways by making the instability of the signifier, its wonderful and multiple transformations, both its effects and its cause.

If the Knight's Tale has implicitly engaged in and played with various misreadings as the effect of the circulation of the signifier, the elaborate literary apparatus of the Knight's Tale already situates its story within a similarly deceptive reading process—acts of revision, appropriation, condensation, and omission—dependent on a set of familiar classical and emerging vernacular traditions. From its opening the Knight's Tale invokes this process with its standard rubric, an epigraph from Statius's *Thebaid*. The pervasiveness of this Statian rubric in the manuscript tradition suggests that the epigraph appeared in the exemplars from which scribes formed some of the earliest and most authoritative of our manuscripts.[58] The implications are thus that it was attached to the Knight's Tale from an early point in the textual tradition, perhaps by Chaucer himself. But Statius is little more than an imaginary source. While his epic history functions to guarantee the status of the Knight's story, Statius's foundational role is really played by Boccaccio's *Teseida*, which itself presumes to emerge from book 12 of the *Thebaid*.[59]

The epigraph's Latinate and written nature produces a literary effect undetectable in the fictional orality of the pilgrimage context—How would a story told on the Canterbury road begin with such a feature? Who could understand this Latin? What about its abbreviations?—disturbing any neat situation of the Knight's Tale in the *Canterbury Tales* even as it announces its classical inheritances.[60] This quotation from Statius may be a survival

---

58. On the consistency of the appearance of the Statian epigraph and its status as a gloss by Chaucer himself, see *The Text of the Canterbury Tales, Studied on the Basis of All Known Manuscripts*, ed. John M. Manly and Edith Rickert, 8 vols. (Chicago: U of Chicago P, 1940), 3.484.

59. Winthrop Wetherbee, "Romance and Epic in the Knight's Tale," *Exemplaria* 2 (1920): 303–28. Wetherbee offers a serious consideration of Chaucer's debt to Statius, mediated through Dante's *Purgatorio*.

60. On the Statian epigraph as a nod to the civic triumph, a scene that in fact opens the action of the Knight's Tale, see Elizabeth Fowler, "The Afterlife of the Civil Dead: Conquest in the Knight's

from the tale's textual existence as an independent romance, a remnant of the earlier "Palamon and Arcite," mentioned in the Prologue to the *Legend of Good Women* (F.420–21). In counterpoise to this Chaucerian remnant, another "remenant" (1.886–90), surely an addition written to purpose, forms the one passage Chaucer added to retrofit the tale to its new fictional environment.[61] In images starkly at odds with the rest of the story's language, the Knight compares his narrative work to plowing a field with a team of weak oxen and recalls the "soper" at stake in the contest. Otherwise the tale makes no outside references to the frame narrative or its concerns.[62]

We might say, then, that the Knight's Tale rereads, even misreads, the former "Palamon and Arcite" in order to attach it more firmly to the *Tales,* even as the story purports to redeploy Statius's *Thebaid* for this same purpose.[63] But instead of looking at Statius or even Boccaccio to find out what the Knight "misreads" in order to produce the story he offers the pilgrim company, this inserted comment already misreads the Knight's story. Early in the tale, he pauses:

> I have, God woot, a large feeld to ere,
> And wayke been the oxen in my plough.
> The remenant of the tale is long ynough.
> I wol nat letten eek noon of this route.
> Lat every felawe telle his tale aboute.
> (1.886–90)

The terms that the Knight applies to his story, the "remenant" of a much longer narrative he cannot tell in full, situates it in relation to the past in the very terms of peasant response (and peasant conflict) coming in the near future (1.3157–66). The signifier circulates both backward and forward in the *Canterbury Tales,* belatedly situating the Knight's Tale as answer to

---

Tale," in *Critical Essays on Geoffrey Chaucer,* ed. Thomas Stillinger (New York: Twayne, 1998), 59–81.

61. This remnant is also treated by Miller, *Philosophical Chaucer,* 50–56, and by Brooke Hunter, "*Remenants* of Things Past: Memory and the *Knight's Tale,*" *Exemplaria* 23 (2011): 126–46.

62. While the Knight makes no explicit references to the pilgrimage or to the other tale-tellers elsewhere in his story, one might argue that Egeus's worldview—"This world nys but a thurghfare ful of wo, / And we been pilgrymes, passynge to and fro" (1.2846–47)—is written in these terms especially for the Knight's storytelling occasion. Theseus's father otherwise has little role to play in the tale.

63. Bowers argues that the Knight's Tale is a cleaned up and moralized version of an explicitly homophobic and anti-Ricardian "Palamon and Arcite." He writes, Chaucer "performed a radical act of rereading his text," purging Boccaccio's focus on male friendship, written "for an Italian mercantile elite possessing far more tolerant, sometimes even supportive attitudes toward male homosexuality" ("Three Readings" 287–88).

the Miller's response. We find the Knight's misreading in a curiously familiar place—one that disrupts the chronology of textual production in a telling way. The misreading characterizing the Knight's Tale is not merely in some previous story or classical exemplar but in the Miller's narrative that follows. As the Knight fictionalizes a backward trajectory to Statius, he also gestures forward with this plowing metaphor. Here is the substitutive structure of the *Canterbury Tales* as a belated (mis)reading of desire in narrative in miniature.[64] Misreadings will not be found in prior tales so much as they will be retroactively interpreted by the tales that follow them in a belated process driving the contest forward.

When Chaucer sought a means of suturing "Palamon and Arcite" into the *Canterbury Tales,* he did so not by altering the romance he formerly wrote but by crafting a particularized response and aggressive reading of it. This strategy marks the ways desire is inscribed in the *Tales* at the level of the signifier and gets carried beyond to generate the relation of stories. The Knight's Tale begins, literally, as a misreading—Statius for Boccaccio, one that misses the point of the "Legend of Ariadne" as well as the anticipated perfidy of Anelida's "fals Arcite"—and it ends as one too in the proliferations of fragment 1. Misrecognizing themselves *in* the Knight's Tale, the pilgrims are located in a chain of narrative substitutions *for* the Knight's Tale. But some of their narrative desires blind them to this relation. Insofar as the Miller consciously appears to take his theme and structure from the Knight's Tale, the Reeve is almost entirely unaware of the origin of his story. He is far too fixated on the insult he thinks the Miller has leveled. But, as we shall see in the next chapter, (mis)reading like the Reeve is a far more dangerous prospect.

---

64. One could also discuss "letten" (to hinder) in this passage. The Knight means he will refrain from delay; he refuses to hinder the pilgrimage journey and its contest. The Miller understands the Knight's potential hindrance in different ways.

two

MISREADING LIKE THE REEVE

Whatever else the conflict between the Knight and Miller is about, their argument is grounded in competing narratives of desire and competing ways of using language. Chaucer's readers have long recognized the way the Miller's fabliau replays the Knight's romance with a difference, making the pair a "comedy of incongruous juxtaposition."[1] The Knight's elaborate symmetrical structure—fully equipped with Latin epigraphs, incipits and explicits organizing its parts, and elevated diction—gives way to the "thrifty" design of the Miller's brisk comedy and its quotidian register. Deploying genres ostensibly suited to the narrators who tell them, these tales pose alternate means of attaining desirable feminine figures; the Miller's Alison has thus stood as "the accessible and sensuous antitype to the distant and spiritualized Emily . . . more animal than goddess."[2] Like the opening sentence of the General Prologue organized around its longing folk, then, the social and narrative contest of the *Canterbury Tales* first emerges as a debate about desire—in fact, a debate about a debate about desire. Because, much like Palamon

---

1. Derek Pearsall, *The Canterbury Tales* (1985; New York: Routledge, 1993), 173.
2. Helen Cooper, *Oxford Guides to Chaucer: The Canterbury Tales* (Oxford: Oxford UP, 1989), 103. In calling the fabliaux "low," I am referring to their setting rather than to their audience. Their oral transmission and the manuscript remains suggest a mixed audience of nobles and townsmen. See R. Howard Bloch's introduction to *The Fabliaux,* trans. Nathaniel E. Dubin (New York: Liveright, 2013), esp. xxi–xxiii.

and Arcite at the beginning of the Knight's story—men who fight over which of them can *say* he loves Emily—what these narrators are really arguing about is language: who can wield the power of the signifier. Of course, each tale witnesses a conflict over a desired feminine object and moves toward a sharper presentation of how desire works, dissipates, or is revealed as something other than it first seemed. Yet the Knight and Miller conflict less over objects and instead focus upon the terms of amorous conflict itself, which is why they have been read as ultimately analogous stories.³

Where this opening pair argues about how to talk about desire, the Reeve's Tale would seem to avoid the subject entirely in its "'adversative' aggressiveness."⁴ In his anger, he tells a dark and bitter version of the Miller's fabliau, corrupting the tale's comedy by trading its erotic focus for a nearly myopic attention to the genre's more vengeful aspects.⁵ Making his tale a personal act of revenge, he disrupts the storytelling contest and sets it down a path of narrative degeneration that ends in silence, with the scurrilous Cook's fragment, too nasty to be completed. Despite what seems the Reeve's insentience to the erotic pressures driving the Miller's Tale, I will argue that his tale plays a pivotal role in the *Canterbury Tales*' discourse of desire. Even further, the simultaneously linear and ultimately disruptive structure formed by the Reeve's addition to the first fragment offers a paradigm of generative misreading governing the rest of Chaucer's poem.

In fabliau the trickster figure (typically an illicit lover and often a priest or cleric) is himself tricked in such a way that the limitations of his cleverness are exposed to laughter. The Reeve zeroes in on the trick in the Miller's story but seeks more brutally to punish its teller for entirely different reasons. The cleverness of tricky Nicholas and the seductiveness of such clerks as he are not so much the issue as the humiliation of the husband, a carpenter named John, whose broken arm and mad raving about a second

---

3. On the ways in which the Knight and Miller share a similar set of assumptions about women, see Elaine Tuttle Hansen, "'Women-as-the Same' in the A-Fragment," in *Chaucer and the Fictions of Gender* (Berkeley: U of California P, 1992), 208–44; and Karma Lochrie, "Women's 'Pryvetees' and Fabliau Politics in the Miller's Tale," *Exemplaria* 6 (1995): 287–304, esp. 302–3.

4. This double quotation testifies to the wide acceptance of the Reeve's negativity. Edward Vasta, "How Chaucer's Reeve Succeeds," *Criticism* 25 (1983): 1–12, at 8, is cited by Bruce Kent Cowgill in "Clerkly Rivalry in the Reeve's Tale" in *Rebels and Rivals: The Contestive Spirit in "The Canterbury Tales,"* ed. Susanna Greer Fein, David Raybin, and Peter C. Braeger (Kalamazoo: Medieval Institute, 1991), 59–71, at 59.

5. Such corruption, like the "low" fabliau itself, is a Chaucerian fiction. The Old French fabliaux are much darker, deeply ironic comedies, more like the Reeve's Tale than the Miller's gamesome fun. See Simon Gaunt, *Gender and Genre in Medieval French Literature* (Cambridge: Cambridge UP, 1995); and Howard Bloch, *The Scandal of the Fabliaux* (Chicago: U of Chicago P, 1986).

Flood provoke more laughter than any "scald[ing] in the towte" Nicholas receives (1.3853). "By cause he was of carpenteris craft," the Reeve is the one pilgrim aggrieved at the end of the Miller's story (1.3861). Understanding it rather narrowly as an insulting representation of carpenters and thus himself, Osewold the Reeve offers his own retaliatory representation of corrupt millers in "deynous Symkyn" (1.3941), a fictional miller who physically resembles Robyn, the Miller described by Chaucer in the General Prologue. This mean-spiritedness has largely been the source of the critical difficulties the story poses. Few would judge it on its own (outside this dramatic context) one of Chaucer's best, and the Reeve himself seems to have forgotten the larger purpose of the tales and the social nature of the game. The storytelling contest fades from view as a very different kind of aggressive competitiveness takes its place.

What *has* been critically appreciated about the Reeve's Tale is the swerve Chaucer makes into character revelation and dramatic interaction. We have been expecting such a response from the beginning of the Miller's Prologue, where the Reeve first made peremptory effort to silence the "legende and . . . lyf / Bothe of a carpenter and of his wyf, / How that a clerk hath set the wrightes cappe" (1.3141–43). Where the Miller's interruption dramatically derailed Harry Bailly's plans, which would have "dutifully organiz[ed] the game according to the conservative program of the three orders," the Reeve's gives the frame story some of its life by taking matters even further away from any such hierarchical plan.[6] The Reeve's offering may have limitations as a tale "of best sentence and moost solaas" (1.798), but in its revealed context, these limitations become legible as the signs of something else. Yet it is hardly the reference to his life, the Reeve's status as an erstwhile carpenter, which does so; rather, it is the force with which he disrupts someone else's design and the new relations among stories such disruptions forge. Most important in this increasingly boisterous set of performances in fragment 1 is the process of change and mutation they chart—each narrator's manner of responding to and thus displacing the tale that has preceded his own. The polite requital or repayment Harry Bailly had in mind, "somwhat to quite with the Knyghtes tale" (1.3119), is nothing like the payback staged by the Reeve. In a story collection framed specifically as a competition, with its terms of "sentence" and "solaas" laid down in advance and its ultimate judgment deferred, each tale transforms what has come before in the very process of adding something new to the sequence.[7]

---

6. Lee Patterson, *Chaucer and the Subject of History* (Madison: U of Wisconsin P, 1991), 244.

7. Helen Cooper also sees the quiting scheme as an implicit act of reading. About the Miller's story she writes, "In 'quiting' the preceding tale it offers a rival reading of the world—a world of

The Reeve responds to the Miller's story in anger, personally insulted by his tale of a naïve carpenter outwitted by a clever young clerk. Chaucer thereby dramatizes more than a competitive reply to the Miller's story in the Reeve's fabliau; he stages a crucial scene of misreading and misrecognition that disables any widespread deployment of a dramatic principle from the very start. The effects of the Reeve's performance have been understood in thematic, characterological, and even political terms, but their effect is also structural. Making a triptych out of the pair that initiate the first fragment and its politics of "quiting," Chaucer offers us an explicit rereading of the Miller's Tale that complicates the linear trajectory in which it is placed, a complication as relevant to the entire *Canterbury Tales* (as a potential round-trip journey) as it is to this first fragment. The direction of the *Tales,* like narrative itself, charts a forward movement that its stories do not simply obey. In this newly formed triptych, the Miller's Tale winds up situated as a tilting mirror, both reflecting the Knight's Tale back to its teller in altered form and, apparently, allowing the Reeve to misrecognize himself in the Miller's story. The figure of the mirror facilitates thinking about the distortions and refractions of these tales' increasingly dark surfaces as well as the imaginary nature of the identifications registered in the Reeve's performance. For in this mirror, as in Lacan's, the image never measures up precisely to what stands outside of it. Occupied by a variety of others, the mirror produces misrecognitions in and on its reflecting surface. When the Reeve responds with his own tale, his narrow focus on the Miller causes him to misrecognize the Other(s) through which that imaginary relation is produced. The Reeve does not realize, that is, that language cannot be narrowly circumscribed and made to refer only to the Miller and his tale, even as he attempts to make a similar point about the ostensibly narrow reference of the Miller's own story. Chaucer ultimately stages a tale about the failure of the Reeve's intent.

The Reeve, we have long known, neglects the human and the humorous desires at the center of the Miller's fabliau and offers, in their place, a spectacle of violence and aggression. But as our previous discussion of desire suggests, these seemingly oppositional poses are intimately related to each other. Rather than merely a localized phenomenon, I would argue, Chaucer thereby dramatizes a scene of misreading crucial to his story collection. In what follows I will show how Chaucer engages the Reeve in a

---

cheerfully amoral disorder, with no metaphysical depth whatsoever." *The Structure of the Canterbury Tales* (London: Duckworth, 1983), 116. And Patterson calls the Miller's appropriation of the Host's request for something to "quit" the Knight's Tale an "aggressive misreading of the Host's words" (*Subject of History* 244).

narrowly subjective mode of reading that he simultaneously disables for the entire project with the very principles the Reeve uses in his focus on the Miller's story. Despite the Reeve's intent to rewrite the desire of the fabliau in other terms, he is ultimately rewritten by desire in that very same place in and through the signifier he would attempt to control. The Reeve's Tale shows how misreading, like the desire that it signals, operates as the *Tales'* engine.

Even as it replays its plot, the Reeve's Tale departs from the Miller's comedy with a shift in tone from its very start. The Miller introduces his protagonist, "hende" Nicholas, with winsome playfulness: "Of deerne love he koude and of solas; / And therto he was sleigh and ful privee, / And lyk a mayden meke for to see" (1.3200–202). The Oxford carpenter is set against this handsome and clever clerk who spends his time pursuing the secrets of "astrologye"(1.3192), an interest in the workings of the stars and the prediction of "droghte or elles shoures" (1.3196), which he ultimately turns to his own advantage. The Reeve little appreciates Nicholas's charm. No such playfulness motivates his clerks even though they too are "lusty for to pleye" (1.4004). A decidedly different kind of game urges them, one that has little relation to "deerne love":

> Testif they were, and lusty for to pleye,
> And, oonly for hire myrthe and revelrye,
> Upon the wardeyn bisily they crye
> To yeve hem leve, but a litel stounde,
> To goon to mille and seen hir corn ygrounde;
> And hardily they dorste leye hir nekke
> The millere sholde not stele hem half a pekke
> Of corn by sleighte, ne by force hem reve.
> (1.4004–11)

Instead these clerks seek their pleasure in foiling the open "sleighte" of Symkyn's outrageous theft during their manciple's illness. Where he had stolen "but curteisly" before, now Symkyn "was a theef outrageously" (1.3997–98), and this situation gives the clerks their opportunity. Unlike the Miller's tale of erotically motivated trickery by "sleigh" Nicholas, the Reeve offers one of nearly gratuitous deception that seeks power for its own sake, turning "pleye" into "force." The clerks are not interested in justice or the pride of their college. They act "oonly for hire myrthe and revelrye" and are given leave to perform their task by desperate necessity. The warden has little confidence in them. Being hicks from the North, identified as such by their ridiculous sounding dialect, they are presented as less than worthy adversaries for Symkyn, who "craketh boost, and swoor it was nat so" (1.4001).[8]

The competition in the Reeve's Tale rescripts the game of fabliau in which town–gown rivals are typically subject to trickery in order to procure sexual goals. In the Reeve's story, Osewold's anger confuses the genre's ends and its means such that its erotic reward is recast as the violent means to the tale's ultimately humiliating end. That is, trickery no longer serves an erotic purpose; instead, sex is the very form of the trick. And rather than displaying the clever antics of a would-be suitor, its characters are confrontational ("testif") from the very start. We might note at this early stage that this inversion of fabliau priorities already shifts the Reeve's satire from its aim, the Miller on Chaucer's pilgrimage, and points to an unacknowledged relation to the Knight to which we will return. Where the Knight's Tale suffered from a lack of a villain, the Reeve's Tale lacks a protagonist—all of its characters are set in antagonistic relationships that satirize everyone, leaving the story with a hole in its center that gets filled by the Reeve's bitterness. Nothing and no one is left out of the narrator's caustic and corrupting purview.

He narrates the story this way intentionally, of course, at the expense of the Miller, who unmistakably resembles the "fictional" Symkyn right down to the physical features and array of blades they share (1.3934). Everything in the story, according to such a logic, represents Symkyn's depraved character, not merely the outrageous thievery and open trickery the clerks hope to forestall but also his haughty wife, "digne as water in a dich" (1.3964); his wife's corrupt father, a vainglorious priest who uses parish tithes for the dowries of his illegitimate offspring; and Symkyn's still unmarried and sexually frustrated daughter, Malyne. So too with the comeuppance Symkyn eventually receives both from within and without. He is counter-tricked by two idiot Northern bumpkins inside his very home, where they are assisted by his daughter, who has thoroughly enjoyed being ruined for the elite marriage her family plots, and he is beaten by his wife, who misrecognizes his bald head for the clerk's "volupeer" in the dark (1.4303), after she has mistaken one of the clerks in her bed for her

---

8. Its representation of dialect has been one of the principal critical interests of the Reeve's Tale. The classic study is J. R. R. Tolkien, "Chaucer as a Philologist: The Reeve's Tale," *Transactions of the Philological Society* 33 (1934): 1–70. Additionally, see Robert Epstein, "'Fer in the north, I kan nat telle where': Dialect, Regionalism, and Philologism," *SAC* 30 (2008): 95–124.

husband and has had the best ride of her life ("So myrie a fit ne hadde she nat ful yoore," 1.4230). No one in Symkyn's family can escape his depravity nor can their suffering mitigate it; every gesture primarily humiliates *him*, in spite of what it might mean individually for each of them. The tale is a formidable achievement as the Reeve turns every detail into an assault on the Miller—or so it has been read.

Despite this rather comprehensive attack, the Reeve cannot fully control either its target or its source because of the very language in which it must be made and the game to which he has submitted, both in the agreement formed in the General Prologue as well as the rules language imposes more generally. The Reeve's story is not exempt from the circuit of desire in language or its Symbolic order that any focus on his intent might suggest. The Reeve's Tale is about desire, in fact, precisely to the extent that its teller believes it is not. Put simply, his attempt to shift the terms of the fabliau away from desire only betrays yet another desire, insofar as desire operates as reparation for an alienation the Reeve knows only too well. But the Reeve's Tale, I want to argue, enters the debate about the debate about desire more directly than its narrator comprehends. In the Knight's Tale, desire led to misrecognition and, in the prayers in the gods' temples, to acts of misreading. In the Miller and Reeve's fabliaux, acts of misreading and misrecognition lead to desire, however distorted and deformed, and thus the larger social world and its imposition of order and law represented by the Knight's Tale, in ways we may not have realized.[9]

Desire appears in the *Canterbury Tales* as a misreading, and nowhere more so than in the Reeve's openly vindictive story. The Reeve threatens us with such misreading from his first appearance.[10] In the Miller's Prologue, the Reeve spontaneously interrupts and tries to derail the Miller's comedy in advance on moral grounds: "It is a synne and eek a greet folye / To apeyren any man, or hym defame, / And eek to bryngen wyves in swich fame" (1.3146–48). With this early gambit, the Reeve hopes to disarm the Miller and his "lewed dronken harlotrye" in advance, offering general rather than particular terms for his distaste (1.3145). He poses a moral resis-

---

9. Here we might collate the distortions of desire and its misrecognitions with the tale's thematic interest in measurement, optics, and perception, or what Susan Yager calls "hindered or restricted sight." See her essay "'A Whit Thyng in Hir Ye': Perception and Error in the *Reeve's Tale*," *Chaucer Review* 28 (1994): 393–404.

10. While I begin with the Reeve's first words in the Miller's Prologue, others might (and have) looked at his appearance in the General Prologue—literally the way he appears with hair "dokked lyk a preest" (1.590) and with his gown "tukked . . . as is a frere" (1.621). This appearance has, for many, set the tone for the Reeve's Tale, especially as he begins with moral disapproval in the Miller's Prologue and sermonizes on age and infirmity in his own.

tance to any such story of "defame," claiming the high ground with his concern for the reputation of wives, who should not suffer "swich fame." But the Reeve's own Prologue reveals a different reason for his resistance. The story annoys him before he even hears it "by cause he was of carpenteris craft" (1.3861). Osewold finds in the Miller's story a personal insult not so covertly directed at him, and this slight has been used to adduce their prior history, some kind of past familiarity between the two "cherles" (1.3917), who are natural professional enemies.[11]

While few have taken seriously the moral contours of the Reeve's critique, preferring instead to see the Miller's Tale in "naturalistic" and amoral terms, some have been all too willing to entertain the idea of the tale's potential as personal insult.[12] A recent essay collating the Reeve's moral self-presentation with efforts to raise his social status assumes that the Miller "mercilessly hon[ed] in on the Reeve's class sensitivites . . . and aim[ed] his ridicule specifically at the Reeve's social presumption."[13] Despite the Host's impatience—"The devel made a reve for to preche" (1.3903)—the Reeve's indignation has largely been taken at face value in discussions of the class-bound animosity of these two figures that posit a professional rivalry to explain in historical terms the narrative and linguistic aggressions that Chaucer has here fictionalized. But whether naturalized into the "truth" of a miller's competition with the reeve of his estate or lamented as a lost opportunity for class solidarity against the aristocracy that oppresses them both, criticism has become comfortable with some animosity between the Miller and the Reeve driving both of these stories and governing their meaning and function, and as such takes for granted the validity of the mode of reading that the Reeve's Tale proffers.[14] Such have been the assumptions, for example, of dramatic readings of the tales, however more or less cautiously tendered. But a very different narrative of desire and aggressivity also drives the Reeve's story and directs its role in the larger collection than the one fictionalized at its surface. Instead,

---

11. Few resist the fantasy of familiarity, despite a general animus to "roadside drama," a phrase coined by George Lyman Kittredge in *Chaucer and His Poetry* (Cambridge: Harvard UP, 1915). For a fuller discussion of the filtration of tales through these individual narrators that refuses the priority of pilgrims over stories, see C. David Benson, *Chaucer's Drama of Style: Poetic Variety and Contrast in the "Canterbury Tales"* (Chapel Hill: U of North Carolina P, 1986).

12. See Frederick Tupper, "The Quarrels of the Canterbury Pilgrims," *JEGP* 14 (1915): 256–70, but the assumption is everywhere.

13. Bryan Carella, "The Social Aspirations and Priestly Pretense of Chaucer's Reeve," *Neophilologus* 94 (2010): 523–29, at 524.

14. Beyond those who have indulged in the narrative of their professional rivalry, see also Lee Patterson, who laments the class nonsolidarity here and chides us for celebrating the "subject" installed as the result of the social loss (*Subject of History* 244–79).

Chaucer portrays the Reeve in an important scene of *misreading* that propels the *Canterbury Tales* forward.

While it is true that the Reeve is angry and has taken the Miller's Tale as a provocation, it is by no means certain that he (or we) should. Derek Pearsall describes the Miller's Tale in distinctly impersonal terms: "The narrative voice is totally absorbed in the narrative, and even the exchange with the Reeve has little or no function in heightening dramatic consciousness: the portrait of John the carpenter is in no way attached to the Reeve."[15] Yet in treating the Reeve's most distinctive features, his animosity and anger that most certainly *are* a response to the portrait of John, we often forget how imaginary their origin and as Imaginary, the misrecognitions it produces in the identification it fosters. One way of going about a more skeptical critical reading of the Reeve and the reading practice he displays is, ironically, to apply it to his own story to see its limitations. The Reeve sees himself as the object of the Miller's Tale because of his former "carpenteris craft." Blinded by his own anger, the Reeve loses sight of the contest and thus his place in the Symbolic order—a situation Chaucer's modern, professional readers would generally wish to avoid. That Symbolic order is on display in the General Prologue, where Chaucer reveals its physical markers (visible physiognomic and costume details, for example) and complicates them with knowledge that is not immediately apparent at the surface, information that must have been revealed in an implicit conversation—details such as the Monk's favorite roast or what he has to say about the rule of St. Benedict. The Prologue includes the Reeve's former "myster" as a carpenter (1.613), presumably because it is one of those details the Reeve mentions in conversation with Chaucer, like the name of his horse, "Scot" (1.617), details that individuate his description and confuse his precise social location even as we learn he's from "Northfolk . . . Biside a town men clepen Baldeswelle" (1.619–20).

The Prologue's details have been confusing and somewhat hard to reconcile with each other. His youthful "myster" may have made him "a wel good wright" (1.614), but it mostly contrasts with his current status as an estate agent who steals, "reve[s]," what he attains (1.608–12). His appearance confuses matters further: "dokked lyk a preest" and with a "long surcote of pers . . . tukked . . . as a frere about," it sends mixed signals (1.617; 621). In this context we would do well to remind ourselves that the Prologue also includes a professional Carpenter, one who sits rather ostentatiously among a set of cloth workers as members of a "solempne and

---

15. Pearsall, *Canterbury Tales*, 172.

a greet fraternitee" (1.364). The Carpenter's unique position among this group calls attention to him and his craft, precisely because it differs from the other four tradesmen, who are more easily grouped together. Should someone be insulted by the Miller's Prologue because it announces his tale will feature a tricked carpenter and what that implies about such craftsmen, it ought perhaps to be *this* Carpenter, whom we have rarely attended. Including "An haberdasshere . . . / A Webbe, a Dyere, and a Tapycer," and their Cook (1.361–62; 679), the guildsmen form an odd grouping some have noticed but few can explain. According to its editorial headnote, "Their great *fraternitee* is probably not one of the craft guilds, which were usually composed of practitioners of a single trade. Instead, they are probably members of one of the parish guilds, fraternal and charitable organizations that were then gaining power" (*Canterbury Tales Complete* 348). Helen Cooper also notes the Carpenter's odd fit with the other guildsmen and echoes these implications: "The four clothworkers Chaucer lists could all belong to a single craft guild, but the inclusion of the Carpenter makes it more likely that Chaucer had in mind a parish guild: an organization in which members associated for acts of piety and mutual welfare."[16] Those very acts of piety and mutual welfare are gently satirized by what we are told of these guildsmen: mostly that their wives parade about the city in their fine clothes, attending vigils, and walking in front of others—a bit like the Wife of Bath in her own parish (1.374–77). The Carpenter has thus been read to help identify the group's historical register, but his singular position among the others—coupled with the craft he shares with the Reeve—begs more attention.

Reading from the beginning of the General Prologue forward, Jill Mann assumes the Reeve rewrites the Carpenter's significance. Ignoring the close ties among the trades of the other guildsmen, she finds "their occupations seem to be arbitrarily chosen and to have assumed no particular significance in the *Canterbury Tales* [because] 200 lines later, Chaucer re-assigns the Carpenter's trade to the Reeve, and it is he who takes offense at the Miller's Tale of the Oxford carpenter."[17] I think we might productively question what (in)significance Cooper and Mann have assigned him because not only does linear reading fail to designate fixed meaning, neither can we be certain, in the context of the poem's unfinished state and its evidence of revision, which of these carpenters came "first" in Chaucer's imagination.[18]

---

16. Cooper, *Oxford Guide*, 47.

17. Jill Mann, *Chaucer and Medieval Estates Satire* (Cambridge: Cambridge UP, 1973), 103.

18. Mann essentially reads them like a set of lines appearing in more than one place, which we tend to assume signals eventual cancellation. In what follows I will detail the ways in which some

The Reeve's former occupation has rendered invisible, or insignificant, the more prominent Carpenter in the General Prologue, when, in fact, the pilgrim Carpenter may function precisely to give the lie to the Miller's supposed insult. Mann and, to an extent, Cooper are here implicitly reading like the Reeve, more sensitive to his past than the present in which the poem engages. But not only do these two carpenters provoke us to question more intently the Reeve's perceived slight, there are also the others implicated in his discourse. Reading the Reeve's language analogously to his way of reading the Miller's shows the complex relation of self and other, subject and social world, constituting this Symbolic order on which the Reeve's very understanding implicitly depends. As short-sighted as the figure he presumes to satirize, the Miller who can see the mote in someone else's eye but in his own cannot see a "balke" (1.3920), the Reeve is blind to the very social world he tries to describe with such precision.

While a general professional enmity could be assumed for the Miller and the Reeve, Chaucer suggests no particular familiarity between these characters. In fact, I would argue, his comedy depends upon their *dissociation.* For one thing, Harry Bailly's dismissal of the Reeve's hypermoralism, "The devel made a reve for to preche" (1.3903), foregrounds the personal nature of the matter and throws it into question. Bailly's admonition assumes that the Reeve's moral response to the Miller's proffered story is unexpected and maybe inappropriate *because* he is a reeve. No one expects moral resistance to the Miller's comedy from such a figure, even one who might be groomed and dressed like a cleric. The slight the Reeve perceives as open hostility is not registered as such by anyone else who has heard the Miller's story, most of whom are laughing.

But this brief interaction also suggests more. Besides indicating a disjunction between the Miller's story and Reeve's response, Bailly thereby also throws into stark relief the Reeve's (in)ability to understand, precisely, the *moral* function of the carpenter figure within the Miller's comedy. That is, in calling attention to the figure of the carpenter in the story—mistakenly seeing it as a reference to himself *and* admonishing the Miller in specifically moral terms—the Reeve's discourse reveals, paradoxically, his blindness to the typological functions of the carpenter driving the Miller's comedy. His immediate turn to a discourse of "synne" (1.3146) adumbrates the very dimension of the Miller's story that the Reeve misrecognizes and misunderstands. John's "carpenteris craft" serves what might be construed

---

of the joke of the Reeve's Tale, which is on the Reeve, depends upon this kind of blindness to what is right in front of him.

as the Miller's "moral" point. But Osewold appears completely unaware of the Biblical humor at the center of this fabliau and nothing so much as its (mis)use of the Noah story for Nicholas's adulterous purposes. The Reeve has not recognized himself in the Miller's fictional discourse so much as *misrecognized* himself and the function of the "carpenteris crafte" in Nicholas's intellectually engineered trick on the common knowledge of the Flood and the Flood play in the Miller's Tale. And it is this very misrecognition out of which the Reeve's Tale is generated.

Within the Miller's comedy, John's profession aligns him with the Biblical Noah, the part Nicholas scripts for the old husband in the drama he is orchestrating in the carpenter's own house. We have always known the Reeve was insensible to the Miller's comedy, failing to "laughen at this nyce cas" (1.3855) like the other pilgrims at its close, but this is literally so in the way John's occupation makes possible the use of the Noah story as the means (and meaning) of the trick in the tale's plot. As Sandra Pierson Prior details, "Both in character and in situation John exemplifies the stereotypical Noah of popular tradition. As an old carpenter who faces the hard work of making and outfitting an ark (or arks in this case), John is nearly identical to the weary Noah who in the Wakefield play tells the audience: 'To begyn of this tree my bonys will I bend' (line 253)."[19] Distinct from the heroic Biblical figure we might imagine, this dramatic character is "the gullible, feeble, henpecked fool Noah had come to be in popular tradition" (Prior 61). Nicholas casts John as this aged Noah when he uses the threat of another Flood to trick the carpenter and attain his goal: "And if so be the game wente aright, / She sholde slepen in his arm al nyght" (1.3405–6). Nicholas can use this ploy because John fails to remember its end: God's promise never to destroy the earth in such a way again. In both doctrinal matters and in their common, popular representations, John shows himself "lewed" to his own detriment and despite the confidence with which he embraces it, "blessed be alwey a lewed man" (1.3455), over and above the intellectual endeavors of the student he houses.

This civic dramatic context matters to the extent John can be blamed for his own ignorant state. Indeed in a number of the extant town cycles, the story of Noah and the Flood was the play assigned to the Shipwrights.[20]

---

19. Sandra Pierson Prior, "Parodying Typology and the Mystery Plays in the *Miller's Tale*," *Journal of Medieval and Renaissance Studies* 16 (1981): 57–73, at 60.

20. Kelsie Harder identifies the shipwrights as carpenters in "Chaucer's Use of the Mystery Plays in the *Miller's Tale*," *Modern Language Quarterly* 17 (1956): 193–98, at 194.

Given the tale's continual attention to the arts of civic drama, we are provoked—nearly from the first moment the Miller begins narrating "in Pilates voys" (1.3124)—to imagine a hypothetical Oxford carpenters' guild responsible for the Noah pageant at the margins of this tale. According to Kelsie Harder, "The pageant plays belonged to the people to such an extent that the performances became a matter of civic pride, trade guilds taking the Biblical stories as bases for expansion and original development until the religious character of the plays became more of a secular spectacle than religious instruction" (194). John certainly seems to be caught under the spell of such a spectacle, forgetting God's promise at the end of the Noah episode. In the Chester Noah play, for example, God speaks:

> And forwarde, Noe, with thee I make
> and all thy seede for thy sake,
> . . . .
> Here I behette thee an heeste
> that man, woman, fowle, ne beaste
> with water whille this worlde shall laste
> I will noe more spill.[21]

Not only is John an ignorant fool for being taken in by the clerk's scheme, he reveals the moral innocence of which he vaunts throughout as simple ignorance, and it marks him as easy prey because this play could have been his own guild's responsibility in the town's festivals.

The Miller's Tale emphasizes the comic nature of this drama and the human emotions it works into the presentation of otherwise historically remote biblical narrative. Further troping on the Flood play, the tale invokes its misogynist tradition in which Noah's recalcitrant wife refuses to board the ark. Nicholas alludes to these episodes when he advises John to build three separate vessels so as to avoid the temptation of sin while they endure God's wrath (1.3589–91), admonishing him: "Hastou nat herd . . . also / The sorwe of Noe with his felaweshipe, / Er that he myghte gete his wyf to shipe?" (1.3538–40). Nicholas here preys on the doting husband's concern for Alison and his misunderstanding of the kind of "sorwe" Noah had getting "his wyf to shipe." Luckily for John, his young wife is no uxor

---

21. *The Chester Mystery Cycle*, ed. R.M. Lumiansky and David Mills, 2 vol. Early English Text Society SS 3 (Oxford: Oxford UP, 1974), 1.301–8. In the York plays, Noah reports a similar promise, located in the symbol of the rainbow: "He sette his bowe clerly to kenne / As a tokenyng bytwene hym and vs, / In knawlage tille all cristen men / That for þis worlde were fynyd þus, / With wattir wolde he neuere wast y[t] þen" (1.284–88). See *The York Plays: A Critical Edition of the York Corpus Christi Play*, ed. Richard Beadle, 2 vol. Early English Text Society, SS 23 (Oxford: Oxford UP, 2009).

Noah, who skeptically argues with her husband about the likelihood of an impending flood. Instead, John finds Alison pliant because she "was war, and knew it bet than he," fully informed of Nicholas's plans from the start (1.3604).

Of course, John is here oblivious to a great many things at the same time that he is quite proud of his own lack of learning, since it keeps him from falling into the "marle-pit," like the philosopher who gazes at the stars (1.3460). No such impractical studies or curiosity, such as Nicholas's interest in "astromye" (1.3457), distract John. He "[can] . . . oonly his bileve" (1.3456); hence his security in citing the virtue of the simple and unlearned from the Beatitudes. So much richer the comedy, then, when Nicholas beguiles this carpenter with an astronomical prediction of a second flood, making him a doting Noah with a far more pliant and knowing wife. Unlike uxor Noah with her "tools to truss," who resists boarding the ark in the Wakefield and York plays, Alison readily participates in the plot John reveals to her.[22] In on Nicholas's plan from the start, Alison plays her part as though "she ferde as she wolde deye" (1.3606). No wonder, then, that the parallels to the Noah play never occur to John since his young wife, the focus of all his attention, is such a very different actor.

Osewold's misrecognitions do not end here, and they continue to depend on the humor to be found via a carpenter's craft and the play upon its figuration in dramatic forms. The compliant status of the wife also suggests yet another biblical intertext for the antics dramatically replayed in the Miller's story. The tale's erotic figural arrangements also parody the Annunciation, invoked by means of yet another popular, artful form. In Prior's words, "Because Nicholas imitates Gabriel in singing the *Angelus ad virginem* (3216), his approach to Alison becomes a type of the Annunciation,"[23] and it installs yet another image of feminine transgression and danger, this time in a scene of divine cuckoldry that also depends upon an aged carpenter husband. John thus plays a second biblical carpenter in the typological narratives woven through the Miller's Tale. Like the Flood deception, this divine adultery plot also has its analogues in civic cycle drama.[24] Replaying biblical history from the Creation to the

---

22. Geraldine Heng notes that "Noah's wife, in the York and Wakefield cycles, for instance, is critiqued for refusing to ascend the ark . . . [;] she is a traditional figure of female disobedience" in *Empire of Magic: Medieval Romance and the Politics of Cultural Fantasy* (New York: Columbia UP, 2001), 200. We are both indebted to the thesis of Jennifer Huth, "'For I have tools to truss': Women in the York Mystery Plays" (University of Texas, 1993).

23. "Parodying Typology" 61.

24. On the ways the situation in the Miller's Tale replays and recalls the drama of the Annunciation see Beryl Rowland, "The Play of the *Miller's Tale:* A Game Within a Game," *Chaucer Review* 5 (1970): 140–46, at 144.

Last Judgment and focusing on the life of Christ, these plays were not without comic interludes. Episodes like "Joseph's Doubts About Mary" invoke contemporary social concerns and engage ordinary human emotions in their skeptical presentation of otherwise remote and serious biblical events.[25] Such episodes milk the scene of angelic seduction and divine adultery implicit in the Annunciation scenario, playing upon the faith of Mary's elderly husband in terms of a rather natural response of incredulity to her miraculous conception. Indeed what is particularly funny, even a bit damning, in the Miller's Tale is the way serious Christian materials repeatedly enter the story, without any strict moralizing framework, in the form of popular culture and communal entertainment.

Musical songs, stories told or depicted in church, biblical history as holiday performance: these are the social means by which moral terms are invoked in the Miller's story defused of their moralizing force over the actions depicted in the tale. At once offering the verisimilar effect of the quotidian world of medieval Oxford, in which religion was woven into everyday practices and "secular" culture, these religious references deflect the kind of firm moralizing gestures we might elsewhere expect them to install. Absalon's turn as Herod on the "scaffold hye" (1.3384), a favorite stock character who rages extravagantly, the Miller himself speaking in Pilate's voice, and the allusions to the Song of Solomon in Absalon's wooing of Alison, his "hony-comb" and "cynamome" (1.3698–99), provide the rich cultural fabric of the Miller's comedy.[26]

Much like the ignorant John himself, then, the Reeve fails to recognize how John's status as a carpenter allows him to play dual roles, both Noah and Joseph, in the alternate biblical dramas Nicholas produces and directs. This figural dimension is an important part of the clever comedy, the way a clerk "koude a carpenter bigyle" (1.3300), rather than any attack on the Reeve. John's "lewed" status, his willfully ignorant failure to know the particulars of the Noah story, has made him into Nicholas's dupe. Unlettered (but also inattentive to narrative details one could expect to encounter as monumental glass, church statuary, or homily), the carpenter misreads the signs of a second flood Nicholas places before him, revealing both pride and selfishness in his willingness to believe in the clerk's story and, particu-

---

25. On the anxious story of Joseph's Troubles dramatized in the mystery plays and the "spectre of adultery that dominates" them, see Theresa Coletti, "Purity and Danger: The Paradox of Mary's Body and the En-gendering of the Infancy Narrative in the English Mystery Cycles," in *Feminist Approaches to the Body in Medieval Literature*, ed. Linda Lomperis and Sarah Stanbury (Philadelphia: U of Pennsylvania P, 1993), 65–95, at 75.

26. See R. E. Kaske, "The *Canticum Canticorum* in the *Miller's Tale*," *Studies in Philology* 59 (1962): 479–500, at 482.

larly, to keep it secret from his servants, Gille and Robyn, whom he "may nat save" (1.3555–56). Similar to the Miller's fictional carpenter, Osewold the erstwhile carpenter misreads this comic story (through the particularity of its signifiers, which I will treat shortly) in the very same way John does. Both carpenter figures misread and thus fail to understand the comic script placed before them in which they should already have learned their part. This dramatic metaphor works even more literally in the Miller's Tale than its fabliau sources since John could have theoretically played some part in the pageant of Noah and the Flood or its production. He has, even more literally than some, neglected his script and misread his text. By contrast, our recognitions are built upon the Reeve's *mis*recognition. The morally conscious Reeve is particularly blind to the spectacularly dramatic force of the Miller's biblical comedy.

But the Reeve's misreading of the Miller's Tale does not end with its typology or his particularly moralizing approach to the story; the tale is full of more local misrecognitions and unwitting ironies that we see specifically in the circulation of the signifier, the intrusion of the Symbolic order into the Reeve's imaginary retaliation at the Miller. The Reeve has imagined the Miller's representation of a carpenter as a reference to himself, but in his retributive fiction he takes up a number of signifiers that refer to other pilgrims, without seeming to notice. In the opening of his story the Reeve describes the villainous Symkyn, positioning him with care. Described first, as are the Knight's Theseus and the Miller's Nicholas, Symkyn is foregrounded in terms that recall the General Prologue portrait of the Miller. Both can "wrastle" (1.548; 3928) and "pipen" (1.565; 3927) on the bagpipes. Neither is particularly attractive: their noses provoke explicit comment (1.554; 3934). Their innate violence and aggression are signaled by the array of weapons they carry (1.558; 3929–33). Both are explicitly labeled as experienced thieves "of corn and mele" (1.562; 3939). Where the General Prologue Miller well knows about "synne and harlotries" (1.561), Symkyn's domestic life is riddled with them; his immediate family relations display the extent of his corruption. His house is literally full of "synne and harlotries," configured as careful social negotiation.

In this myopic focus on Symkyn, Osewold displays an imaginary association with the Miller at the cost of other symbolic relations, which is another way of saying that his purpose overwhelms any concern with the others his slander of the Miller might implicate. Dylan Evans defines misrecognition (*méconnaissance*) in terms of the ego and thus the imaginary, a "self-knowledge (*me-connaissance*) [that] is synonymous with misunderstanding," what amounts to "a misrecognition of the symbolic determinants of subjectivity."²⁷ It is precisely these symbolic determinants that return to disrupt the Reeve's imaginary view of the Miller, whom he describes so carefully and with such venom. His descriptions of his principal characters early in the fabliau uncannily wind up referring to a number of the pilgrims' occupations—not only the Miller, whom his tale is clearly intended to abuse, but also a Wife, a Parson, a Manciple, and two Clerks. One could also extrapolate a Nun (from the nunnery in which the Miller's wife was "ynorrissed" [1.3948]), a Yeoman (from Symkyn's desire "to saven his estaat of yeomanrye" [1.3949], through this marriage), and possibly a Knight or a Squire (given Malyne's family's machinations "to bistowe hire hye / Into som *worthy* blood of auncestrye" [1.3981–82; my emphasis], a term the General Prologue uses repeatedly to describe the Knight [1.43; 47; 50; 64; 68]). The number of pilgrim occupations mentioned or implied by this opening is impressive, and its sheer density turns the reader's focus from Robyn the Miller, clearly portrayed in the fictional Symkyn, toward everyone else within earshot. Thus, reading the Reeve's Tale in the same overly focused way the Reeve has read the Miller's Tale, we find a host of insults the Reeve can hardly mean to issue alongside his focused rebuke.

Part of Chaucer's comedy, then, arises from the Reeve's *lack* of understanding about how his own language is potentially misdirected and insulting in the process of so particularly directing it *as* a specific insult. All of the details he offers to insult Robyn through his portrait of Symkyn— a false sense of nobility; marriage to an illegitimate daughter of a priest; plans to endow his own daughter with ill-gotten goods stolen from the Church's needy; being hoodwinked by two idiot "intellectuals" that get to him merely by the incapacity of their college's manciple—do more than assassinate the character of the Miller at whom they are directed. These bitterly sardonic details about Symkyn/Robyn operate simultaneously for and beyond the trajectory Osewold intends. And the more he stabs at the Miller and presumes to tell us about the pilgrim riding with the company to Canterbury, the more Osewold winds up talking about others, ironically the others Chaucer has described in the General Prologue, and thus about himself. The Reeve provides an exceptionally good example of the social nature of psychic relations—he can't talk about the miller without talking about all the others in the story, as he addresses the Other, an agency fit to judge (and who wants to hear from him) toward which his tale is ultimately directed. In the imaginary focus on the Miller, an imaginary identification

---

27. Dylan Evans, *An Introductory Dictionary of Lacanian Psychoanalysis* (London and New York: Routledge, 1996), 109 *s.v.* "méconnaissance."

of Symkyn with Robyn, the Reeve reveals his dependence on the Symbolic, what comes rushing to the fore in the terms, literally, found in the General Prologue's portrait gallery and as a system of judgment beyond the Host's limited authority. For the judgment on the Miller that the Reeve seeks has little to do with any storytelling contest or prize.

To read the Reeve's Tale in the same terms by which the Reeve reads the Miller's Tale is to miss much of both stories, but it is also to learn something important about the fiction of reading in Chaucer's poem and the performance of its negations, that is, the way the poem both stages and disables models of reading and interpretation. Implicitly in the course of fragment 1, we are taught, in effect, *not* to read like the Reeve, *not* to identify completely the figures in the tales with the pilgrims, fiction with "reality," even as the Reeve specifically makes Symkyn into a hyperbolic version of Robyn. Such a mode of reading and its overidentifications is posited as a mode of misreading and misrecognition, away from which we are urged to turn. The attractions of such identifications outside of the fiction, in the way models for the pilgrims might be found in the historical register, speaks to the deceptive and rather productive power of these fictional effects.[28] As I have argued elsewhere, the power of the *Canterbury Tales* lies in the "transgressive turn" fueling both fragment 1 and its critical tradition. That power "originates . . . not from a revelation of what the tales *are* . . . but from a disclosure of what they *are not* . . . [a] situation [that] suggests that how we should read the poem is always different from the way the poem is being read at any given moment."[29] In terms of the Reeve's rather dramatic performance, we should not be reading the tales dramatically, as if they were direct responses cordoned off from all else. That does not mean, of course, that the tales are not responding to each other at all. Indeed, the genre relations of the tales are some of their most interesting aspects. But the fiction of reading that the Reeve displays disrupts this strictly dialogic sense of the tales as contrastive pairs, spectacularly so when he aligns his own with the Miller's in an imaginary duality. The Reeve cannot see, in effect, something crucially important to Chaucer's readers: that signifiers (here principally the professions that act as names in the *Canterbury Tales*) operate in various ways and circulate beyond fixed boundaries, hence the number of repeated names in Chaucer's stories that evoke previous figures even as they push matters forward. These occur in, between, and across tales; notably, the cuckolded husband, John, whose

---

28. See John Matthews Manly, *Some New Light on Chaucer* (New York: Holt, 1926).

29. Elizabeth Scala, "The Deconstructure of the *Canterbury Tales*," *Journal x* 4 (2000): 171–90, at 180.

name reappears as one of the Reeve's clerks and returns, continually, as the name of rather able and dexterous clerics. This kind of repetition, coupled with the commonness of the name generally, would seem self-explanatory as Osewold rehabilitates the husband with whom he has overidentified as one of his tools of revenge. But Osewold's other clerk, Aleyn, also possesses a name that inscribes him in the tale's symbolic economy. Coupled with Malyne lexically as well as in the vengeful plot, "Aleyn" plays with the very ideas of alignment and misalignment, association and disruption, central to the Reeve's story, even as it disrupts the Reeve's point—which is always the corruption of Symkyn—entirely from another place. Here at the level of the signifier, the Reeve both attempts to wield control and finds himself subject to other determinations.

The circulation of such signifiers is far more important than any one reference back to a source, as the "meaning" of the name John in clerical context will show. Its appearance in so many places in the *Tales* could be shrugged off as mere commonness, and probably has been, a simple name that works at various social levels: an Oxford carpenter, a Cambridge clerk, but also a nun's priest, a friar (in the Summoner's Tale), a monk (in the Shipman's), the youngest of the Wife of Bath's five husbands. As a name of both kings and simple servants, we have hardly noticed how far it circulates. It might apply to anyone, and as such works as a pure signifier, like Poe's "Purloined Letter" whose content remains unknown and whose power resides in its effects.[30] It designates nothing on its own, unlike more socially resonant names some figures possess (the Prioress's "Eglentyne"), but forges associations and distinctions, taking its meaning from the place it holds. When Harry Bailly, "with rude speche and boold," calls on the Nun's Priest in this way: "Com neer, thou prest, com hyder, thou sir John!" (7.2767–69), we think the name is derisive. According to the editorial notes, sir John is "A common and rather contemptuous designation for a priest but apparently the Nun's Priest's actual name," and they specify the "familiarity" with which Bailly addresses him "in the use of the second person singular" (*Canterbury Tales Complete* 456n 2810). Calling the Nun's Priest "sir John" might be rude, but the exact source of its condescension is hard to track.[31]

---

30. Poe's story is, of course, the subject of one of Lacan's best known essays, "Seminar on 'The Purloined Letter'," in *Écrits: The First Complete Edition in English*, trans. Bruce Fink (New York: Norton, 2006), 6–48.

31. The *MED* (*s.v.* "John" (n.)) suggests that with "sir" John is "used as a familiar name for a priest" and, separately, that it is "used as a contemptuous name for a person of mean station." Compare the way the Host addresses the Parson early in the contest for his overly moral aversion to swearing: "O Jankin, be ye there? / I smelle a Lollere in the wynd" (2.1172–73), where the diminutive appears more condescending.

The ordinary nature of the name, fabliau assumptions about clerics, and the lack of formality with pronouns collude to make it seem so. If Chaucer wished to dignify the Nun's Priest, he would have given him something more distinctive, like Huberd (1.269). Yet, when Bailly addresses the Monk, in the tale directly preceding the Nun's Priest's, he says:

> Ryde forth, myn owene lord, brek nat oure game.
> But, by my trouthe, I knowe nat youre name.
> Wher shal I calle yow my lord daun John,
> Or daun Thomas, or elles daun Albon?
> (7.1927–30)

Nothing in the Host's words to the "lord . . . Monk," for whom he uses the formal "ye" (7.1924–25), suggests a similar derision despite first calling him "John." There is little in the name itself that does such work. Any derision toward "sir John" is produced by the circulation of the signifier in the *Canterbury Tales* through all the other Johns and Jankyns he can thus be associated with, many of which are rather sexually adept clerics.

Unlike "John," "Aleyn" remains closer to home, circulating within the Reeve's Tale rather than beyond it. No other Aleyn inhabits the *Tales*, but a similar name appears inside the Reeve's story. Aleyn and Malyne are spelled and pronounced similarly, and both are quite common. Indeed their commonness would seem their most important feature. Aleyn is a name of French (and originally Breton) origin that arrives in England with the Conquest. Malyne, according to the editorial notes, is a diminutive of Maud (L. Matilda), similar to Molly or Malkyn, both of which appear elsewhere.[32] The similarity of these names draws our attention to them as signifiers circulating in relation to each other, both up and down the social register. Malyne may never have seen Aleyn before this visit to her father's mill, but her name knows his as its negative inversion, and their close relation nearly draws these figures together. Malyne's name has provoked comment from early on, causing scholars to consider what kind of ironies might be located there. Citing *Promptorum Parvulorum*, an early Latin–English Dictionary, Walter W. Skeat shows that "malin" was a term for a dishcloth,

---

32. Malkyn appears in the introduction to the Man of Law's Tale (2.30) and in the Nun's Priest's Tale (7.3384), which also features a sheep named "Malle" or Moll (7.2821). The *Chaucer Name Dictionary*, ed. Jacqueline DeWeever (New York: Garland, 1987) cites W. W. Skeat's edition, *The Works of Geoffrey Chaucer* (Oxford: Clarendon, 1900), 5:126, for this information. P. H. Reaney, *A Dictionary of British Surnames* (London: Routledge, Kegan & Paul, 1958), cited by Timothy O'Keefe, defines it as "a pet name for Mary" ("Malin, Malins, Malin"). See O'Keefe, "Meanings of 'Malyne' in *The Reeve's Tale*," *American Notes & Querries* 12 (1973): 5–7.

which kept conversation grounded in whether she was being marked as a low and possibly promiscuous figure (Skeat 5.126). More recently, Timothy O'Keefe offers a direct English etymologizing of Malyne's name, "mal" and "line," which Chaucer attends to elsewhere as a concern with "lynage" to emphasize "her rather dubious ancestry. Literally the name means 'bad line,' which contains ironic significance since Malyne's mother is the illegitimate offspring of the parson."[33] He concludes, "the most outstanding irony of Malyne's name . . . is the implication that her lineage or line is tainted" (6). Both readings would suggest that the Reeve is satirizing the girl, as well as mocking her parents' aspirations for her marriage, and thus work within the Reeve's intentional orbit.

But a more complex sense of Malyne's name circulates in the text as well, and in relation to the man who deflowers her, which makes mere satire harder to maintain. Norman Hinton has analyzed Chaucer's use of Malyne specifically in coordination with Aleyn, arguing for a close connection to "a set of bilingual puns with two old French words," *alignier* and *malignier*, signaling the fabliau's French origin as well as its signature wordplay.[34] Seeking the meanings of his puns in Godefroy's *Dictionnaire de L'Ancienne Langue Française,* Hinton writes:

> Godefroy defines *alignier* as *arpenter* [to survey, stride along, pace], *accoupler* [to couple, unite], *couvrir* (used of animals) [to cover, smother], and *peupler* [to people, populate]. All these meanings apply directly to Aleyn's activities of the night. *Malignier* means *machiner* [to conspire], *tramer* [to hatch a plot], *tromper* [to deceive, mislead, be unfaithful to], *être trompeur* [to be misled or tricked], and *user de fraude* [to use deceit or fraud]. These terms likewise apply to Malyne's part in the story, since she has helped her father trick the students out of their corn, and confesses it here, just after she is named. (120; translations mine)

The way these meanings themselves align so perfectly with the ambivalent actions in the Reeve's story is outdone only by the way Chaucer's Middle English names would be pronounced much like these fourteenth-century French terms, suggesting that the adaptation of "align" and "malign," from Anglo-Norman to Middle English, was occurring in spoken language at this time. The *OED* first records usage for each of these verbs as circa 1425. But Chaucer may here provide, only about thirty years earlier, their first

---

33. O'Keefe, "Meanings of 'Malyne,'" 5. On the signature wordplay in the Old French fabliaux, see Bloch, *Scandal of the Fabliaux,* 101ff.

34. Norman Hinton, "Two Names in *The Reeve's Tale,*" *Names* 9 (1961): 117–20, at 119.

recorded usage as proper names, which the *OED* could not be expected to register.

The play of these signifiers across languages betrays the desires coursing through the Reeve's Tale, desires both to malign and to align simultaneously. The signifier announces in advance the forces to which these figures are subject. If Malyne's name carries her family history with her in her "line," it also foreshadows her actions: a duplicity in her behavior both to the clerks and to her father, since she will ultimately betray his theft of flour and offer her lover the cake it was used to make. Given the French meanings Hinton uncovers (both *tromper* and *être trompeur*), it is unclear whether her name signifies her actions or her condition, as the one who assists her father in his theft or the one fooled, mistaken in taking the clerk's vengeful assault as lovemaking. The signifier claims these senses simultaneously and in no particular hierarchy. And while the Reeve may little care about the difference, as both senses reflect poorly upon the target of his insult, others have found the difference important, as it engages our sympathies in the tale and shifts them about.[35]

The proximity of the names Aleyn and Malyne, and the words "align" and "malign" proximate to them, is of course telling, since Symkyn's father-in-law, the parson, hopes to align ("allye," 1.3945) himself with more noble bloodlines through Malyne's marriage. Aleyn's name is a variant spelling of the ME verb "alyne," descending from the twelfth-century Old French meanings Hinton adduces, "to arrange in a line," "to put (a naval fleet) into formation," and "(of a male animal) to copulate with (a female)" (*OED*, s.v. "align" (v.), etym.), meanings literally appropriate to Aleyn's actions, creeping into her bed: "This wenche lay uprighte and faste slepte, / Til he so ny was, er she myghte espie . . . And shortly for to seyn, they were aton" (1.4194–97). The specific sense of animal copulation dates from the fourteenth century and appears in English for the first time circa 1425 in Edward, Duke of York's *Master of Game*. Yet the emphasis on order and proper formation in strategic military and sexual senses is wickedly appropriate to the damage the Reeve gladly allows Aleyn to perform in Symkyn's home.

In this story aligning and maligning (both mis-aligning and mis-speaking or speaking ill of someone) are intimately connected. One cannot align oneself without maligning something, and often oneself, and this may be as

---

35. Malyne, and to an extent Symkyn, have become subjects of critical sympathy. See Tamara Kohanski, "In Search of Malyne," *Chaucer Review* 27 (1993): 228–38; and Nicole Nolan Sidhu, "'To Late for to Crie': Female Desire, Fabliau Politics, and Classical Legend in Chaucer's *Reeve's Tale*," *Exemplaria* 21 (2009): 3–23.

true for the Reeve as it is for the figures about which he speaks. This modern sense of malign is alive in the Anglo-Norman origin of the word, which would be pronounced, with its silent "g," nearly identically with Malyne's name. Earliest uses of the word in English date from precisely the same time as "align." The *OED* cites Lydgate's *Troy Book* (c. 1425) and *The Fall of Princes* (c. 1439) where "malign" means "to plot, contrive" (*s.v.* "malign" (v.), def. 4), senses relevant, of course, to Chaucer's Malyne. Anglo-Norman *malignier* means "to plot, deceive, act wrongly" and descends from twelfth-century Old French and postclassical Latin (*malignare*), where it means "to act evilly, scheme, maltreat" (*OED, s.v.* "malign," etym.). The scheming, deceptive nature of alignments and misalignments in the Reeve's Tale make the "accidental" connotations of these names unlikely and more than simple irony. The play of signifiers in the tale suggests both more and less than Osewold intends in his narrow and focused satire. Throughout the story, and not just in this episode, then, "Malyne" is the signifier the Reeve wants to control, naming the nature of his very project in its widest scope. But it would seem difficult if not impossible to malign the Miller without aligning himself with some point in the Symbolic, the social order he otherwise manipulates to criticize the figures in the tale.

The Reeve's use of common names to do some rather uncommon work in his tale (to rehabilitate or empower John, to familiarize Aleyn and Malyne) is at one level rather clever, as it works to tighten the grip he holds upon the story as a mode of revenge. But it also prompts us to look beyond and to see something the Reeve has clearly missed, and possibly misses here too in the very act of making his point. The Reeve may have put the character with whom he has overidentified (and aggresses against) in the form of John so that he can punish the Miller, but the Miller has already put himself into his own story in the act of naming John's servant, Robyn. In other words, what happens within the Reeve's Tale with these names takes some of its meaning from what happens between the tales through such names. The conduits they trace signify more than what appears an "intentional" reference or rewriting. Or in Lacanian terms, imaginary identifications are not separate from but already embedded in symbolic structures. John has little in common with the "sklendre, choleric" Reeve, but his burly servant Robyn, who heaves doors off their hinges, appears a lot like the Miller described in the General Prologue (1.550; 1.3470–71). Unlike the others, Harry Bailly names the Miller, "Robyn, my leeve brother," in his Prologue (1.3129) as he tries to quiet him down and prevent his interruption of the game: "Som bettre man shal tell us first another. / Abyd, and lat us werken thriftily" (1.3130–31). With self-deprecating humor, then, Chaucer's Miller names his carpenter's servant after himself, mentioning it twice in the story (1.3466; 3555), even as the Reeve *misrecognizes* his own figuration in the Miller's Tale. Imagining himself maligned in the Miller's story, he recognizes little else. What we have called the Reeve's lack of a sense of humor more emphatically reveals the Miller's comedy, in which the Miller himself is all too willing to participate. In this minor figure's name, the "author" has signed his story, making a bit of fun at his own expense in the tale.

As a name for his principal intent, "Malyne" is a signifier the Reeve thinks he knows. He has aligned matters to malign matters, suggesting a neat and tidy set of formulations with which he controls the (mis)alignments and maligned plans of his satiric target. But this control is disrupted from within; like Robyn's name in the Miller's Tale, the signifier betrays other meanings. Circulating well beyond the Reeve's Tale and the narrowness of its slights upon Symkyn's family, Malyne signifies as a Chaucer family name. In yet another redoubling of this gesture, Chaucer puts *himself* in the Reeve's story through the circulation of the signifier—undoing from the very beginning and in the same manner as the Miller the strict intention the Reeve works so hard to effect. Malyne is a rather awkward name for a daughter one hopes to push up the social ladder, as scholars discussing both linguistic and social history have shown, and trying to pin down its precise significance has given them some trouble. The girl hardly appears important enough to name, a fact that has provoked a scholarly search for some other kind of historical reference to a figure somewhere outside the poem. But the possibility that Chaucer employs the name "Malyne" as a joke at someone's expense is slight, for one of the few historical figures scholars have uncovered is the John Malynes in the Subsidy Rolls for Putnam, Warwickshire in 1358, and "as far as is known, Chaucer had no connection with him."[36] Indeed, John M. Manly, whose *New Light on Chaucer* was a veritable textbook indicating the possible contemporary figures and acquaintances Chaucer may have fictionalized in the *Canterbury Tales*, also failed to find any London associates with this name and was forced to conclude that "the miller's daughter is probably drawn from real life," an emptiness of reference linking her to the other proverbial Malkyns and Mollys in cultural discourse.[37]

Such a turn to "real life" had been a means of rescuing Chaucer from misnaming Malyne, where a too lowborn name might endanger her moral status and disrupt the social aspirations in which understandings of her had

---

36. O'Keefe, "Meanings of 'Malyne,'" 6.
37. Manly, *New Light on Chaucer*, cited in O'Keefe, "Meanings of 'Malyne,'" 7n5.

been embedded. But in looking so far afield for Malyne's possible meaning, scholars have missed a more proximate source that works precisely in terms of social movement that the Reeve's rebuttal to the Miller charts, which opens the tale to a much larger frame of reference. In a distant echo of the Miller, another author covertly signs his story by giving a fictional character his own name, and this signature disrupts all the control the Reeve supposes he has. Robert Malyn, Chaucer's grandfather, was the upwardly mobile Ipswich taverner whose son, John, changed the family surname to "Chaucer" upon their move to London. In fact, "Whenever a Malyn moved from Ipswich to London, he changed his name to Chaucer."[38] A deeper irony, if we would even call it that, than the Reeve's pervades the scene and the extent to which Malyne's name plays the part of a signifier tracing the desire for upward mobility—and it is not Symkyn's or the Miller's. Chaucer's names display the power of the signifier, which can always also be located somewhere else, especially whenever the Reeve tries to fix its referent.

Proper names in the Reeve's Tale provide a spectacular show of the signifier's mobility in ways its narrator does and does not understand, making us read (and reread) beyond the fiction of the Reeve's intent. But it also moves more generally through the proverbial language wielded by the story's figures, so much so that the tale seems to be about the conscious control of and unconscious subjection to its power. At the center of the story, Symkyn and his houseguests spar over the practical wisdom that is to rule the situation and the upper hand such wisdom affords. The brevity of the tale enhances the density of its proverbial discourse—a feature it shares with both the Miller's and Knight's Tales to a lesser extent—making us feel that such language provides its very texture rather than a clever summation it might deliver at the end. From the moment of their arrival, Symkyn sees that the two clerks are trying to prevent him from stealing any of their grain, as they stand and watch the hopper as it "wagges til and fra" (1.4039). Their amusement at his machinery is performed as a means of prevention. But the miller thinks little of their wit: "Of al hir art counte I noght a tare" (1.4056). With the help of his wife, he easily confounds them by loosing their horse "Toward the fen, ther wilde mares renne" (1.4065). The horse's natural, animal desire sets his deception in motion and offers an easy means of manipulating Aleyn and John. They must leave the mill

---

38. See Lister M. Matheson, "Chaucer's Ancestry: Historical and Philological Re-Assessments," *Chaucer Review* 25 (1991): 171–89, at 177. More generally for some of this account, Matheson depends on Donald Howard, *Chaucer: His Life, His Works, His World* (New York: Dutton, 1987).

and chase the horse down, allowing Symkyn to steal "half a busshel" in no time, which his wife quickly bakes into a cake (1.4093). But the clerks are not to be outdone so easily and entreat Symkyn by playing upon his greed with some proverbial knowledge of their own:

"Now, Symond," seyde John, "by Seinte Cutberd,
Ay is thou myrie, and this is faire answerd.
I have herd seyd, 'Man sal taa of twa thynges:
Slyk as he fyndes, or taa slyk as he bryngs.'
But specially I pray thee, hooste deere,
Get us som mete and drynke, and make us cheere,
And we wil payen trewely atte fulle.
With empty hand men may na haukes tulle;
Loo, heere our silver, redy for to spende."
(1.4127–35)

The proverbs quoted relate to proximate concerns as well as to matters more generally and thus operate beyond the immediate situation. Asking for some dinner and a night's lodging after their hard labor, John offers the Miller cash: "Loo, heere our silver, redy for to spende." But his request also says far more, as the admission of their need lures him with the possibility of more gain.

Stranded at the mill after spending the afternoon chasing their horse, the clerks must beg Symkyn's hospitality: "But for the love of God they hym bisoght / Of herberwe and of ese, as for hir peny" (1.4118–19), a situation the miller enjoys too much. His response taunts them for and with their academic pursuits. His house is small, but he is sure they can turn it into a more roomy place with their philosophical arguments: "Myn hous is streit, but ye han lerned art; / Ye konne by argumentes make a place / A myle brood of twenty foot of space" (1.4122–24). The clerks have been well used by the time they make their request, and Symkyn seems to be feeling his power over them. The proverb John invokes here, "Man sal taa of twa thynges . . . ," plays on the difference between one who is content merely to "fynde" whatever comes his way and the one who goes out and gets ("bryngs") something for himself, and it applies both to the clerks themselves and to Symkyn, to whom it is presumably directed. Both clerks and miller have been gaming matters from the very start, less content with what is had and trying hard to make something more out of it. John's words thus operate as concession *and* challenge. He admits Symkyn's success thus far, "Ay is thou myrie," in his request for lodging. Symkyn is sitting pretty at the moment, and John suffers his sarcastic reply (1.4120–26). The clerks know they can get nothing, no dinner, no lodging for the night, unless they have something to offer. In one sense, then, these lines admit to their defeat and acknowledge what they are willing to pay "trewely atte fulle." However, while John notes that no hawks can be lured ("tulle[d]") with an empty hand, that very proverb also makes Symkyn into a bird of prey under the control of the clerks who lure him and make possible the opportunity for their revenge.

The direction of the proverbial wisdom in the Reeve's Tale is thus uncertain. The payment John promises quickly turns to a different kind of repayment and revenge once the clerks are given access to Symkyn's home. Place and position, insofar as they offer opportunity, thus mean everything, both in the tale, for the tale, and with the proverbs themselves. The Reeve conveniently compresses everyone into a single bedroom for the night, a topography that exposes Symkyn to payment of a different order, changing the directionality of these words. The "mete and drynke" the clerks buy subjects the entire family to their late-night shenanigans because Symkyn enjoys his victory a bit too much: "Ful pale he was for dronken, and nat reed" (1.4150). By allowing them into his bedroom and sharing the wine for which he makes them pay, Symkyn is quite literally repaid for his theft of flour. The luring of the hawk John mentioned seems a much different business read from this vantage. We do not know for sure who operates the lure and which figures are its gulls. Similarly, John's reference to "Seinte Cutberd," surely a comical Northern pronunciation of St. Cuthbert as its editor notes, also signifies as part of the vengeful economy escalating in this scene, as well as between the Reeve's and Miller's fabliaux. The clerk's oath is supposed to guarantee his earnestness (and display his scornful accent), and surely it does, even as it advertises his trickery: "cutbeard" announces itself in this context as a portmanteau term for a thief, much like a "cutpurse."[39] Symkyn explains the very idiomization at stake in John's reference to "Seinte Cutberd" and thus unwittingly remarks on the danger of housing a couple of tricky cutbeards in his house as he watches the clerks run after their horse: "I trowe the clerkes were aferd. / Yet kan a millere make a clerkes berd, / For al his art; now lat hem goon hir weye!" (1.4095–97). Once he had fooled them and "ma[d]e a clerkes berd," Symkyn would have done well to heed his own words by making the clerks go their way, back to the college that night rather than enjoying the ridiculous spectacle of "thise sely clerkes ren[nynge] up and doun" (1.4100).

---

39. Catherine Brown Tkacz, "Chaucer's Beard-Making," *Chaucer Review* 18 (1983): 127–36, notes this pun.

Of course, the power of outwitting or fooling someone in terms of manipulating a "berd," playing a joke, circulates outward from the close of the Miller's comedy. Nicholas cries "A berd! A berd!" (1.3742) as Alison plays her prank on Absalon "put[ing out] hir hole" so that he might "kis[s] hir naked ers" (1.3732–34). But the joke, the "berd," is even more literal as Absalon realizes something has gone amiss with his kiss, "for wel he wiste a womman hath no berd. / He felte a thyng al rough and long yherd" (1.3737–38). In the Miller's Tale the joke itself (what Absalon perceives as a "berd" on Alison's face) is the word for the joke (a beard, making one's beard), or in other words, the joke is *in* the signifier. It returns in displaced form in this oath to St. Cutberd, even when its narrator seems to have missed the jokes in the Miller's Tale entirely.[40] And it perhaps gives meaning to the Reeve's close-shaven face, which is nearly the first thing the narrator mentions about him: "His berd was shave as ny as ever he kan" (1.588). In more ways than one, the "berd" is anywhere but on the Reeve.

Circulating through these signifiers, desire is not something "in" the Reeve's Tale that must be exposed so much as the structure of fragment 1 itself, a relation to lack and privation, in which its participants are located and defined.[41] Despite the fact that the Reeve seems to have forgotten the tale-telling game in his revenge upon the Miller, the game—and the Symbolic order on which it depends—has not forgotten him. Much of what I have written on the Reeve's imagined insult and quite palpable resentment may sound at times rather intentionalist, grounded in the way he means for his audience to understand his story. But in critiquing the Reeve's intent and showing the ways his language works beyond it because of the position he occupies, we see Chaucer's representation of his failure to recognize his relation to larger Symbolic structures, or what appears as the way the *Canterbury Tales* recognizes the subjection of his alienated position, "hyndreste of our route" (1.622).

We need not even look to the back of the pilgrimage company in the General Prologue to see the Reeve's alienated posture; it is already inscribed in his speaking position in fragment 1. Situated as a third term in its struc-

---

40. Also "in" this joke, we see that desire inheres in the signifier even when it is extinguished by it. After Alison's trick, "His hoote love was coold and al yqueynt" (1.3754). Absalon is healed of his lovesickness—his hot love goes cold and is completely quenched—when he finally possesses what he had been seeking all along. See V. A. Kolve, *Chaucer and the Imagery of Narrative* (Stanford: Stanford UP, 1984), 196. This play reveals desire's location (and dislocation) in the signifier.

41. This nice formulation is adapted from Sarah Kay's, "Desire and Subjectivity," in *The Troubadours: An Introduction,* ed. Simon Gaunt and Sarah Kay (Cambridge: Cambridge UP, 1999), 212–27, an excellent introduction to historicist uses of Lacan.

ture, the Reeve takes up a crucial place in the scene of analysis at work quietly generating tales. Where the Miller offered just such a scene of analysis in his response to the Knight, both repeating and revising its normativizing narrative gestures, the Reeve offers "an act of analysis of the act of analysis," showing the transformations wrought by taking up his position in relation to this structure.[42] The Reeve's Tale displays the energy circulating between and among tales as those stories are shaped and driven by each other, not merely by particular tellers and their intents. Overly, even obsessively, focused on the Miller, the Reeve's Tale shows what can only be returned to the Knight, a figure that stands for the larger set of concerns and conventions underwriting the Miller's disruptive response. Fixated on not getting tricked, keeping one's eyes open, and the means of compensating oneself against loss, the Reeve hardly understands his debts.

As with Barbara Johnson's attention to the readings of Poe's "Purloined Letter" by Derrida and Lacan I invoked in the quotation above, so too with the Miller and Reeve: "In all three texts, it is the *act of analysis* which seems to occupy the center of the discursive stage, and *the act of analysis of the act of analysis* which in some way disrupts that centrality" (110; emphasis in original). That the critical discourse on Lacan's "Seminar on 'The Purloined Letter'" should make sense of Chaucer's project should not completely surprise us, given the power of repetition in this first fragment and the itinerary of the signifier Poe's story and these first three tales trace. Like Poe's story and Lacan's reading of it as an allegory of the itinerary of the signifier, fragment 1 is produced by and in a series of structural and linguistic repetitions we too often explain as mere parody. But the connectivity between tales exceeds any simple imitation of plot or action and instead engages a structure of reading and retelling from which no position outside can really be called safe. Johnson gives us a new model for comprehending the Reeve's position in fragment 1. His is not merely the (near) final blow to a degenerating social discourse or some blotch on the comic form he attempts to deploy but an analytic position that emerges from within the very tales to which he responds. The Reeve is not outside the structure of desire and language but deeply within it. As such, the Reeve makes us aware of the importance of place, not merely from his "hyndreste" position, the place of the unseen seer, but within his tale itself.

His "Cambridge counterblast to the Miller's Oxford tale" begins with such an emphasis on place, a precise topography for the thieving miller's locale "in Trumpyngtoun" that has been taken as a near set of directions:

---

42. This phrase comes from Barbara Johnson, "The Frame of Reference: Poe, Lacan, Derrida," in *The Critical Difference* (Baltimore: Johns Hopkins UP, 1980), 110–46, at 110; emphasis in original.

"And this is verray sooth that I yow telle" (1.3924).[43] The university town setting of his tale rivals the Miller's Oxford, locating aggressivity in "place" and from the place from which he narrates. Place has long been read as a central feature of the Norfolk Reeve's fiction, part of his aggressive "Northern" character.[44] Lacking the refinement associated with England's south, the Reeve's northernisms depart from a more central London diction and style characterizing the rest of the tales. This style, of course, is part and parcel of the Reeve's location in the poem, both socially and professionally. Not just a "Northfolk" (1.619) man, he is an outsider who has gained an inside vantage. This structure emphasizing place and position is both a historical distinction and operates as a narrative and interpretive strategy. In Poe's story, a letter is stolen in plain sight, a theft made possible by the blind eye of an authority figure, like the Reeve, who never doubts his control over what he sees. Crucially he misses the significance of what occurs right in front of him. The letter as pure signifier (it is never read; we never find out what it says) confers its meaning only according to its position in the circuit of subjects who hold it. Power is distributed according to the subject's position in relation to this signifier. So too the Reeve's Tale marks the importance of place, both in his northern orientation and its plot, in which everything takes on its meaning because of the position it holds.[45] We have always read the tale in such terms: what could the Reeve's Tale mean dislocated from this opening set of three? His story at once fits into the compulsive set of repeated narratives *and* disrupts the symmetry of the Knight's romance and Miller's fabliau. The Reeve makes odd what had been, between the Miller and the Knight, a simple game of getting even.[46]

In its focus on place and placement, the Reeve returns us to the place of the Other by reworking the importance of the place the other occupies in the Knight's Tale. Where Palamon and Arcite each fantasize that the other is enjoying in his place, the violence of the Reeve's Tale is provoked by a similar fear. John *knows* Aleyn is enjoying in his place, in fact, a place

---

43. The phrase is Pearsall's, *Canterbury Tales*, 186.

44. On the Northern dialect see Tolkien, "Chaucer as a Philologist." For its historical significance to the way the North situates English identity, see Joseph Taylor, "Chaucer's Uncanny Regionalism: Rereading the North in *The Reeve's Tale*," *JEGP* 109 (2010): 468–93. According to Taylor, the Northern cast to the Cambridge clerks not only figures the disruptive powers of regional difference and their aggressions but also powerfully configures national identity. On the Norfolk character of the Reeve himself, see Alan J. Fletcher, "Chaucer's Norfolk Reeve," *Medium Aevum* 52 (1983): 100–103.

45. On the importance of spatial positioning, see William Woods, *Chaucerian Spaces: Spatial Poetics in Chaucer's Opening Tales* (Albany: State U of New York P, 2008).

46. This neat formulation echoes Johnson, "Frame of Reference," 118.

Aleyn has constructed for himself by applying a law of "esement" to take the place of a different loss (1.4179–82). But John is also afraid that when the tale is told another day, he will be called "daft" (1.4208) because he got nothing for his "harm" (1.4203). Imitating Aleyn's daring advance on the miller's daughter, John moves the cradle so that Symkyn's wife gets into his bed. Less for any pleasure he might derive from her, John appears to "priketh" (1.4231) the miller's wife because of the competitive anxiety provoked by Aleyn and the foolish position in which Aleyn's action places him:

> "Allas!" quod he, "this is a wikked jape;
> Now may I seyn that I is but an ape.
> Yet has my felawe somwhat for his harm;
> He has the milleris doghter in his arm.
> He auntred hym, and has his nedes sped,
> And I lye as a draf-sak in my bed;
> And when this jape is tald another day,
> I sal been halde a daf, a cokenay!
> I wil arise and auntre it, by my fayth!
> 'Unhardy is unseely,' thus men sayth."
> (1.4201–10)

The ethical nature of this behavior is no concern for John. Instead, he looks to change the position Aleyn's audacity assigns him as "coward" (1.4267), which he does literally by repositioning things: moving the cradle in the dark that confuses everyone's place in the room. Not only will John get what Aleyn "auntred," his easement will come to him by her own mistaken volition. These details charge the actions of the Reeve's story with their meaning. Symkyn will be humiliated by the "swyvyng" of daughter and wife, as well as the wife's complicity in the act. But they are even more important to the extent that they are signifiers as well, to be "toold another day." John and Aleyn are well aware that what happens at Symkyn's mill won't stay at Symkyn's mill. Having come for no other reason than to best him, the clerks take their "esement" not merely in competition with each other but so that they can report it to the Other. In thinking about those who will hear this story and judge, they literally perform for the Other, even as each clerk seems to act in more narrow competition with his fellow. Here we see the Reeve's Tale again imitating the Knight's, as these rivals perform for the Other. Indeed, Palamon and Arcite first fight in the grove for the Other, as neither has any possible means of attaining Emily through this secret conflict. If the Knight put his knights into private battle—

dressing each other so that they could fight to the death in a purely symbolic register—the Reeve's Tale more darkly unveils the competitive desires for prestige and recognition behind such self-aggrandizing gestures, even in the absence of a real audience.

At stake in the Reeve's Tale and, one might say, throughout the Reeve's performance, is recognition; both the Reeve's desire for the Canterbury pilgrims to recognize the Miller in his maligned portrait within his tale, and the Reeve's own unacknowledged desire for recognition among the pilgrims as well. Such a claim seems rather counterintuitive since the Reeve rides "the hyndreste of oure route" (1.622). As the unseen seer of the others, such attention is the last thing he might seem to want. And, at the level of the Reeve's intent, this much is true. But the desire the subject seeks in taking up language, in the desire of the Other, is of an entirely different order. The Reeve claims to be motivated by revenge, which emerges as a desire to accuse the Miller of everything he can possibly hurl in response to the insult he perceives in his tale. But the Reeve's answer far exceeds its supposed cause, the implication of cuckoldry, which the Miller comically disables in his Prologue. The Reeve is motivated not merely by this insult but by a desire to make himself into what he takes the Other to want from him, which makes some sense of his specifically moralizing cynicism and its renunciations in the fabliaux prologues of fragment 1. These gestures would appear to get desire out of the way, but as we shall see more fully in chapter 4, these moralizing gestures are not an escape from desire so much as a violent transformation of its terms.

The Knight's Tale reveals desire's transformative logic, both in terms of the individual figures changed by its workings (Arcite's physical transformation into Philostrate) and in terms of the narrative transformations that desire motivates. The Reeve's Tale rewrites that transformation in almost unrecognizably transformed terms. In this way it both repeats the Knight's story as it replays the Miller's Tale and disguises itself in doing so, using the paradox of age to perpetuate a desire he can't even attempt to satisfy but can only describe. Fragment 1, like the *Canterbury Tales* as a whole, thus writes a disfiguringly transformative narrative of desire. The violent and oppressive aggressions of the Reeve's Tale do not banish desire so much as disguise it once more, written over, but not undone, by the disturbing machinations of the Reeve's fiction. The end result of these observations might be that the Reeve, yet again, tells the same story as the Miller and the Knight, a story of erotic competition and competitive recognition, despite the tale's lack of love and his own retreat into the safety of age and impotence.

In his treatment of the women in his tale, the Reeve, of course, does not intentionally echo or gloss the Knight's story—in this they could hardly look more different. Emily is set at a remove from both Theban knights and admired from afar. The women in the Reeve's Tale are handled far more roughly. Yet in his blindness to the desires for (and certainly of) Emily and Alison, the Reeve inadvertently repeats what he does not remember—here, especially, the awkward way Malyne imitates Emily's transformation to become a willing participant in the romance. For it is only like Malyne, after the fact, that Emily "caste a freendlich ye" upon Arcite, thus calling for the Knight's famed "aside" to explain her changed behavior: "For wommen, as to speken in comune, / Thei folwen alle the favour of Fortune" (1.2680–82). The Reeve would hardly see Emily's action here as the origin of Malyne's pathetic lament to her aggressor-lover. In fact, the Reeve could hardly recognize the Knight's Tale as ultimate source for his own story—and this is part of Chaucer's comedy. Since his entire motive lies in avenging himself upon the Miller, Malyne's rape *cum* wooing merely inflicts a punishment upon her father, the fictional miller, Symkyn, adding insult to his injury. To that end, every sordid detail of his story has been aimed at the miller's (and thus *the* Miller's) humiliation, making the Miller's Tale the sole origin of his story at the cost of the rest of the social Symbolic order.

His daughter (as his goods) may be "disparaged" (1.4271) in these acts but, more disparaging still to the repute of Symkyn, she understands this furtive sexual contact as a form of wooing. The next morning she tears up at the departure of her so-called "lemman" (1.4240), at what reads as Aleyn's ridiculous imitation of the traditional courtly "aube."[47] The Northern clerk departs with this promise to her: "Fare weel, Malyne, sweete wight! / The day is come; I may no lenger byde; / But everemo, wher so I go or ryde, / I is thyn awen clerk, swa have I seel!" (1.4240; 4236–39). Such a dawn song would, of course, be far more appropriate to the Knight's romance or perhaps even the Miller's parody, as a courtly form the clever Nicholas might knowingly exploit in his seduction of his landlord's wife. In the Reeve's story the aubade is simply out of place. Signifiers, as this mobility shows, never hold definite and unitary meaning—even when they follow stable sequencing. They make meaning, often in multiple ways, by connotations and associations with other signifiers not immediately apparent, as when the terms of Malyne's lament draw upon the language of romances like the Knight's. Of course the Knight's Tale does not properly contain this

---

47. See R. E. Kaske, "An Aube in the *Reeve's Tale*," *ELH* 26 (1959): 295–310, and some short remarks in his "*Canticum Canticorum* in the *Miller's Tale*" (498).

linguistic feature—no dawn song separates any pair of lovers in his story—yet the Knight's courtly romance is almost certainly the place from which Malyne's aubade derives its fantastic incongruity.

This pathetic departure scene has been triggered by the travesty of courtly language and behavior in the Miller's Tale, of course. It takes its source from the Miller's sophisticated mockery of the courtly discourse of the Knight's romance in Nicholas's winking deployment of Arcite's words in new contexts. Arcite is slain both figuratively and literally by Emily's beauty: "The fresshe beautee sleeth me sodeynly . . . And but I have hir mercy and hir grace, . . . / I nam but deed; ther nis namoore to seye" (1.1118–22). So too is Nicholas nearly killed by his secret love for Alison. Addressing her face to face while holding her "harde by the haunchebones," Nicholas pleads: "For deerne love of thee, lemman, I spille / . . . love me al atones, / Or I wol dyen, also God me save!" (1.3277–82). His language strains the kind of death, "the little death," or spilling he might soon experience due to his desire. Taking the wooing strategies of romance more seriously, Absalon attempts to imitate those conventions with various gifts (1.3375–82), a performance that ends with an offer of cold hard cash ("meede" 1.3380) for Alison's affections: "For som folk wol ben wonnen for richesse, / And somme for strokes, and somme for gentillesse" (1.3381–82). Such deployments of courtly convention repeat the division of the Knight's Tale between spiritual and creaturely aspects of love in a new context, which makes the choice between suitors in the Miller's Tale rather simple business. In one fell stroke, the Miller is able to dispose of and use to his own advantage the putatively elegant terms of knightly discourse. But these knowing and naïve imitations of courtly "wooing" trigger the Reeve's even more appalling travesty of romance as ex post facto sexual phenomenon in the Aleyn–Malyne plot. And even further, when John "priketh" the Miller's wife, an act that imitates and somewhat inverts the horse's wild ride with the mares in the fens that instigates the trick in the first place, one might say his action also travesties the *chevalrie* exalted by the Knight's Tale as well.[48] The social and conventional relations between the Reeve's and Knight's stories are a function of symbolic systems well beyond any particular intent.

The Miller's medial position between the Knight and Reeve makes his story more than the object of the Reeve's savage satire; it is also a conduit

---

48. Not merely riding associates this gesture with the *chevalrie* but the "priking" a knight errant performs in romance that the Tale of Thopas parodies. For a lengthy discussion of the horse in the Reeve's Tale, see Kolve's chapter in *Chaucer and the Imagery of Narrative*, esp. 248–56. He does not connect it to the Knight or his concerns.

for the Reeve's unwitting desires upon the Knight's discourse, itself a figure for the larger stakes of the game in Chaucer's poem. It also simultaneously makes the Knight the address of his appropriation of the signifier. Nothing has been quoted, yet the Knight's Tale is surely the point from which Malyne's emotional lament to her "lemman" originates, even and especially because the Reeve doesn't know it. Part of the humor of the Reeve's Tale, then, might be put this way: setting his tale so firmly and directly against the Miller, the Reeve's language aligns him with and attaches him to a Symbolic law (here figured as the concerns of the Knight's Tale) in ways he cannot see and other than he intends, a more complex connection than mere irony has been able to describe. The Reeve's language positions him in a larger social order and exposes the desire for recognition he does not know he has.

In such alignment with the Knight, we could register the social-climbing aspect of the Reeve that others have observed and located in his clerical appearance. But this explanation leaves a number of matters opaque, including the Reeve's representation of the Northern clerks in his story. The tale is full of disdain for them, even as it uses them as tools of punishment and revenge. As such ambivalent figures, the clerks could provide a fitting point of identification for the Reeve, who clearly enjoys through their actions ("Now pleye Aleyn . . . ," 1.4198) and, at the same time, who distances himself from such behavior ("Ik am oold, me list not pley for age," 1.3867). The Reeve's alignment with Aleyn and John in the tale originates in his self-perception and a self-loathing expressed in terms of a stoic moral injunction and the withering effects of old age as well as the regionalism that they share. The Reeve himself is from Norfolk, even if not as "fer in the north" (1.4015) as he claims the clerks originate. Here we find the aggressivity toward himself that is the source of his aggression toward everyone else.

When the Reeve assumes the signifier and moves forward at the end of the Miller's Tale, what we hear most emphatically from him is his desire: a desire to be free of desire and thus to control and contain the Miller's terms, a desire to malign him completely. As he explains the privilege of older men: "whan we may nat doon, than wol we speke" (1.3881). This sentiment is part of the Reeve's longer preface to his story, which seeks to differentiate itself from the Miller's erotic play in one of the most self-deflating representations that any of the pilgrims offer:

> Gras tyme is doon; my fodder is now forage;
> This white top writeth myne olde yeris;
> Myn herte is also mowled as myne heris,

> But if I fare as dooth an open-ers—
> That ilke fruyt is ever lenger the wers,
> Til it be roten in mullok or in stree.
> We olde men, I drede, so fare we:
> Til we be roten, kan we nat be rype;
> We hoppen alwey whil that the world wol pype.
> For in our wyl ther sticketh evere a nayl,
> To have an hoor heed and a grene tayl,
> As hath a leek; for thogh oure myght be goon,
> Oure wyl desireth folie evere in oon.
> For whan we may nat doon, than wol we speke;
> Yet in oure asshen olde is fyr yreke.
> (1.3868–82)

While the grouchy sentiment of these lines has been noted, their exact sense is elusive and their relation to the tale unclear.[49] Anger provokes him to retaliate, but he denies the power to do so. Avowing his age and infirmity, he stumbles upon an image that licenses his aggression: old men are like medlars, not ripe until rotten (1.3875). This paradoxical image gives him a chance to assimilate desire to his powerlessness, which emerges in speech: "For whan we may nat doon, than wol we speke" (1.3881). This sermonizing on age is largely a logical diversion, located between a disavowal of his desire to retaliate and a slight apologia in advance of doing so. But it is also a point at which the Reeve raises the issue of his own relation to a desire his tale putatively neglects. If desire still burns in the lingering embers of old men, defined as "foure gleedes . . . / Avauntyng, liyng, anger, coveitise" (1.3883–84), half of these live coals are explicitly verbal, though all four may be verbally expressed. The powers ("sparkles") of age are not physical ones so much as verbal ones licensing the "leveful" Reeve's story of "force [with] force of-showve" (1.3912). The Reeve wants to legitimate his revenge and aggression and he does so by turning the persistence of desire ("wyl") beyond bodily strength into the force of speech. He thereby shifts matters from the "folie" old men still want but cannot perform to the mean violence and aggressivity that "longen unto eelde" (1.3885), making a paradoxical attempt at recognition and self-aggrandizement in the guise of diminution.

---

49. Much of the discussion of agedness in the Reeve's Prologue has sought to find a consistency between the speaker and the figure described in the General Prologue. See Carol Everest, "Sex and Old Age in Chaucer's *Reeve's Prologue*," *Chaucer Review* 31 (1996): 99–114. Susanna Greer Fein argues for the importance of the issue of age and youth in the tale itself in "'Lat the Children Pleye': The Game Betwixt the Ages in the *Reeve's Tale*," in Fein, Raybin, and Braeger, 73–104.

Aggressivity and its attendant violence are foregrounded to an unusual degree in the Reeve's Tale, and so too are his acts of misreading. But what the Reeve is really looking for is compensation, which, as we have seen, is never an easy thing to calculate. Like Aleyn and John, he will have to apply a "law" of easement that balances inequivalent things: "gif a man in a point be agreved, / That in another he sal be releved" (1.4182–83). Aleyn knows his corn, once ground, cannot be restored; he must look for something else: "the flour of il endyng" (1.4174). In a remarkable *sotto voce* pun, Aleyn substitutes Malyne's flower for his stolen flour, getting his compensation in and through the signifier.[50] But lest we forget the difficulties of compensation and its substitutive logic, the flours exchanged here remind us of the excess of such measures. Aleyn may seem to have made equivalencies for himself when there were none to be had, but he also seems to have taken far more than was stolen from him, flour that was not even his in the first place. The only kind of equivalence that is possible between Malyne's flower and Aleyn's flour resides in the way he will retell the tale.

At every narrative level, as well as the signifier grounding its discourse, the fabliaux more forthrightly acknowledge the aggressivity at the heart of desire. Both within the fictions that they tell and also within the competitive narrative gestures of the Miller and the Reeve, aggressivity almost completely overwrites the tales' depiction of desire and moves far beyond the socially productive sublimations of the Knight's chivalric order. We can easily read the Miller's Tale as a desublimation (and thus more open replaying) of the Knight's, with a heroine who knows which suitor she wants and a clear distinction between the practical and manipulative Nicholas (Arcite) and the effeminately lovelorn clerk whose name rhymes with Palamon. The nature of the plot of the Miller's Tale makes this structure even easier to see, as well as the Reeve's exploitation and aggravated heightening of the Miller's competitive aggression in a gameful adultery turned to near assault. Romance stages its conflict as a form of heroic proof (the desert of its heroes before other men) and as a means of writing its sexual interests in more elegant terms. Not so with either the action or the language of the fabliaux, where embodied eroticism takes center stage. Conflict in the fabliaux does not substitute for and sublimate sexual pursuit; instead, it prepares for it and makes it happen. With John away at Osney as often as he is, Nicholas and Alison have plenty of time for their amorous dalliances. There is hardly a need for the Flood plot at all. Like desire itself, a demand for something beyond need, Nicholas and Alison behave in excess of the

---

50. This pun is similarly located in an identical form in the Wife of Bath's Prologue. She vaunts: "The flour is goon; ther is namoore to telle; / The bren, as best I kan, now moste I selle" (3.477–78).

exigencies of their situation. The tale (and the erotic desires it elaborates) are so much more pleasurable when augmented by the trickery plot the two lovers fabricate. Where Nicholas and Alison "rage and pleye" at their leisure, they also delay and defer until she can "slepen in his arm al nyght" (1.3406). The tale is somewhat cagey about whether they have had sex. Alison says that they must "wayte wel and been privee" (1.3295) because of her husband's jealousy. But once Nicholas agrees to this caution, he "thakked hire aboute the lendes weel, / He kiste hire sweete and taketh his sawtrie, / And pleyeth faste, and maketh melodie" (1.3304–6). Music in the *Canterbury Tales* almost always comes with a sexual suggestiveness. After the music of the "smale foweles" sleeping "al the nyght with open ye" (1.9–10) one need only recall the "stif burdoun" (1.673) carried by the Summoner for the Pardoner in the General Prologue.[51] It is unclear at this point whether they are arranging another (even greater) opportunity or they are putting off their initial consummation until John can be present for his blinding humiliation. In the symbolic economy of "mak[ing] melodie," it hardly matters.

The desire violently disclosed by the Reeve's Tale, then, turns out to be a circulation of desire among the tales, a desire we see most clearly in the acts of misreading and the open hostilities both inside and between stories. The Reeve's Tale is about misrecognition, not only the misrecognitions in the bedroom—the wife in bed with John having "a murie fit" and then beating her husband's bald head thinking it were the clerk's "volupeer"—but also the misrecognition of the tale's social satire and trajectory. It is yet another way the tale is about, and driven by, desire as surely as those told in differing registers by the Miller and Knight.

---

51. See my essay "Yeoman Services: Chaucer's Knight, His Critics, and the Pleasures of Historicism," *Chaucer Review* 45.2 (2010): 194–221. On the "sexual suggestiveness" of music in the comedies, see Derek Pearsall, "The *Canterbury Tales* II: Comedy," in *The Cambridge Companion to Chaucer*, ed. Jill Mann and Piero Boitani, 2nd ed. (1986; Cambridge: Cambridge UP, 2003), 160–77, at 165.

three

SYMPTOMS OF DESIRE IN CHAUCER'S WIVES AND CLERKS

The Reeve's vengeful "quiting" of the Miller is written on the bodies of the women in his story and glossed by their unwitting enjoyment, a spectacular scene throwing into relief the competitive desires of wives and clerks witnessed in fabliaux and other comic tales of an economic cast. According to the logic of Chaucer's first fragment, married women attract clerks as well as provoke their ire and ridicule, and this situation forms the normative and normalizing universe that the genre's quotidian comedy projects.[1] We see its contours as the Miller details the erotic interest clerks Nicholas and Absolon naturally display for Alison, the carpenter's young wife. Absolon's role as parish clerk places him in the company of such wives regularly as he "Gooth with a senser on the haliday, / Sensynge the wyves of the parisshe faste; / And many a lovely look on hem he caste" (1.3340–42). "Sensynge the wyves," he carries the censor that blesses his church's congregation, but, of course, Absolon also indulges in other sensory pleasures. As readers of the Miller's adulterous comedy know, such innocent "sensynge" provides no limit to clerks' "daliaunce" (1.211) with wives, and it does not always result in pleasing ends. Absolon later emerges as the butt of the joke when he kisses the "naked ers" of the wife he has been courting in ridiculous fashion, unaware

---

1. See Mark Miller's chapter on the Miller's Tale, "Naturalism and its Discontents," in *Philosophical Chaucer: Love, Sex, and Agency in the "Canterbury Tales"* (Cambridge: Cambridge UP, 2004), 36–81.

that she has already taken another clerkly lover (1.3734). That kiss cures him of his lovesickness, prompting violent dreams of revenge with a hot coulter upon his would-be "lemman" that is ultimately visited on his rival, Nicholas, the much-preferred lover who boards in the carpenter's home. Though aimed at the former object of his affections, Absolon's aggression also comes from within, functioning as a kind of self-mutilation, since it is a more successful, rivalrous version of himself that he ultimately punishes. Only with such self-purgations can he truly have "his hoote love . . . coold and al yqueynt" (1.3754). But the fast and sharp turn that his feelings for Alison take is telling, and reveals the complex contours of desire between wives and clerks rather than any simple interest clerks seem to have in women.

These antics appear obliquely in any number of comic stories, satires, and farcical scenes. For instance, the friar in the Summoner's Tale knows Thomas and his wife of old, and not only because he's been working on Thomas to attain donations for his house. Such clerks are always on the lookout for the "fair[est] . . . wyf / In al the chirche" (3.1808–9). Like the Friar who is described in the General Prologue carrying pins and knives in his "typet" (1.233) as little gifts for the women in his jurisdiction, "freer John" (3.2171) in this tale has visited this home before where he was "refresshed moore than in an hondred placis" (3.1767). We intuit his familiarity from the manner in which he shoos away the cat from the most comfortable spot on the bench (3.1775) and kisses Thomas's wife (3.1803–5). But their apotheosis appears in the Shipman's Tale, a story that was likely attributed to the Wife of Bath at an earlier state of the *Tales*' composition.[2] This fabliau is unique in Chaucer's collection for its lack of violent retribution, and as such it is the very antithesis of the Reeve's story. In the end, no one is humiliated. The circulation of words follows (and explains) the circulation of money, itself a signifier, such that the wife can return symbolic capital to her husband by scoring it "upon [her] taille" (7.416). Not only do such transactions cause all to turn out well, they force the competitiveness of the wife and clerk to take center stage, where they substitute for the competition between men that formerly seemed to be the locus of fabliaux attention. Even as they are attracted to each other and arrange their liaison for when her merchant–husband will be away at Bruges, this pair is also engaged in competition with each other, duping each other more fully than they dupe the wife's husband.

---

2. Yet for an essay that overturns this common assumption about the Shipman's Tale and also complicates our assumptions about the cohesiveness of the genre of fabliau, see Joseph Dane, "The Wife of Bath's Shipman's Tale and the Invention of Chaucerian Fabliaux," *Modern Language Review* 99 (2004): 287–300.

Their flirtatious play begins with a dirty joke, a provocation that emerges from a situation of friendship and intimacy the tale carefully cultivates. Their flirtation starts with subtle aggressivity when the merchant retreats to his counting house in order to balance his accounts before a business journey. His withdrawal leaves the wife and monk alone. Seeing that the monk, daun John, has risen early one morning, the wife asks after his health. In response, he slyly defends his early walk in the garden by taking the opportunity to criticize the laziness (or luxuriousness) of married men. This jovial conversation affords the monk and the wife further intimacy. Their dalliance has, of course, been noted, but it has also prompted readers to argue over which of them is the instigator of the affair. On the one hand, the monk is the first one to suggest a sexual innuendo in his characterization of "thise wedded men" (7.103) who spend too much time abed. Such ideas prompt him to say how much he hopes she has not been "labour[ing] sith the nyght bigan" with her husband (7.108): "And with that word he lough ful murily, / And of his owene thought he wax al reed" (7.110–11). By laughing and blushing, the monk gives away his thoughts of being in bed with the wife, of which she is quick to take advantage. But others have read the wife's quick-wittedness as more deliberate, seeing her initial question as to the monk's health in more aggressive terms. John Hermann describes the scene as a predatory seduction on the wife's part: "The merchant's wife steals up on him to ask whether or not he is ill, apparently the only explanation she can adduce for his rising so early."[3] Calling the monk's answer a "gentle sally in response to the wife's raillery," he locates the engine of "the risqué conversation" that follows: "Of course, she did not really think he was sick, but wished to imply that he was not the sort of monk who rose at the proper canonical hour to recite his office" (303). Hermann reads the wife's language critically and aggressively, somewhere between a conscious seduction of daun John with her disingenuous question and a more simple baiting of him into licentious thoughts. Already the aggressiveness of the desires of wives and clerks are felt long before they become entangled in the deception over the hundred franks.

Once the subject is broached, however, their sexual attraction for each other emerges fast. She disavows any such interest in her husband, "lasse lust . . . to that sory pley" (7.116), because of the financial troubles plaguing her. Her distress is measured by thoughts of desertion and death (7.121–22). Vowing their secrecy to each other, as well as their "love and affiance" (7.139), the monk and wife set each other up as they make an alliance

---

3. John Hermann, "Dismemberment, Dissemination, Discourse: Sign and Symbol in the *Shipman's Tale*," *Chaucer Review* 19 (1985): 302–37, at 303.

against the merchant. The wife confesses to a debt she is dangerously close to defaulting in order to entice him to her aid. The monk takes advantage of the situation by borrowing from the merchant to procure the wife as his lover. We could characterize this scene as an economized dramatization of the way clerks like the Miller's Nicholas "fil with this yonge wyf to rage and pleye" (1.3272). What the Miller describes in summary fashion—he "spak so faire, and profred him so faste, / That she hir love hym graunted atte laste" (1.3289–90)—is more fully shown in the Shipman's fabliau. From this beginning, each of these figures in the Shipman's Tale believes (s)he is getting the better of the other and at no cost. Daun John rides off in the end having had his fun with her and acting as the conduit for more generous financial exchange between marital partners that the wife will repay to her husband "in trade." Neither husband nor wife understands at the time what John is doing with the money; each believes it's a token of John's esteem, thus leaving the integrity of their friendship—here punningly expressed as "cosynage" (736), both familiarity and trickery, indeed a trickery only possible between familiars—intact. In these neat transactions, then, the Shipman's Tale reveals a rivalrous attraction of wives and clerks in one and the same gesture. Without any turn to blinding anger or resentment toward each other, the wife and clerk in this least violent and humiliating of Chaucer's fabliaux reveal the aggressivity of desire itself, here as a means of gaining power and potency.

The familiarity of wives and clerks, as well as their rivalrous attraction to each other, is writ large in the *Canterbury Tales* by the dramatic interaction of the Wife of Bath and the Clerk in the so-called marriage group, a set of textual relations and argumentative postures in the poem's frame that have long held critical attention.[4] The tales leading up to and contained within fragments 3 and 4 especially position the Wife of Bath and the Clerk within a "naturally" aggressive, competitive, and desiring framework. Indeed, their aggressions and competitions are shaped by the desires that the fabliaux witness in distinction from authoritatively academic or ecclesiastic discourse about women, which the Wife of Bath's Prologue reframes anew.

When the Wife of Bath takes on the defense of women from the ravages of such clerical authority, she attacks on a number of fronts, both

---

4. The "marriage group," a heuristic collocation of tales that respond to the ideas about gender in Jerome's *Adversus Jovinianum*, is typically attributed to George Lyman Kittredge's essay "Chaucer's Discussion of Marriage," *Modern Philology* 9 (1912): 435–67, but originally comes from Eleanor Prescott Hammond, *Chaucer: A Bibliographical Manual* (New York: Macmillan, 1908), 256. For a fuller discussion of this conflation, see my essay "The Women in Chaucer's Marriage Group," *Medieval Feminist Forum* 45 (2009): 50–56.

from the experience of her unique "scoleiyng" (3.44f) and from the perspective of the object of representation portrayed from "withinne [clerical] oratories," asking "Who peyntede the leon, tel me who?" (3.694; 692). But beyond her argumentative Prologue, the Wife's and Clerk's Tales seem to engage overtly in a debate over the correct (feminine) form of desire in their nearly oppositional narratives of marital conflict and reconciliation. The Wife of Bath's Tale addresses feminine desire explicitly by subjecting a recreant knight to the task of finding "what thyng is it that wommen moost desiren" (3.905). The Clerk more cannily deflects this question in his exemplification of patient Griselda, the wife who can subordinate herself completely to the desire of another. These ideal images in the Wife's and Clerk's Tales, the magical old woman and the humble, desire-less wife, figure ideal self-images imagined and projected by the Wife and Clerk, respectively. Each of these narrators clearly identifies with this figure in his or her story.[5] But this Imaginary scenario can be in no way complete; the Symbolic intrudes upon it at each and every turn, and most emphatically at each tale's end when its narrator must return to the sociality of the group. The tales may make neatly oppositional claims about the object of desire, but desire's structuring force relates the stories in unexpected ways.

The Wife of Bath herself explains the naturalness of the charged desires between wives and clerks in more scientific terms in her Prologue. She uses the same "astromye" that Nicholas studies to explain the forces leading to their opposition:

> And thus, God woot, Mercurie is desolat
> In Pisces, wher Venus is exaltat,
> And Venus falleth ther Mercurie is reysed.
> Therfore no womman of no clerk is preysed.
> The clerk, whan he is oold, and may noght do
> Of Venus werkes worth his olde sho,
> Thanne sit he doun, and writ in his dotage
> That wommen kan nat kepe hir mariage!
> (3.703–10)

Cosmic determinism naturalizes a rivalry between clerks and wives, which then gives way to more practical explanations in the sexual frustration of

---

5. On the identifications of these narrators with their heroines, see Warren Ginsberg, "The Lineaments of Desire: Wish-Fulfillment in Chaucer's Marriage Group," *Criticism* 25 (1983): 197–210. On the Clerk's identification with Griselda, see Carolyn Dinshaw, *Chaucer's Sexual Poetics* (Madison: U of Wisconsin P, 1989), 135–36.

the older clerk, his inability to "do / Of Venus werkes worth his olde sho." Such physical desire and the impotence preventing its fulfillment provoke the stories about women found in texts like Jankyn's "book of wikked wyves" (3.685). Where stories like that of "Hercules and of his Dianyre" (3.725) or "Clitermystra . . . / That falsly made hire housebonde for to dye" (3.737–38) would appear to show the desire for a wife to be an illogical and self-defeating enterprise, the Wife's logic betrays the aggressivity of desire underwriting those very claims: "For trusteth wel, it is an impossible / That any clerk wol speke good of wyves, / But if it be of hooly seintes lyves, / Ne of noon oother womman never the mo" (3.688–91). These clerical writings are never unmotivated. In her explanation of their sexual frustrations, the Wife has suggested that discourse like the Clerk's is propelled by desires he fails to acknowledge. No wonder, then, that the Clerk's Tale posits an avatar whose simple and unspoiled nature lacks all desire and avoids its temptations at every turn. His complimentary description of Griselda, "no likerous lust was thurgh hire herte yronne" (4.214), confirms by implication the condemnation of others.

Readers have taken the Clerk's Tale as a direct rebuttal of these assertions, which are made especially pointed when he refers to the Wife by name in his Envoy. If the Wife's statement stands as a challenge, the Clerk's Tale frustrates her claims with the story of an impossibly good wife in patient Griselda. Both the Prologue and Envoy to the Clerk's Tale make the Wife's "impossible" quite possible as they locate the story in a particular "clerkly" origin, "Frauceys Petrak, the lauriat poete" (4.31), and address the Wife of Bath "and al hire secte" respectively (4.1171). The conflict between Wife and Clerk in this matter is, perhaps, largely overdetermined. Not only does the Wife's idealization of the crafty old woman and cannily judicious Guenevere contrast sharply with the Clerk's perfectly passive Griselda, the conflict begins even before her Prologue. Chaucer sets the Wife and Clerk at odds through their contrasting descriptions in the General Prologue as "mirror opposites" which are from the beginning "destined to clash."[6] This rivalry has greater stakes than the dramatic context or competitive narrative of the pilgrimage alone, because what we are talking about here is something that happens in the Wife's and Clerk's stories, not some private

---

[6]. See John A. Alford, "The Wife of Bath Versus the Clerk of Oxford: What Their Rivalry Means," *Chaucer Review* 21 (1986): 108–32, at 109. Even further, Alford argues, they must be understood in terms of each other and each other's discourse, not as characters. They "come directly from the tradition of the allegorized liberal arts" in which the Clerk is "Logic personified," while the Wife speaks as "Dame Rhetoric herself" (110). Thus, Alford concludes that "the conflict between the Wife and the Clerk is not personal but historical. It is rooted in the recurrent tension between two modes of discourse, rhetorical and philosophical" (109).

animosity driving the relationship between two narrative genres.[7] It is as much a rivalry between wives and clerks within various stories as between two narrating figures. The desire of clerks and wives witnessed in these tales—desire that appears in such radically different forms—figures the very desiring discourse and its dislocations that produce the *Canterbury Tales* in the first place. A shift from the ordinary sense of desire to the more linguistically constitutive one at stake here makes the significance of the particular object of desire give way to the persistence of desire itself and the telling symptom in which it is manifested. This means that despite the fact that the Wife and Clerk have such oppositional things to say about women, desire, and women who desire in their tales, their language will also say things about which they are unaware.

Given that they are positioned against one another by so much of what has come before as well as by the Wife's elaborate anticlerical Prologue, the similar ways in which they end their tales is striking, even if it has long gone unnoticed. Desire's symptom arises as this structural similarity, which has been largely overshadowed by their argumentative posture. With their different social locations as well as the differing concerns and operations of their genres, it is little surprise these tales sketch idealized representations of female behavior dramatically at odds with each other. The Wife depicts an actively aggressive woman who takes responsibility for the redemptive and transformative power of "magic" in her tale. Indeed she seizes it. She appears magically before the tale's questing knight, demanding to know his purpose: "Sire knyght, heer forth ne lith no wey. / Tel me what that ye seken" (3.1001–2). The Clerk, on the other hand, idealizes a passive woman whose inhuman constancy is rewarded in the end. Griselda could hardly be more different from the old woman of the wife's romance. Yet the Wife and Clerk respond to their tales in surprisingly similar ways. Both pilgrims' closing gestures withdraw from the powerful position of mastery each of their tales has achieved, and both narrating figures speak anxiously, well beyond the simple conclusion their stories eventually reach.

The recoil of these two narrators is striking and has been magnified by various critical attempts to explain the end of each performance. The Wife

---

7. In an essay on the Clerk's Tale, Andrea Denny-Brown repositions its rhetoric in relation to the Wife of Bath and her "sumptuous material world," to show how he argues against it in increasingly subtle ways. She reads the dressing and undressing of Griselda in the context of the historical significance of material goods and objects, and particularly sartorial legislation and infraction, to the ultimate critique of the "superfluity, frivolity, and love of novelty with not only the common 'peple' of his tale but also the *nouveaux riches* [sic] merchant class and its spendthrift 'arch' wives"— a critique pointedly relevant, in yet another way, to the Wife of Bath. See "*Povre* Griselda and the All-Consuming *Archewyves*," *SAC* 28 (2006): 77–115, at 80.

of Bath's diverse arguments for the beneficence of female dominance culminate, for instance, in a fairy-tale ending from which she withdraws back into belligerence in the space of a mere eight lines (3.1257–64). Likewise, the Clerk proffers an idealized image of female submission that proves heroically dominant at the end of his tale. In a more prolonged fashion, he recoils from the power Griselda exerts over Walter in eleven stanzas of Petrarchan apology and allegorization. Even more excessively, the Clerk adds an antifeminist harangue that closes the debate in his ironically caustic Envoy (4.1142–1212) by redoubling the Wife's closing aggression. In these conclusions, the Wife's and Clerk's Tales both reveal a form of narrative *jouissance,* an ecstasy of pleasure that abruptly turns to unpleasure, provoking their aversion and a retreat to the safety of the stereotyped Symbolic once more.

Attempts to explain the tales' closing gestures have treated them in isolation, thus the critical misrecognition of the shared structure of these performances. Opposed in philosophic ideas and feminine ideals, these tales both work to conceal a similar recognition. In René Girard's formulation, both tales "defend the same illusion of autonomy," or what the Wife and Clerk call sovereignty, by means of tracking the kind of feminine or feminized power each tale is most interested in exalting.[8] But in offering a particular account of sovereignty, each tale depends on a mastery that ultimately disrupts any neat identification with these ideal heroines. Into the imaginary fiction of autonomy that each figure has offered, such mastery inserts an other that gives the lie to the fantasy of sovereignty each story proffers. In their structural similarity, then, the Wife's and Clerk's Tales momentarily reveal a desire—much like the Franklin's Dorigen discussed in the introduction—for what each speaker seems most desperate to deny. The Wife's rhetoric of mastery and exemplary female sovereignty covers over a wish to submit to masculine power, while the Clerk's ideal of passive suffering, Christ-like in its exemplification, is driven by a disavowed desire to dominate, seemingly unchristian in its very aspiration.[9] For all their supposed differences, the Wife and the Clerk reveal the same divi-

---

8. Girard's quasi-Hegelian formulation of mimetic desire and triangulation looks to account for the way desire arises through social relations rather than in imitation of one's originary and imaginary relation with the other, the *objet petit a*. See René Girard, *Deceit, Desire and the Novel: Self and Other in Literary Structure,* trans. Yvonne Freccero (Baltimore: Johns Hopkins UP, 1965), 16. In distinction from Lacanian accounts, Girard makes desire an instantaneous and entirely social (and thus symbolic) formation.

9. Lynn Staley, "Chaucer and the Postures of Sanctity," in David Aers and Lynn Staley, *The Powers of the Holy: Religion, Politics, and Gender in Late Medieval English Culture* (University Park: Pennsylvania State UP, 1996), esp. 233–59.

sion in the structure of desire, the desire for (and thus to be) the Other's desire, that unravels the neat close of their fictions and provokes a number of ironic readings of those endings. This shared structure suggests an analogy between the two figures and between their tales that rewrites our conception of the marriage group as a simple debate in these fragments. This analogy, in turn, disrupts the very opposition between wives and clerks that readers of Chaucer's poetry have all too easily accepted and shifts our attention to the productive value of desire—even if desire means lack—for the *Canterbury Tales* as a whole.[10]

Where Chaucer's *Tales* originate in a human desire embedded in and obfuscated by the artifice of its opening sentence, the individual tales' conclusions typically resound with the satisfaction of a narrative crescendo like the one the Miller's comedy offers. Its narrator's voice comes crashing down upon his conclusion—"This tale is doon, and God save al the rowte!" (1.3854)—much like the carpenter hanging from the rafters at the climax of the Miller's comedy. The Wife's speedy ending appears less a departure from the Miller's tidy conclusion than the Clerk's multiple endings, which include Petrarchan moral and antifeminist song. We know these tales have ended, not least because the Host likes to give his opinion and resume control as soon as possible. The Wife's Tale closes with the transformation and happy marriage of beautiful, young, and faithful lady with reformed knight (3.1250–58), a world improved by the ministrations of women: not merely the old woman whose request challenges and tests the knight's understanding of the superior wisdom she has demonstrated, but also Guenevere, whose justice outstrips the rule of law that Arthur would impose.[11] The Clerk's ends with the re-exaltation of Griselda and her emotional reunion with her children (4.1079–1127). Griselda is thus restored "and ther she was honored as hire oghte" (4.1120) in a "revel" and "feste" that is "more solempne" and more costly than her wedding (4.1125–27). Both endings bring their protagonists reward and satisfaction, and, we might imagine, their narrators too. They seem to have accomplished their

---

10. See Kristyn Gorton, *Theorising Desire: From Freud to Feminism to Film* (Basingstoke and New York: Palgrave Macmillan, 2008), for a recent discussion of the unhelpful opposition staged between Deleuzian and Lacanian accounts of desire.

11. The Wife's Tale has been dramatizing the answer to the question of feminine desire from its very beginning. When Guenevere asks Arthur for the right "to chese wheither she wolde hym save or spille" (3.897), she has already shown the knight the answer he sets out to find.

narrative and argumentative goals. But the Clerk's Tale has always been invested in broader concerns than those we might attribute to Walter or Griselda. His interests are abstract and political rather than personal. His tale's prospective vision goes so far as to suggest the future happiness and security that motivated the tale in the first place. Walter's son, we are told, eventually "succedeth in his heritage / In reste and pees, after his fader day" (4.1135–36). These endings are conventional in that they resolve the conflicts each tale stages. Problems arise, then, only from their narrators' own doing. Much like the Franklin's Dorigen, whose travail emerges from an excess of words uttered after she had already given her refusal, these narrators speak in excess of their meaning, beyond the conclusion each tale had carefully orchestrated. The Wife and Clerk continue to speak as if fearful that their points have not been made clearly enough. But we might also read them as anxious acknowledgments that they have been spoken all *too* clearly or directly. Like Dorigen's words uttered "in pley" (5.988), words that assuage the harsh refusal of Aurelius's suit, these conclusions have provoked, even necessitated, discursive intervention.

While these endings are foregrounded by critical attempts to supervene them, such evasive readings only repeat the tales' own evasive and resistant gestures.[12] For instance, just as the Wife offers the transformative, happily-ever-after ending—"And thus they lyve unto hir lyves ende / In parfit joye" (3.1257–58)—she returns, even before she can finish the sentence, to the Prologue's masterful terms she had finally seemed to transcend:

> . . . and Jhesu Crist us sende
> Housbondes meeke, yonge, and fressh abedde,
> And grace t'overbyde hem that we wedde;
> And eek I praye Jhesu shorte hir lyves
> That noght wol be governed by hir wyves;
> And olde and angry nygardes of dispence,
> God sende hem soone verray pestilence!
> (3.1258–64)

---

12. Charlotte Morse and William McClellan, in very different ways, challenge us to rethink our response to and what we supposedly know about the Clerk's Tale. In its uncanny scene of domestic violence, we have to avert our eyes, and this aversion leads to highly critical responses to the tale: we historicize it, we allegorize and dehumanize it, as we make it into something "as for oure excercise" (4.1156). See Morse, "The Exemplary Griselda," *SAC* 7 (1985): 51–86; and McClellan, "'Ful Pale Face': Agamben's Biopolitical Theory and the Sovereign Subject in Chaucer's *Clerk's Tale*," *Exemplaria* 17 (2005): 103–34. As a last resort, I suppose, we might ironize the Clerk's narration—even before the satiric Envoy—or Chaucer's depiction of the Clerk himself and so release him from all authority.

The happiness produced at the end of the Wife's Tale as proof that female sovereignty makes for perfect male felicity in marriage is short-lived. What could be a two-line conclusion (by ending, that is, at line 1259's "fresh abbede," or even earlier in "parfit joye," at 1258) runs on for almost ten, following an associative chain of thought that brings us back to the marital reality the Wife knows firsthand. Her characters' perfect joy, it would seem, inspires thoughts of her own intimate pleasures: "Housbondes meeke, yonge, and fressh abedde." Forgetting something of the corrective goal of the tale, her language recalls other aspects of marriage retailed in her Prologue. Similarly, the continuation of such joy "unto hir lyves ende" is an "end" with which the Wife is only too familiar: "Welcome the sixte, whan that evere he shal" (3.45). Her comic prayer to outlive these "meeke, yonge, and fresh" husbands raises the specter of death, which is what she wishes on those men resistant to her superior knowledge. At one point the Wife calmly concluded her Breton lai with the mutual satisfaction of reformed knight and transformed lady: "A thousand tyme a-rewe he gan hire kisse, / And she obeyed hym in every thyng / That myghte doon hym plesance or likyng" (3.1254–56). But the account of such bliss, contingent finally upon female obedience, quickly moves to the kind of pre-emptive curse in terms more familiar from her Prologue.

The situation is not particularly hard to explain given the resemblance of the Wife to the wily old woman of the tale. As a projection of the Wife's ideal self-image, the old woman can position herself, through shrewd argumentation (or the enchantments of fiction), to be transformed by the "maistrie" ceded to her by her new husband (3.1236), a transformation much harder to effect at the level of the Canterbury pilgrims and their competition. Attaining mastery over the man in deed, rather than in mere word, and in earnest, rather than in naïve repetition of what she "rowned . . . in his ere" (3.1021), produces the best marital arrangement in this fictive world. It consolidates their marriage, guaranteeing her love and fidelity: "we be no lenger wrothe, / For, by my trouthe, I wol be to yow bothe— / This is to seyn, ye, bothe fair and good" (3.1239–41). Much as she expects, the reward delights the husband: "For joye he hente hire in his armes two. / His herte bathed in a bath of blisse" (3.1252–53). Such physical affection also delights the Wife/wife, who has entered into the terms of conventional marriage in idealized form. Giving women what they want will always end in men's happiness: "happy wife, happy life," she might more economically say. But the ideals espoused here are also placed into conventional terms harder to assimilate after the Wife's pragmatically knowledgeable Prologue. Miming the wedding vows themselves, which solicit a promise to love, honor, and obey from the woman, and which ensure the legal rights a husband attains in marriage, she promises to love and "be also good and trewe" (3.1243) in a way that returns to him ultimate power over her: "Dooth with my lyf and deth right as yow lest" (3.1248). These words appear as a heightened expression of the exchanged affections at the end of the story. The old woman has cornered the knight with her demand for marriage in payment for her lifesaving answer to Guenevere's question and traps him once again in the choice she offers him on their wedding night:

> I prey to God that I moote sterven wood
> But I to yow be also good and trewe
> As evere was wyf, syn that the world was newe.
> And but I be to-morn as fair to seene
> As any lady, emperice, or queene,
> That is bitwixe the est and eke the west,
> Dooth with my lyf and deth right as yow lest.
> Cast up the curtyn, looke how that it is.
> (3.1242–49)

Her life, and his very power over it, provides the guarantee against the possibility that she is tricking him again here. When he wakes up tomorrow morning she will be just as beautiful as she is now when he lifts up the curtain and just as faithful "as any lady, emperice, or queene." Offering this power over her life would seem an appropriate gesture for such a lowborn figure, who must clearly find a way to align herself with these aristocratic feminine types. So too does the humble Griselda offer her life to Walter under far less joyful circumstances. She claims that she and her child are his to do with as he pleases: "ye mowe save or spille / Youre owene thyng; werketh after youre wille" (4.503–4). Her marriage and all her actions are produced under the sign of his "luste" (4.659–65). Indeed she would do his will before he asked it of her if she "hadde prescience / [His] wyl to knowe" (4.659–60). Even more explicitly, she offers: "wiste I that my deeth wolde do yow ese, / Right gladly wolde I dyen, yow to plese" (4.664–65). Griselda's willingness to die because "Deth may noght make no comparisoun / Unto [his] love" (4.666–67) delights her husband with near embarrassment. He must "cast adoun / His eyen two" for the shame and delight they betray (4.668–69). Such delight also affects the Wife's knight, rendering him speechless (3.1252–54).

The Wife's Tale's expression of the knight's joy in her transformation and the power it affords him is inscribed with the Wife's name: his heart *bathes* in a *bath* of bliss at this critical juncture in which the woman answers in proper wifely fashion: "And she *obeyed* hym in every thyng / That myghte doon hym plesance or likyng" (3.1255–56; my emphasis).[13] Occurring in the signifier, "bath," the odd discrepancy between the very conventionality of this ending and the unconventional Wife who narrates it has led to various arguments about the impact of the wish-fulfillment aspect of her story.[14]

The end of the Wife of Bath's Tale thus shifts from argument and opposition ("we be . . . wrothe"), from a marriage won through guile and female mastery, to elaborating man's "real" happiness in marriage. The image of the tale's characters with which the Wife closes also forms the conclusion to her argument: the formula for happy, contented husbands. We end not with female mastery or sovereignty but with an image of *male* bliss, *his* "plesance or likyng." One can massage this tale's conclusion in terms of mutual sovereignty or shared mastery, but the Wife's Tale more strategically shows men what they need to relinquish so as to gain complete happiness and obedience from their wives. If she reveals the conditions under which men and women ultimately give up their claims of mastery over each other, as Dorigen and Arveragus attempt by means of their courtly marital contract, she ends somewhere deeply uncomfortable: with the lady offering the power of life and death to the knight. The Wife has made us attentive to the masterful terms of worldly and spiritual matters, sharpening the rhetoric of romance and its subjugations at the end of her own story. We have been prompted to laugh at the Wife's annoyed response to her idealized romance story, chalking it up to Chaucer's sophisticated characterization. As with many of the digressions, illogicalities, and falsehoods used locally and to comic effect in her Prologue, this obstreperous and abrupt ending characterizes her discourse as stereotypically "feminine" precisely because self-contradictory and thus works in accord with what we see elsewhere in her Prologue and Tale. It makes her sound like "herself," a characterization that may, in fact, obscure our realization of how much

---

13. This uncharacteristic lexical redundancy, "bathing in a bath of bliss," reinscribes her name, perhaps testifying to the fiction of identity at stake here.

14. For critiques of the rather commonplace reading of the Wife's shift at the end of her tale, see Louise [Aranye] Fradenburg, "The Wife of Bath's Passing Fancy," *SAC* 8 (1986): 31–58, at 55; H. Marshall Leicester, *The Disenchanted Self: Representing the Subject in the "Canterbury Tales"* (Berkeley: U of California P, 1990), 155; and Ginsberg, "Lineaments of Desire," 197–98.

like *every* self she sounds, since desire is located and revealed, precisely, at such points of discontinuity and contradiction.[15]

If we enjoy the comic reversal by which the Wife of Bath's Tale returns to the forceful rhetoric heard in the Prologue, the ending of the Clerk's Tale provokes a more heated debate about its endgame and one that has been posited in terms of a very different characterization as well. As one reader puts it, multiple "closing frames of the *Clerk's Tale* offer shifting evaluations . . . [that] are marked by changes in the clerkly voice of the narrator, and his ostensible audience of address."[16] In far more dramatic fashion, the Clerk's Envoy has provoked a variety of critical responses, not the least of which concerns the textual status of its ending. Long read as caustic irony within the frame narrative of the *Tales,* and, to its critical admirers, "a passable display of wit . . . a heartily ironic tribute to the Wife of Bath, . . . and a vivacious and sarcastic song," the Clerk's Envoy has complicated our responses to the unobtrusive pilgrim Harry Bailly has introduced *as a wife,* "ryd[ing] as coy and stille as dooth a mayde / Were newe spoused, sittynge at the bord" (4.2–3).[17] Thus the wife–clerk friction is clearly something bigger than just a provocation between two pilgrims. It already circulates in the discourse of the Host.

The standard printed version of the Clerk's Tale in the *Riverside Chaucer* and its derivatives displays its ambiguous textual situation through a number of formatting choices that make for a story with a markedly different *mise-en-page* than the majority of other Canterbury tales. It is broken into sections with Latin incipits and explicits, and it has a prologue and formal envoy in different verse forms with at least one rubric. The Envoy also remains problematic at the level of structure and narration as well. Readers have found its tone glib and far out of character for its otherwise erudite and somewhat unassuming speaker.[18] But the Envoy might also be too easily read as an addition to the story that ruins its elegant allegory. Sepa-

---

15. See, for instance, the discussion by Judith Butler in *Subjects of Desire: Hegelian Reflections in Twentieth-Century France* (New York: Columbia UP, 1986), 186ff.

16. Lesley Johnson, "Reincarnations of Griselda: Contexts for the *Clerk's Tale?*," in *Feminist Readings of Middle English Literature: The Wife of Bath and All Her Sect,* ed. Ruth Evans and Lesley Johnson (London: Routledge, 1994), 195–220, at 209.

17. Steven Axelrod, "The Wife of Bath and the Clerk," *Annuale Mediaevale* 15 (1974): 109–24, at 112. Axelrod's essay recuperates the Clerk "for the witty, spirited, flawed and attractive human being he is" (113). Dinshaw has also made much of the Clerk's position as a newly "spoused" (4.3) wife (*Chaucer's Sexual Poetics* 135).

18. The Clerk's Envoy has been reckoned a problem by a number of readers including Thomas J. Farrell, "The 'Envoy de Chaucer' and the *Clerk's Tale,*" *Chaucer Review* 24 (1990): 329–36; and Howell Chickering, "Form and Interpretation in the *Envoy* to the *Clerk's Tale,*" *Chaucer Review* 29 (1995): 352–72.

rated from the tale by a rubric, this feature puts the Envoy's textual status in doubt even as it attempts to clarify its status.[19] And if the Envoy's final line—"And lat hym care, and wepe, and wrynge, and waille!" (4.1212)— were not immediately picked up by the Merchant and transformed into the opening of his own prologue—"Wepyng and waylyng, care and oother sorwe / I knowe ynogh, on even and a-morwe" (4.1213–14)—it might have long been cancelled by editors as a crudely antifeminist interpolation.[20] The scribes of the manuscript tradition may perhaps be warding off just such a cancellation by marking the passage now at 4.1177 as "Lenvoy de Chaucer," signing its author's name.

The change in verse form in the Envoy may also make necessary that authorial signature. Introducing "a song to glade yow" after the "ernestful matere" of his tale (4.1174–75), the Clerk switches from his elevated rhyme-royal stanzas to the form of the double ballade (six-line stanzas with only three rhymes).[21] Formally different from most others in the Canterbury collection, the Clerk's Tale's differences from itself are most illuminating. These differences are embodied in the name of the author, signed as rubric to the Envoy's beginning, a signature ostensibly offered to guarantee the authority of the text. But the imposition of an authorial signature, even if only in the manuscript apparatus, here works the opposite way as well by breaking the fiction of the speaking character and marking all too clearly the absence of a consistent voice in the Clerk's performance.[22] Ironically, if the scribes were looking to preserve an authentic part of the Clerk's speech at the end of his story—a desire in which the modern editor also indulges—they do so by indicating Chaucer's name rather than the fictional speaker's. Preserving the text as Chaucer's, they disrupt the Chaucerian fiction of the Clerk's discourse.

---

19. The rubric introducing the Clerk's Envoy is attested in most of the base manuscripts of the *Canterbury Tales*; see Farrell, "Envoy de Chaucer," 329, and John M. Manly and Edith Rickert, eds., *The Text of the Canterbury Tales, Studied on the Basis of All Known Manuscripts*, 8 vols. (Chicago: University of Chicago Press, 1940), 3:534–35. According to their view Chaucer revised the ending of the Clerk's Tale, at which time he added the Envoy to link directly to the Merchant's Prologue.

20. Following line 1212 stands what is called "the Host's stanza," which, according to the *Riverside* textual notes, "is generally held to have been written early and canceled when Chaucer wrote new lines for The Merchant's Prologue containing an echo of 1212 [see Manly and Rickert above, n23]. It is found in Ellesmere, Hengwrt, and 20 other MSS" (*Riverside Chaucer* 884). John Ganim finds "the evidence seems to indicate that the envoy was added after the tale itself was originally written, perhaps much later," possibly expanding on Manly-Rickert's presentation of evidence. See *Chaucerian Theatricality* (Princeton: Princeton UP, 1990), 80.

21. The most elaborate analysis of these metrics, particularly in the Envoy, is found in Chickering, "Form and Interpretation." See also Ganim, *Chaucerian Theatricality*, 86–87.

22. On the textual tradition of the Envoy and the Chaucerian signature by which it is introduced, see Farrell, "Envoy de Chaucer."

Despite these problems, the Envoy remains, and it remains to be explained by readers of the Clerk's allegory. Beyond the various arguments preserving, assimilating, and nullifying the Envoy are those justifying the Clerk's sarcasm and integrating its ironies into the argument of the tale as a whole. John Ganim, for instance, argues for "the festive nature of the envoy," part of a critical trend that separates the Envoy from the tale.[23] Reading it as independent lyric, Ganim returns it to the conditions set by the Clerk's own Prologue. In the Envoy, filled with "comic sexual reversals, . . . Harry's mastery of the proceedings and his sense of how stories are meant to be understood is made fun of, certainly as much as the Wife of Bath's ideas on marriage are ironically praised" (82). Ganim reads the Envoy as a decided shift to the sort of performances, "song, minstrelsy, student prank—[that] dramatize th[e] failure" of the tale for the contest's judge (84). It is too difficult and demanding for the likes of Harry Bailly, who wants no preaching or scholarly terms but only "pleyn" language (4.12–19). Separating the Envoy from the tale, then, Ganim attaches it more securely to the Prologue and changes its immediate audience from that named, "for the Wyves love of Bathe / . . . and al hire secte" (4.1170–71), to the Host. If such a separation is meant to allow us to read beyond the dramatic principle or a marriage group—beyond a conflict with the Wife herself—this reading only widens, by including the rest of the pilgrim company, its dramatic context. Even as a separate poem, then, the Envoy is directed toward a larger dramatic audience.

Registering a similar difference at the end of the Clerk's Tale, Elizabeth Salter hears the voice of the tale's conclusion *as* the Clerk's. In her extremely influential study Salter writes, "If, during the *Tale*, we have sometimes been uncertain about the exact identity of the narrator, we are now clearly intended to understand that the voice we hear is that of the Clerk, speaking familiarly to his fellow pilgrims, and establishing a second *raison d'être* for his story—an outer frame of reference."[24] The two voices Salter hears in the Tale echo the two registers, allegorical and verisimilar, in which Chaucer seeks to write and which he sets in open competition. The Clerk's story emerges, in Salter's words, as caught "between two worlds" and two very different styles, demanding opposing kinds of audience response that cannot be reconciled: "the one expressing itself in austere modes, with controlled religious echoes, the other in lively language, critical, sentimental, dramatic" (62). In this way she explains the Envoy's humor and

---

23. Ganim, *Chaucerian Theatricality*, 82.
24. Elizabeth Salter, *Chaucer: The Knight's Tale and The Clerk's Tale* (London: Edward Arnold, 1962), 62–63.

the Clerk's self-abasing ending to his story as a "skillfully managed return to the miscellaneous crowd of pilgrims on the road to Canterbury" (64). The Envoy continues with its humor by "recommend[ing], tacitly, those very virtues and behaviour [prudence, humility, innocence, reverence] they seem to scorn" (Salter 65). Thus, according to Salter, if Griselda cannot be believed in any realist sense, the Envoy makes her "a more acceptable, less preposterous creation than the Wife of Bath and 'archewyves' of her kind" (65). Yet we might note even further that, much like the ending of the Wife of Bath's Tale, the Clerk's humor and shift in tone return us to its narrator's own anxious uncertainty. Read as a continuation of the tale, a reinscription into the marriage debate, or part of the linking framework of the entire poem, the Envoy has made Chaucer's readers uncertain as to what it *is* as well as the Clerk's control over its discourse.

Also a bit out of character like the Clerk's *volta face* shift in tone, the Wife's bid for mastery and her practical argument for its foundation in nature and divine creation are complicated by the tale she chooses to tell. Her Prologue makes an openly hostile rebuttal to clerical judgments about women that borders on diatribe, but the unexpectedly nuanced and idealist Arthurian romance she tells offers a more sophisticated articulation of the mutual bliss made possible through women's sovereignty in marriage. In these claims I have very consciously moved from one of the Wife's operative terms, "maistrie" (mastery), to another, "sovereynetee" (sovereignty), because of the importance of both words and their sometimes unexamined relations.[25] The elision of sovereignty and mastery emerges from the general discourse of power and the hierarchies it generates. A sovereign has power or mastery over others, as does Arthur in the Wife of Bath's Tale or Walter in the Clerk's over their subjects. But no one holds power over the sovereign, who has complete self-determination. This is why the old woman in the Wife's Tale must clarify the power she has gained from the

---

25. In "The Semantics of Power: *Maistrie* and *Soveraynetee* in *The Canterbury Tales*," *Modern Philology* 84 (1986): 18–23, Donald C. Green discusses these terms and four others (servage, servyse, governaunce, and assente), with particular attention to the Wife and Clerk, to reread sovereignty (*contra* the Wife) as subordination to a role and/in a proper order. He writes, "Chaucer has made a careful distinction between the individually defined relationships of *maistrie* and *servyse* on the one hand and the role-defined relationships of *soveraynetee* and *servage* on the other" (23). The Wife, who conflates mastery with sovereignty, performs a heresy in Green's reading: "It is significant, then, that the term *maistrie* does not occur in the *Clerk's Tale*. Walter's sovereignty is acknowledged from the beginning, and the story is not about winning or losing mastery; rather, it is about assent to that higher sovereignty whose yoke, if Griselda's example is to be believed, may not be blissful at all times but which leads to the ultimate bliss" (23). For a more skeptical reading of the Tale, see Susanne Sara Thomas, "The Problem of Defining *Sovereynetee* in the *Wife of Bath's Tale*," *Chaucer Review* 41 (2006): 87–97.

knight: "Thanne have I gete of yow maistrie . . . / Syn I may chese and governe as me lest?" (3.1236–37). Her control in this situation is actually self-control, the ability to "chese" herself over and against the privilege marriage affords to men. As her husband has shown: "For as yow liketh, it suffiseth me" (3.1235). So too in the Clerk's Tale, Walter's subjects try to explain marriage as something other than constraint, "soveraynetee, noght of servyse" (4.114), an explanation that is clearly more difficult. Because the "yok" (4.113) of wedlock "streyne[s]" him and is set against the "liberte" (4.145) he previously enjoyed, Walter's acceptance of this bond "of soveraynetee" must be immediately turned into a dramatization of his self-determination in the scenes of subordination (of his subjects and of Griselda) to his will.

The ease with which the idea of sovereignty (self-determination) slides into a discourse of mastery (control over another) has always been a problem in and for the Wife's story. Her critical readers have found it difficult to define the sovereignty the Wife advocates because it looks so much like mastery over another plain and simple.[26] Similarly difficult for readers, and for the Clerk himself, is Walter's compulsive desire for mastery over his wife.[27] While "some men preise it for a subtil wit" (4.459), the Clerk finds Walter's trial of Griselda both unnecessary and unendurable, and therefore he interjects some rather glaring first-person commentary into the tale: "But as for me, I seye that yvele it sit / To assaye a wyf whan that it is no nede, / And putten hire in angwyssh and in drede" (4.460–62). While "mastery" is a word that neither the Clerk nor Walter uses to describe his desires or Griselda's subjected condition, the idea of Walter's mastery looms large over the tale and Griselda's sworn obedience to him.[28] It is heard when Walter assents to the idea of marriage, an idea to which he claims "I nevere erst thoughte streyne me" (4.144) in the tale's beginning, as well as in the testing scenes in which he invokes Griselda's promises of perfect obedience by reminding her of the state to which he has raised her. He begins:

---

26. Not that the knight doesn't deserve a bit of feminine mastery after his behavior with the "mayde . . . maugree hir heed" (3.887). See Thomas, "Problem of *Sovereynetee*," 89, and Susan Crane, *Gender and Romance in Chaucer's "Canterbury Tales"* (Princeton: Princeton UP, 1994), 123–26.

27. For an extensive study of this situation as one reflecting the issue of Lombard tyranny with which Chaucer came into contact on his Italian voyages, see David Wallace, *Chaucerian Polity: Absolutist Lineages and Associational Forms in England and Italy* (Stanford: Stanford UP, 1997), 261–98. A more general discussion of the tale's commentary on tyranny in relation to English politics can be found in Carol Falvo Heffernan, "Tyranny and *Commune Profit* in the *Clerk's Tale*," *Chaucer Review* 17 (1983): 332–40, as well as Staley's "Postures of Sanctity."

28. Significantly, the Clerk uses the term "maistrie" only once, just before the Envoy, when he speaks specifically about the Wife of Bath herself, "Whos lyf and al hire secte God mayntene / In heigh *maistrie*" (4.1171–72; my emphasis).

> Grisilde ... that day
> That I yow took out of youre povere array,
> And putte yow in estaat of heigh noblesse—
> Ye have nat that forgeten, as I gesse?
> (4.466–69)

Walter's mastery over Griselda, his people, and the institution of marriage itself are woven into the first movement of the story in which the Marquis's loving subjects suggest a marriage in order to ensure the continuity of his lineage and rule.[29] As many critics have elaborated in the material already cited, the analysis of marriage in the Clerk's Tale never fully escapes its political function. Marriage remains consistently *un*related to personal pleasure (in sharp distinction to what the Wife of Bath claims) and stands in opposition to the "lust present" (4.80) upon which Walter's youthful attention is fixed. The Clerk thus blames him for a failure to consider "in tyme comynge what myghte hym bityde," as Walter instead focuses on immediate enjoyments, "for to hauke and hunte" (4.79; 81). Divorced from pleasure, marriage, for Walter, signifies prudence and responsive responsibility to his people.

However, marriage also gets framed as a pledge of obedience *from* his people and is therefore implicated in the sovereignty he holds over them. Much as he will with Griselda, Walter exacts a promise "agayn my choys ... neither [to] grucche ne stryve" from his subjects (4.170). In fact, in the story's opening Walter's subjects foreshadow the humble position Griselda will assume in the very next part of the tale, when they promise their obedience to his pleasure upon their knees:

> With hertely wyl they sworen and assenten
> To al this thyng—ther seyde no wight nay—
> Bisekynge hym of grace, er that they wenten,
> That he wolde graunten hem a certein day
> Of his spousaille, as soone as evere he may;
> For yet alwey the peple somwhat dredde,
> Lest that the markys no wyf wolde wedde.

---

29. In this way Walter demonstrates the paradoxical operations of what Fradenburg calls "sovereign love," which offers "a relation of social and economic 'necessity' ... refigured as volitional." See Louise [Aranye] Fradenburg, *City, Marriage, Tournament: Arts of Rule in Late Medieval Scotland* (Madison: U Wisconsin P, 1991), 85. I am indebted here to Fradenburg's analysis of the Song of Songs and her conception of the uses of marriage for the articulation of sovereignty, particularly her chapter on "Sovereign Love."

> He graunted hem a day, swich as hym leste,
> On which he wolde be wedded sikerly,
> And seyde he dide al this at hir requeste.
> And they, with humble entente, buxomly,
> Knelynge upon hir knees ful reverently,
> Hym thonken alle; and thus they han an ende
> Of hire entente, and hoom agayn they wende.
> (4.176–89)

This kneeling throng, "with humble entente" and "buxomly" as a wife, presages Griselda's actions before the Marquis only one hundred lines later:

> The markys cam and gan hire for to calle;
> And she set doun hir water pot anon,
> Biside the thresshfold, in an oxes stalle,
> And doun upon hir knes she gan to falle,
> And with sad contenance kneleth stille,
> Til she had herd what was the lordes wille.
> (4.289–94)

The Marian imagery of buxom maid on knees waiting to hear the Lord's will has overshadowed the secular and ideological dimension of Griselda's state, her reproduction of (and symbolic substitution for) the people's political position in relation to Walter's governance. William McClellan reads the Clerk's Tale "enact[ing] a kind of primal scene of sovereign power, showing how it exerts itself over those it subjects."[30] Reading Walter and Griselda quasi-allegorically in Giorgio Agamben's terms of "sovereign power" and "bare life," respectively, McClellan shows how their marriage translates Griselda into a political subject. "At the same time, Walter subjects Griselda to the most abject treatment and outrageous demands, to which she gives silent 'assente'" (107), illuminating the paradox of sovereignty and the agency of its subject(ions). Such a reading also makes the Clerk's Tale into an explicitly political drama. Insofar as Griselda's promise to obey her husband and to follow his will figures the assent of Walter's people to his rule, marriage in the Clerk's Tale forges perfect, idealized political relationships—or at least it should.[31]

---

30. McClellan, "'Ful Pale Face,'" 107.
31. McClellan also returns to this point, "the secret contract of obedience between sovereign and subject.... As Agamben maintains, the oldest secret of sovereign power is that obedience

More than mere romance such as the Wife offers, then, the Clerk's Tale presents marriage as always signifying something beyond itself. Individual motives drive no figure in this story, save Walter's strange desire to test his wife. His people, on the other hand, desire only political continuity and stability, what they call living "in sovereyn hertes reste" (4.112). Similarly, Griselda marries the Marquis for no personal gain or pleasure but out of obedience to her "Lord," which variously refers to her father, to Walter as Saluzzo's ruler, and to God. Marriage thus figures, quite literally, Walter's relation to his people and his right to rule. In both Walter's assent to his peoples' concern for an heir and in the choice he makes for a wife, the Clerk dramatizes the political figurations of marriage that exceed the pleasures or personal desires anatomized by romance and the Wife of Bath's Prologue.

But within the Clerk's political economy, Walter's choice not only displays his benevolent rule, it also exacts a price from the audience for whom it is publicly performed. Even before revealing Griselda as his chosen bride, he demands a promise of obedience from his subjects:

What wyf that I take, ye me assure
To worshipe hire, whil that hir lyf may dure,
In word and werk, bothe heere and everywheere,
As she an emperoures doghter weere.
(4.165–68)

His choice of a simple, lowborn maid not only appears prudent, it also offers the opportunity for testing his subjects' loyalty and obedience. Indeed, the choice is staged as such for his subjects as the "retenue [of] the bachelrye" (4.270) follows Walter into Griselda's village, while she, around whom the drama is constructed, waits unaware of her role in his elaborate wedding plans. Griselda's consent to follow Walter's will, "in werk ne thoght . . . [never to] disobeye" (4.363), is only as important as the consent of his people to "swere . . . [never] / Agayn [his] choys shul neither grucche ne stryve" (4.169–70). In fact, the parallel terms in which each must make its promise to Walter, by full assent, only renders the political function of marriage all the more visible. To Walter's demands Griselda must:

be . . . redy with good herte
To al my lust, and that I frely may,

---

precedes every institution of power. . . . Chaucer shows us how the sovereign coerces the human subject to 'assente' to the demand of obedience" ("'Ful Pale Face'" 126).

As me best thynketh, do yow laughe or smerte
And nevere ye *to grucche* it, nyght ne day?
(4.351–54; my emphasis)

In similar terms, Walter exacts the same promise from his subjects before he consents to wed: "this shal ye swere: that ye / Agayn my choys shul neither *grucche* ne stryve" (4.169–70; my emphasis). Thus, Walter marries to satisfy *and* to subdue his subjects. He turns their request for his marriage from a constraint placed upon his will into an exercise of that same will. And in the end, his correction of his subjects, the "stormy peple" (4.995) who shift their sworn allegiance from Griselda to the idea of a new wife, shows how much they stand in need of such correction.

Not so with Griselda herself. Instead, as a number of feminist readers have recognized, she subdues Walter.[32] Indeed, as we shall see, the satisfaction Griselda offers to Walter's curious desire "hir sadness for to knowe" (4.452) results in a similar alignment of satisfying and subduing her husband. Such a performance contravenes the Wife's discussion of marriage, particularly her subtle understanding of the economics of desire governing its operations. For the Wife, marriage turns upon someone's desire, typically her own. The Clerk's abstract ideas of marital union and its figural significance, played out not only in the allegorizing ending of the tale but also at the literal level of the story—in the signifier—in the political figurations elaborated above, could not be further from the Wife's completely human and corporealized assumptions about marriage and its relation to personal desire.

Of course it is the human actions of Walter at the tale's literal level that provide the most difficulty for the Clerk and that trigger his well-known interjections of opinion into the fiction. Walter's "lest / To tempte his wyf" causes embarrassment for the Clerk, even as it fuels the story of Griselda's unendurable and exemplary patience (4.619–20). But Walter's monstrous acts—dramatized child murders and spousal abandonment—are matched by the unfathomable monstrosity of Griselda herself, whose maternal and human feelings have been called into question.[33] In fact, one could charge

---

32. See Elaine Tuttle Hansen, *Chaucer and the Fictions of Gender* (Berkeley: U of California P, 1992); and Jill Mann, *Geoffrey Chaucer* (Atlantic Highlands: Humanities, 1991), 203 and *Feminizing Chaucer*, rev. ed. (Cambridge: Brewer, 2002), 119. All quotations from Mann are from the revised edition.

33. Modern readings of the Clerk's Tale criticize Griselda's behavior as much as Walter's. See Robert Emmett Finnegan, "'She Should Have Said No to Walter': Griselda's Promise in *The Clerk's Tale*," *English Studies* 75 (1994): 303–21; and J. Allen Mitchell, "Chaucer's *Clerk's Tale* and the Question of Ethical Monstrosity," *Studies in Philology* 102 (2005): 1–26. Even McClellan's reading of the

the Clerk's recoil from his tale, his speedy transition into the satiric song of the Envoy, upon her as well. But to see Griselda as the monster rather than Walter, the Wife "and al hire secte" (4.1171) might argue, amounts to a form of feminist heresy as well as the vanishing point of the tale's figural and thus moral significance. Whether an allegorical success or a failure, the Clerk's exemplum of patience extols its virtue by taking the narrative to the limit, perhaps even threatening to exceed such limits and thus to know no limit at all. She "wol no thyng, ne nyl no thyng" (4.646); she will do and say nothing, no matter how gross the cruelty of Walter's design. But at this limit Griselda explodes the very concept of limits; her passivity in the face of all Walter can devise for her, becomes, like Christ's, the greatest *action*, as an act of will, to which the tale can bear witness.³⁴

Because the Clerk's Tale works to argue for passive suffering as the more powerful role for women in marriage, and because it figures the most sublimely heroic model of human behavior possible, we might find even more shocking the Clerk's recoil from its achievement. The Clerk's success, it would seem, comes at a heavy price. Griselda's strength in the face of her own rejection, Walter's request that she "voyde anon hir place" (4.806), as well as her forbearance to arrange his new bride's accommodations, quickly becomes a machinery that threatens to permit the most heinous and inhuman of actions: an incestuous union of father and daughter. Though Griselda is completely unaware of the drama Walter scripts (much as she was in the beginning of the tale when he processed up to her door and chose her as his bride), the narrative tension staged for the Clerk's audience is almost palpable. In these final moments, we see Walter continually upping the ante "to the outtreste preeve of hir corage" (4.787). Beyond murder and divorce, the Marquis would also have Griselda return as the servant of a new bride, who also happens to be her daughter. Like the dramatic spectacle staged for Walter's wedding, but with far more of an uncomfortable effect, these intricated plans are set to bring final resolu-

---

"aenigma of Griselda" as a Lacanian "negative subject," one "who cannot say no," falls back upon this distinction when he writes that her inability to say no, her power to be completely obedient to the will of another even to the point of death, was "meant to show us just how monstrous the situation really is" ("'Ful Pale Face'" 130). The critical tradition of reading the tale in terms of the monstrosity of its characters is long-standing and has been assessed as such. See, for example, James Sledd, "The *Clerk's Tale*: the Monsters and the Critics," *Modern Philology* 51 (1953): 73–82.

34. On the modern (largely Protestant) inability to understand Griselda's passive power of assent, see Linda Georgianna, "The Clerk's Tale and the Grammar of Assent," *Speculum* 70 (1995): 793–821. Lynn Staley compares Griselda specifically to the intimidating Jesus figure of the mystery plays. She writes, "His silence, his dignity under torture, his willing assumption of suffering, and his understanding of the dynamics of power are attributes of absolute authority" ("Postures of Sanctity" 254).

tion to matters in Saluzzo and restoration to Griselda and to the audience watching her perform.

Griselda's refusal to break her promise of perfect obedience to Walter's will propels him to potentially horrific ends. Refusing to stand in the way, she will assist in Walter's union with his own daughter. Griselda's monstrosity, should the tale be said to contain this, has been configured as a lack of womanly or maternal resistance to Walter's designs. Caught between virtue and neglect, her lack of resistance drives Walter to the altar of incest and provokes an impending scene of pollution that he alone must forestall. Walter stops matters with the very same words he used earlier in the tale to exact Griselda's promise of obedience in marriage: "This is ynogh, Grisilde myn" (4.1051; cf. 4.365), marking an explicit connection in the signifier. Where such a statement once halted the flow of her words, a promise "in werk ne thought, I nyl yow disobeye, / For to be deed, though me were looth to deye" (4.363–64), by the end of the tale those words must stop more than speech. They must prevent the act that would prove the absolute limitlessness of Walter's power by violating one of human civilization's primary laws.

If Walter is finally satisfied with Griselda's constancy, despite or actually because "he so ofte had doon to hire offence" (4.1046), that satisfaction subdues—and conquers—him as it positions him to do the unthinkable in making his daughter his bride. Griselda's patience forces him to curtail his will and to relinquish his fiction of remarriage before it becomes a different story entirely. At the end of the incestuous fiction staged before her, Griselda triumphs over Walter's plot by making him relinquish the position of complete mastery he has so confidently exercised at all other points throughout the story. Griselda thus gives the lie to "sovereignty," the Marquis's absolute self-determination, by turning Walter's power inside out, extending its limits beyond his own seemingly "limitless" desires.

In the midst of this, Griselda's greatest trial, the Clerk unleashes an animus (possibly against Walter as much as Griselda herself) on the "stormy peple" (4.995), who were so easily swayed by the allure of a new and more noble bride. One could say that their responses throughout the tale were the ones Walter had been tempting his wife to exhibit:

> O stormy peple! Unsad and evere untrewe!
> Ay undiscreet and chaungynge as a fane!
> Delitynge evere in rumbul that is newe,
> For lyk the moone ay wexe ye and wane!
> Ay ful of clappyng, deere ynogh a jane!

Youre doom is fals, youre constance yvele preeveth;
A ful greet fool is he that on yow leeveth.
(4.995–1001)

The steadfast Griselda, "sad and constant as a wal" (4.1047), provides the contrast for this image of the jangling and changeable "peple," "ful of clappyng." But they also bear an archetypically feminine resemblance to the "archewyves" in the Envoy, who are urged to "clappeth as a mille" (4.1200). Even more, besides the noise of "clappyng" common to both passages, the image of the moon with its changeable cycle is one of the most persistent images of femininity, elaborated early in the *Canterbury Tales* in the Knight's depiction of Diana's temple (1.2077–78). Much like the gossiping of wives seen in the Wife of Bath's Prologue, the crowd's "rumbul" echoes women's language, heard when Midas's wife "bombleth in the myre" (3.972) to satisfy her irresistible urge to tell his secret. In the elaborate circulation of these signifiers, this subtle feminine characterization of Walter's people refigures them into the image of a bad wife, one that specifically recalls Alison of Bath, who stands as an ostentatious and hyperbolic version of the wife Griselda refuses to become.

The Clerk's Tale unleashes a number of transferred effects here, at the point at which Griselda turns from victim of Walter's tests to victor over his incestuous plot. This movement shapes the Clerk's proof of his implicit argument, ostensibly setting to rest all the division and discord unleashed by the tale and the fictions maintained by Walter's repeated testing of his wife that is reinscribed as a test of his people. Conflating ideas of passivity and passion, Griselda's passive suffering triumphs in an intently active way.[35] About this paradox Linda Georgianna writes, "For all of his seeming

---

35. On this conflation, see Georgianna, "Grammar of Assent," esp. 803–5. Georgianna's stricter historicism articulates the active will of Griselda's passive suffering and also uncovers a latent protestant critical ethic in readings of Griselda. In her view, the Clerk fails to understand Griselda's story and reads it, much as modern critics have, in too rational terms. Georgianna calls for an emotive, numinous experience of reading the tale's pathos, an articulation that leaves the higher historicist claim somewhat troubled. Georgianna would see the critical (mis)reading of passivity in negative terms (i.e., the critical rebuke of Griselda for neglect of her children) as a purely historical problem: "Passivity as a psychological abnormality found especially in females is a modern, post-Freudian usage" (803n22). But the narrator's own misunderstanding of his tale, which she posits on 814–15, makes it less so. The Clerk's Tale appears to dramatize the difference between such renderings of passivity, showing Griselda's passive will as different from itself. A similar deconstruction of the idea of "sadness," a term, like "passive" here, strongly policed by philologists as completely separate from its modern emotional signification, would also seem in play. And, of course, what Georgianna's historicism can nowhere address is the salvific fantasy of symbolic plentitude such a reading offers via identification with Griselda herself.

power and authority, Walter becomes increasingly *reactive*, following rather than directing Griselda's assent" (815; emphasis in original). Even further, Griselda's passion amounts to a mastery that the tale formerly seemed to resist; in the telling words of Lynn Staley, "Griselda appears less victim than master of the man who apparently masters her."[36]

We might wonder here why the Clerk does not end on the note of triumph he has worked so hard to orchestrate. Was this not "ynogh"? Even further than the Wife's, the Clerk's Tale reaches beyond fairy-tale endings, which see a "pitous day" result in a "blisful ende" (4.1121):

> For moore solempne in every mannes syght
> This feste was, and gretter of costage,
> Than was the revel of hire mariage.
> (4.1125–27)

Much of this close to the Clerk's Tale repeats with excess the opening drama of Walter's wedding, retranslating Griselda from yet another "provre estaat" (4.473) back into "swich richesse" (4.385), "ther she was honured as hire oghte" (4.1120). In referencing the opening "revel of hir mariage," this "moore solempne" close must also exceed its "costage" to form a fitting and final conclusion. It must repeat with a difference: as a renewal of the politico-marriage drama it marks both points of origination and conclusion as such.[37] Yet as a final end, it must also denote its singularity, its unrepeatability—it "ys ynogh" and more. This should be his tale's proper end, and yet, the Clerk continues beyond this point to assure us, with the certainty of history, that all turned out for the best.

In this elaborate allegorizing, the Clerk may position marriage far beyond personal pleasure or desire, but not so for the Clerk's performance. His unstoppable speech and nervous "song" reveal a number of desires in his narrative both proclaimed and disavowed. Even as he offers a broader reason for Griselda's testing, which fills the lack the story answers, his proliferating words betray their insufficiency. More information than seems needed follows: their daughter's marriage, Janicula's death, their son's succession are all foretold. But the factuality of these events cannot conclusively interpret and guarantee the story. He then offers the meaning Griselda's story does *not* hold:

---

36. Staley, "Postures of Sanctity," 254.
37. On the way repetition must repeat with a difference, see Shlomith Rimmon-Kenan, "The Paradoxical Status of Repetition," *Poetics Today* 1.4 (1980): 151–59.

> This storie is seyd nat for that wyves sholde
> Folwen Grisilde as in humylitee,
> For it were inportable, though they wolde, . . .
> (4.1142–44)

But the Clerk's disavowed reason for telling the story provides no final word or conclusive *raison d'être*. And that lack of finality or conclusion, it seems, propels him to keep speaking, to beg for another word, just a bit more of his audience's attention: "But o word, lordynges, herkneth er I go" (4.1163); "I wol . . . / Seyn yow a song to glade yow" (4.1173–74); "Herkneth my song that seith in this manere" (4.1176). These pleas to his audience repeat, and thus ultimately show the failure of, his invocation of Petrarch's purpose, which is itself introduced in similar terms: "Herkneth what this auctour seith" (4.1141). With a more opaque motive than would appear for the Wife's, perhaps because of his quiet and reserved character, the Clerk's Tale also nervously withdraws from its own triumphant end. These self-fracturing endings are not some symptom of a failure with these idealizations; indeed, on its own each succeeds brilliantly. But the recoil of these momentarily triumphant narrators ultimately articulates the desire, and thus the lack, that drives them toward narration in the first place. In this sense, then, the Clerk's aggression against the Wife in the Envoy to his tale is not so much a hostility to the content of her tale as much as it is his attempt to control the circulation of the signifier between them and who properly "owns" it. Seeking the recognition always at the heart of desire, he speaks as if he wants to be sure of having the last word.

Yet where the Wife's and Clerk's Tales offer radically different idealizations of femininity, to an uncanny degree they work and speak alike within their fictions. If a hideous, undesirable (yet magical) crone in a fanciful Arthurian romance appears too distinct from the exemplary Griselda, we have only to turn to the powerful mobility of these figures to see their connection. The old woman changes her own form, appearing repulsive on her wedding night only to reward her husband with what she knows he wants in a mate. We are even led, retrospectively, to attribute to her the abrupt vision of dancing ladies that lures the questing knight into her company in the first place. Similarly mobile, Griselda is "translated" (4.385) by marriage to Walter out of her inferior social position and filthy clothes at the opening and close of her tale. Her transformation differs from the magical old woman's as much as the genre of the Clerk's story trumps the ostensible frivolity of romance. Yet, Griselda's translation ultimately marks an essential lack of change, her stability from her first words out of the "oxes stalle" in which she is found, throughout her trials by Walter's cruel design, to the tale's final denouement. Griselda's initial translation works as a kind of revelation, a shift in appearance (much like the old woman's) that articulates an essential, if misrecognized, inscription of value. In this Griselda appears as a living figure of the wife's pillow lecture on the illusions of "old richesse" (3.1110) and the origin of "gentilesse [that] cometh from God allone" (3.1162). The Wife's old woman might as well be describing in advance the virtue of Griselda herself.

Despite what may *seem* to us their differences, in the end Griselda and the old woman offer the very same argument in their tales; the fairy does so explicitly in her pillow lecture while Griselda does so implicitly by her constancy. These female figures, of course, give the lie to the assumed value of inherited wealth and station. Both subvert the social conditions of aristocratic privilege upon which so much of the discourse of the *Canterbury Tales* is founded. They offer in its place a moral order of heritability: "Crist wole we clayme of hym oure gentillesse" (3.1117). As the hag puts it to the knight she rebukes: "Looke who that is moost vertuous alway, / Pryvee and apert, and moost entendeth ay / To do the gentil dedes that he kan; / Taak hym for the grettest gentil man" (3.1113–16). Much like the narrators recoiling at the end of their respective tales, we may be shocked to learn that, in more ways than one, the Wife and Clerk, misreading both themselves and each other, have told the very same story.

The desires of the Wife of Bath have always been easy to discern from the way she openly acknowledges them in her Prologue and Tale. Not so for the Clerk. In a tale where the limitless desire for sovereignty must be curtailed by one who lacks any desire whatsoever, his story provokes a number of questions about its narrator's desires and those of his presumed audience. With whom should we align the Clerk's desire? Although the question orients us toward the figures in his tale, to a choice between Walter and Griselda, the real answer appears to be the Wife of Bath. To attain the narrative sovereignty and autonomy to which the Wife and Clerk aspire (and which anyone engaged in Bailly's competition implicitly seeks), they must lay themselves open to the mastery they have supposedly abjured. In this way they define themselves not by sharing any similar appetite (in this they remain opposed), but by and through the Other's desire—the working of the Symbolic order to which they must submit.[38] Both narrators align

---

38. We might note the way the self-sufficient Walter paradigmatically assumes the desire of the Other in the Clerk's Tale. Walter's desire to marry, we will recall, comes from elsewhere; it originates with his people's desire and their concern for the "tyme comynge" (4.79). He claims to have "nevere erst thoughte streyne me," but Walter immediately orchestrates a wedding that proves his

themselves with feminine heroes idealized by their tales, the old woman/ young and beautiful lady and Griselda, figures that inhabit the place of the Other's desire for each of them. And each tale ultimately narrates the assumption of this desire for the Other. Desiring an other they imagine and formulate in radically different terms, the Wife and Clerk desire to be the object of the Other's desire.

These terms undo the confusion between sovereignty and mastery at the end of the Wife's Tale and rescript them into a fiction of subjectivity and its attendant (mis)recognitions. Given the "sovereynetee" to decide for herself, the old woman asks her husband to qualify his choice: "Thanne have I gete of yow maistrie" (3.1236). The wife/Wife defines her sovereignty in terms of mastery over her husband, and thus gives the lie to the subject's simple fiction of autonomy and self-determination. Gaining sovereignty, the power of self-determination, is a fiction of subjectivity, which demands far more mastery, as well as the others mastery necessitates. To become a "self" one must also become a subject—and endure subjectification—which means recognizing and identifying with the Other. In fact, the misrecognition of the conditions of mastery *as* sovereignty is one of the primal fictions of the subject out of which desire, and the language that aims to fulfill it, emerges.

Such a reading thus turns the Clerk, through his identification with Griselda's desire, into one who desires complete mastery: "But as ye wole youreself, right so wol I" (4.361). It also turns the Wife into the one subjected to an absolute master to whom she relinquishes all control. Seen in this way, the Wife and Clerk come to inhabit the desires of each other's stories insofar as the raped maiden who has to submit "maugree hir heed" (3.887) functions as a version of the passive Griselda and as Walter appears as a more exalted exemplar for the bachelor knight who deserves redemption. If the Wife's and Clerk's Tales center on ideal images, then, these projections come at a cost, which is the fundamental alienation that the assumption of identity and language incurs. Particularly for the Clerk— who so wishes to universalize his ideal as a model for human rather than feminine or wifely behavior—this cost is pressing. Difficult to calculate, these costs do not appear as such on the surface but stalk these ideal images in abjected form as raped maiden and voracious husband, respectively.

Ultimately, it may be no surprise to find out that the Clerk envies Walter's sovereign will, particularly insofar as it can be admired in the opening

---

beneficence and forethought. Walter similarly constructs his choice for a wife as other to the desire of the people for one "born of the gentilleste" appropriate to his "honour" (4.144; 131, 133). He works according to a logic beyond the aristocratic form by which his people presume to find him a suitable match.

scene of the tale, before Griselda demystifies its lack. Such power subtends the meek and threadbare Clerk's desire.[39] More shocking is the recognition of the Wife's analogous fantasy of submission to a worthy man, a desire that positions her somewhat uncomfortably as the silent maiden and accounts for the rape opening her unique version of this traditional story.[40] Such associations (and the extreme versions of the desire they articulate) make it all that much clearer why the Wife and Clerk recoil from what they have accomplished in their tales. Their fictions witness the structure of desire underwriting them, their so-called rivalry, and the storytelling game more generally, putting the desires of safely moral tales more closely in line with those of romance. Yet, as we will see in the next chapter, the desires of such stories are anything but what they seem in their disfiguringly ascetic religious form.

---

39. We might read the Clerk's one resounding criticism of the noble Walter in this context. After delineating his conventionally noble attributes the Clerk abruptly objects: "I blame hym thus: that he considered noght / In tyme comynge what myghte hym bityde" (4.78–79). Such a curiously, even awkwardly, articulated evaluation in the Clerk's own voice amounts to the kind of performative utterance that does and means far more than it says. Not only symptomatizing the Clerk's veiled desire to dominate in advance of the story, his "blame" aligns him further with Walter's power, much of which operates in terms of performative utterances and orchestrated dramas Walter stages for an internal audience.

40. In her discussion of the sources and analogues to the Wife of Bath's Tale, Helen Cooper writes, "The rape that opens the tale has no parallels in these other English versions, though similar adventures are on occasion credited (or discredited) to Gawain in some French romances" (159). Cooper, *Oxford Guides to Chaucer: The Canterbury Tales* (Oxford: Oxford UP, 1989).

four

DISFIGUREMENTS OF DESIRE IN CHAUCER'S RELIGIOUS TALES

When the Clerk offers his Petrarchan tale of patient Griselda in response to the Host and at least partially as rejoinder to the Wife of Bath's performance, he shifts the terms of desire along the lines of a political and depersonalized definition of marriage. Technically, he avoids the category of "hooly seintes lyves" (3.690), foiling the Wife's claims about clerks who supposedly have nothing good to say about women. She knows that such specifically religious tales do not count as speaking good about wives, that their assumptions would obviate the economic principles by which real women live. Thus, with completely different reasons for doing so, the Wife and Clerk both avoid a specific kind of religious story, even if they engage moral terms within their fictions. And, for the most part, critical readers of the *Canterbury Tales* have been all too happy to follow suit, avoiding the religious tales assiduously. They have been called "the most marginalized of the works of Geoffrey Chaucer."[1] Actual saints' lives and virgin martyr stories couched as political history (influencing and related to the kind of exemplary narratives of feminine virtue the Clerk himself narrates), a considerable number of religious stories inhabit the *Canterbury Tales*. Hard to define with precision, these tales have been the most difficult to include in discussions of the "entire" poem

---

1. C. David Benson, introduction to *Chaucer's Religious Tales,* ed. C. David Benson and Elizabeth Robertson (Cambridge: Brewer, 1990), 1–7, at 1.

where "religious" has become a kind of catchall term for those stories that are hardest to assimilate to the poem's more playful register.[2] Most studies attending to the work's overall design and, ironically, those particularly with a moral focus, tend to neglect some of the most serious of them—the Second Nun's Tale, the Physician's Tale, the Monk's Tale, and the Tale of Melibee—as "givens": stories in little need of interpretation.[3] Indeed, the governing assumption with these tales has been that their meaning is self-evident and self-evidently moral.

One of the few essay collections to deal explicitly with the religious stories in the *Canterbury Tales*, as well as the critical aversion to them, repeats it anew by focusing almost exclusively on the four rhyme-royal poems of devotional piety: the Man of Law's Tale, the Clerk's Tale, the Prioress's Tale, and the Second Nun's Tale.[4] The first three of these are fairly well-appreciated contributions to the storytelling contest and enjoy lively critical traditions—the Clerk's Tale especially, with its Petrarchan source, its romance plot, and perhaps most importantly, its dramatic location within the debate on marriage. The Prioress's Tale's anti-Semitism has kept that story in critical view, offering modern readers both access and resistance to its pieties for the Virgin as well as its teller's imitation of the innocence of "a child of twelf month oold, or lesse" (7.484). The Second Nun's Tale has inspired less critical rapture than we might expect for a story unanimously praised as a superior example of Middle English hagiography.

---

2. On the difficulty, and usefulness, of the category of "religious tale," see Derek Pearsall, "Chaucer's Religious Tales: A Question of Genre," in Benson and Robertson, 11–19.

3. The better part of critical studies of the *Canterbury Tales* finds the religious tales intractable. Paul Ruggiers's *Art of the Canterbury Tales* (Madison: U of Wisconsin P, 1967) is broken into two sections, one on the comedies and one on the romances. Of the tales under consideration, only the Man of Law's Tale, the Clerk's Tale, and the Prioress's Tale appear in the latter category. Robert Burlin's *Chaucerian Fiction* (Princeton: Princeton UP, 1977) attends four pairs of Canterbury tales as "psychological fictions," one of which is the Monk and Prioress, and the "philosophic" Clerk's Tale. In *The Strumpet Muse: Art and Morals in Chaucer's Poetry* (Bloomington: Indiana UP, 1976), Alfred David offers a full reading of only the Prioress. The way he accounts for the Second Nun's Tale is telling for such studies. Her tale comes up in the opening of the conclusion, "Some Last Views of Poetry," in which he treats the Canon's Yeoman's Tale and Retraction, but hagiography, despite its importance, does not warrant a chapter of its own. He sees the saint's life as a simple form with its moral significance at the surface, which helps Chaucer anticipate the end of the collection and his return to the Pilgrim's Way. Perhaps most ironically, given its overt interest in morals, Bernard Huppé's *A Reading of the Canterbury Tales* (Albany: State U of New York P, 1964), tenders a full Robertsonian reading of the entire poem, neglecting all the religious stories other than Man of Law's and Clerk's Tales.

4. See the various essays in *Chaucer's Religious Tales* above. Benson makes clear that the four "tales of transcendence" are the ones that "most obviously fit our title" (1), an overt preference for the rhyme-royal narratives but one that ignores the aesthetic power of that feature in determining that "fit."

That exaltation of genre has, in fact, been a stopping point—as if remarking on its superlative status were an interpretation in itself. No such acclaim falls to tales like the Physician's or the Monk's, stories that are even more problematic once contextualized in the Canterbury frame. The General Prologue description of the Physician offers little assistance and provides almost no context for his Roman tale of female virtue, if indeed that is its main focus. The tale's shift in attention to the criminal judge, Apius, and the domestic cruelty of her father, as some have recognized, may ultimately usurp Virginia's story. And despite its explicit exaltation of virginity, its status as a religious tale is in no sense certain. It is far from the kind of Christian exemplarity exalting God's power offered by the Man of Law. The Monk is even more of a disappointment. His General Prologue description prepares us for a very different kind of narrative—a tale of the greenwood or a romance perhaps, given his aristocratic tastes, sylvan pursuits, and love-knot pin. Even the Host appears to have held similar expectations of this "manly man" (1.167). When the Monk is finally interrupted by the Knight and stopped from narrating what threatens to become "an hundred" of such tragedies (7.1973), the Host would have him "sey somwhat of huntyng, I yow preye" (7.2805), but the Monk refuses.[5] The religious tales continually appear only to disappear, an act we mime even within our critical conversations.

In blaming (and somewhat distancing ourselves from) their piety, we have avoided the uncomfortable emotions these tales generate. These are not simply moments of dangerous identification in, for instance, Cecilia's hectoring of authority; the Prioress's visceral anti-Semitism; or Virginia's lament to her father before accepting her sacrificial death, but uncomfortable locations of violence and aggression—and thus desire that implicate the tales' audience. These tales center on figures who are supposed to be the bearers of moral meaning for which such an audience—sometimes an audience depicted within the story itself—hungers, but which instead generate a violence that reveals the aggressivity at desire's core. We may pretend that these scenes and their drive toward death were less uncomfortable for medieval readers, but a look at the responses of the Canterbury pilgrims suggests otherwise. Most are struck silent by these performances. After the Prioress's Tale, for example, "every man / As sobre was that wonder was to se" until the Host begins to "japen" at Chaucer himself (7.691–93).

---

5. The Prioress's Tale is similarly surprising given the lady's General Prologue description. Her quasi-aristocratic background leads an audience to expect a form of romance from the French-speaking nun named Eglentyne. Yet no such disappointment as the Monk incites characterizes the collective response of the pilgrims to the Prioress's Tale.

Similarly, the Physician's Tale finishes with a call for "triacle, / Or elles a draughte of moyste and corny ale" (6.314–15)—the recuperative medicinal value of a stiff drink. The averted critical gaze of Chaucer's readers repeats these deflective responses beyond the poem's fictional borders. If Harry Bailly has to fortify himself after this story or his "herte is lost for pitee of this mayde" (6.317), then desensitization is his recommended course for the sharp surprise of exemplary violence, a drive to death that is far more direct and less cautiously deferred than we are used to.

These religious stories share more with the rest of the *Tales* than we realize, particularly in the manner in which they are driven by desire. Though differently inflected than the romances and fabliaux, the religious stories are marked by a desire we can track through the threat of misreading. In the Second Nun's Tale, for instance, Cecilia's rebuff of her new husband's amorous attentions and the Roman prefect's misconception of his own worldly power—what he claims is a control over life and death—sit at the center of the saint's exemplary life. Seemingly the very opposite of the renunciations such a tale ought to exalt, these scenarios are turned to a spectacular exemplification of hagiographic power. Such trials of desire—the unwanted sexual advances of Apius threatening Virginia; the near rape of Constance in the Man of Law's Tale; even the delighted tormenting of Griselda by her overcurious husband—provoke the moral crisis for each of these stories and direct a kind of exemplary reading of each tale's terms. Through such trials, these religious stories urge an even greater desire (for God) that recasts and redefines the terms of life and death, political power and familial relations. Such happens through the disturbing desires these tales spectacularly disavow. Desire thus performs its own appearance in a scene of misreading and misrecognition, in which various figures in the story come up hard against signifiers over which they struggle to exert control. Even more, the religious tales inspire scenes of misreading: in the way the significance of these stories is dramatically processed in the frame and in the textual tradition that situates the tales in Chaucer's collection. No less than the Canterbury comedies and romances (with which some religious stories share generic features), these narratives pay witness to the circulation of the signifier, pivoting upon particular turns of phrase and the variable significance of words.

This final chapter addresses the problematic category of the religious tales by paying particular attention to two very different stories suffering from critical neglect. The Physician's Tale and the Second Nun's Tale are two of the most abject poetic pieces in Chaucer's collection and are often dissociated, when not completely forgotten, from the rest.[6] One is a much-admired (yet little read) saint's life, an authoritative and orthodox religious genre; the other is a tale that has been more difficult to pin down. A virgin martyr story, it can be described as a classical exemplum adapted to the Physician's purpose (whatever we might take that to be). But neither story much occupies Chaucer's readers or stakes a claim to the center of any of our many interests in the *Canterbury Tales*. As an unlikely pair—one strictly Christian, the other seemingly less so—they help define the loose parameters of the category of religious tale I mean to invoke here, one that can contain both the formal rigor of hagiography and the flexible moralism of secular exemplum. Instead of arguing for a tight connection between them of the kind seen in the previous chapter between the Wife's and Clerk's Tales, I will work to tether these particularly resistant stories more loosely and then show how they are embroiled in the conversation engrossing the tales in the rest of the collection. Thus their difference from each other is one of the principal reasons I will use them as examples of Chaucer's religious tales, defined as a problematic yet productive category rather than a strictly thematic one. More often than not, those categorized as religious tales are those most readily resisted. I will also make recourse throughout to various other stories in an effort to keep an eye toward the signifiers circulating in ways we have not always attended. Part of the goal will be to challenge our tendency toward isolation by remaining alive to the ways these religious tales speak as well as listen to the others in the collection.

The isolation plaguing these stories emerges from a textual tradition grounding their anomalous status. These founding narratives of Roman virtue have been relegated to the status of "early work." Both tales, of course, are situated in prior Roman history.[7] The Second Nun's hagiography is an overtly Christian account of the martyrdom of St. Cecilia; the Physician's exemplum a more ambiguously moral story, tenuously linked to Christian ethics.[8] Strong ties to Chaucer's larger poetic project, as well as the other

---

6. Only the Monk's Tale might give these two a run for their money. As an interrupted/unfinished story (and who knows for how long the Monk might have gone on with his litany of tragedies), it might be more difficult to confront the Monk's story and problematic to classify it as "religious." The manuscript tradition has partially arranged the religious and hagiographic narratives: see the collocation of tales in Harley 2382 and MS Cheltenham, where they are included with other saint's lives, miracles, and pious works of Lydgate.

7. On the Roman sites of civic disorder and political corruption uniting these two tales, see John C. Hirsch, "Chaucer's Roman Tales," *Chaucer Review* 31 (1996): 45–57, as well as Kathy Lavezzo "Beyond Rome: Mapping Gender and Justice in *The Man of Law's Tale*," SAC 24 (2002): 149–80.

8. For an argument that the Physician's Tale is "virtually a modern and secular rewriting of the Second Nun's," see Hirsch's "Modern Times: The Discourse of the *Physician's Tale*," *Chaucer Review* 27 (1993): 387–95. According to his analogy, "where the *Second Nun's Tale* presents a central

tales, have also seemed lacking, even when one of these stories has been mentioned in his previous works. The "lyf of Seynt Cecile" appears in the Prologue to the *Legend of Good Women* (F. 426), offering evidence that Chaucer had written the story before the plan for the *Canterbury Tales* was fully formed and without any concern for a female speaker.[9] As such, the tale might be a completely independent production. The Physician's Tale, by contrast, has merely seemed too simplistic and disjointed to be the product of the late Chaucer.[10] Neither possesses an introductory prologue incorporating the tale into the Canterbury frame and the fiction of its pilgrims. Beginning without introduction—only manuscript rubrics announce who is speaking—they are positioned in what editors have labeled "headless" fragments. Given that both are imperfectly fitted to their particular location in the larger poem and that neither is forcefully attached to its pilgrim speaker, "headless" seems an appropriate moniker for these tales, not least because of what happens to both of their heroines. Yet both stories witness intense and disruptive desires despite their valorization of a different kind of chastising discipline.[11]

---

and motivating image of chastity informed by religious zeal and devout commitment, chastity in the *Physician's Tale* is an end in itself, tenuously connected to social order, but really at the service of the patriarchy. The choice of death in each case also shows both the connections and the differences between these two related but unrelated tales" (390). The Physician's Tale thus reads as a secularized hagiography of a particularly classical cast. Hence the many comparisons to and attempted connections with a similar effort at secularization in the *Legend of Good Women*.

  9. David Raybin calls the placement of the Second Nun's Tale into the *Canterbury Tales* a "double translation," as he "explores what it means for the sacred tale to have been translated into a profane context" (196) in "Chaucer's Creation and Recreation of the *Lyf of Seynt Cecile*," *Chaucer Review* 32 (1997): 196–212. This comment about the place/placing/placement of the religious tales in the poem restages the interpretive problems witnessed in the opening of the General Prologue in which we are uncertain how to take the pilgrimage as a context for the stories and/or spring as a context for the pilgrimage.

  10. But unlike "Palamon and Arcite," also mentioned in the *Legend* (F.420), few consider the Knight's Tale, by this same logic, an "immature" piece. Alternately, nothing alluding to or resembling the Virginia story has appeared in Chaucer's canon, and offers little hard evidence for its "early" status, other than its unpopularity. The *Riverside* textual notes give it a *terminus ad quem* of 1390 because the tale evinces little influence of Gower's version in the *Confessio Amantis*, though this logic, as its editor C. David Benson admits, is flawed. For one thing, this claim assumes that if Chaucer had read Gower, he would make it known by adapting some portion of his tale over and against materials in his principal source, Jean's continuation of the *Romance of the Rose*, and second, that the influence of Gower would show up as some form of agreement with his version. Given Chaucer's intimate familiarity with Gower registered in so many other places, I find it hard to believe he did not know his tale of Virginia from book 7 of the *Confessio*. In the pages that follow, I will make a number of comparisons between these two texts that suggest that Chaucer knew Gower's version and chose explicitly to diverge from its details. The Physician's Tale is written in the same decasyllabic couplets of Chaucer's later period, and, along with the Second Nun's, is thematically related to other stories that were written at a late point in the development of the *Canterbury Tales*.

  11. Given these Roman and hagiographic connections, which we might also extend to the Man of Law's Tale, we have perhaps neglected a continued interest of Chaucer's here.

For Chaucer's readers, a major problem with the religious tales is that they seem to be about other things. They are located beyond earthly desires, the erotically playful language and worldly concerns with which the pilgrims are otherwise engaged. Distanced in this way, they seem always to be moving beyond their own terms. The Prioress, for example, with her exquisite table manners and "amyable port" (1.138), appears to want "to banish the body . . . to conquer the natural messiness of appetite and consumption."[12] Thus her efforts to "countrefete cheere / Of court" as well as her self-identification with the voice of "a child of twelf month oold, or lesse" as she begins her story (1.139–40; 7.484). Some tales also encourage us to read beyond the signifier, to take these stories at something other than their word(s) and to transcend their language as quickly as possible. We could look at what the Second Nun does with Cecilia's name in her Prologue (8.85–119). The Nun's "expown[ding]" of the signifier finds multiple ways to "declare . . . what she highte" (8.86; 119) and what we might "seye" (8.86; 87; 92; 99; 104; 110) with it, moving from earthly to heavenly things, and away from Cecilia herself. In proffering spiritual values, they look to dispense with worldly interests, even as they indulge in their description (here music, color, flowers) and call for their explicit rejection. This narrative strategy also governs the quasi-hagiographic story the Man of Law tells. Despite offering a tale that shares much with popular romances like *Emaré*, one of its likely sources, he is embarrassed by its more worldly aspects.[13] He wants to avoid this kind of material, both the details of the wedding celebration as well as its necessary act of physical consummation. He resents what we might consider the verisimilar elements typically enjoyed in romance:

> Me list nat of the chaf, ne of the stree,
> Maken so long a tale as of the corn.
> What sholde I tellen of the roialtee
> At mariage, or which cours goth biforn;
> Who bloweth in a trumpe, or in an horn?
> The fruyt of every tale is for to seye:
> They ete, and drynke, and daunce, and synge, and pleye.
> (2.701–7)

---

12. Merrall Llewelyn Price, "Sadism and Sentimentality: Absorbing Antisemitism in the Prioress," *Chaucer Review* 43 (2008): 197–214, at 209. Price's focus on the Prioress herself, a boundary for a narrative of vexed boundaries, prompts us to consider the embodied and cloistered religious in similar terms.

13. On the structure of such didactic and homiletic romances, see my "The Texture of *Emaré*," *Philological Quarterly* 86 (2006): 224–46, at 225–26.

These ceremonial details include the very "manere necessaries" (2.711) forced upon Custance (and that the Man of Law is forced to include) for reasons of legitimation, in regard both to her union with King Alla and to the birth of her "knave child anon" (2.715), who will eventually inherit the title "Emperour" (2.1121). Rhetorically, the Man of Law aligns his narrative endurance with Custance's physical endurance of those activities "as been plesynges / To folk that han ywedded hem with rynges" (2.711–12), as well as the more straightforwardly difficult aspects of her ordeal. He passes such matters over quickly and in summary fashion because "it may no bet bitide" (2.714). Calling attention to what he finds inappropriate and uncomfortable—too material or too embodied—the Man of Law, as if speaking for the religious tales as a whole, wants to get to the moral point.

Yet narrators like the Prioress and the Man of Law cannot avoid the body or desire, even in tales seemingly well beyond any pleasure principle of most fiction, tales, that is, full of difficulty, tribulation, suffering, and disaster—and typically ending with death rather than any pleasant "happily ever after." Their hardships and frustrations are not avoided for some kind of transcendent pleasure. Instead, they are indulged and extended, as if suffering itself held its own delights.[14] In the Prioress's Tale, her Marian miracle "cannot make bodily concerns go away"; instead, they resurface in her story of a murdered clergeon and his devotion to the Virgin. In this brief and economical narrative, one of the shortest in the Canterbury collection, the messiness of the body is literally what speaks. Not only through the murdered child's throat—both the conduit of song and the bloody "ykorven" wound—but the tale itself, which is equally obsessed with bodily mess and waste in its fixation on the "wardrobe" into which he is thrown "where as thise Jewes purgen hire entraille" (7.611; 572–73). In the Prioress's miracle, physical perfection characterizes virtue only in relation to the way the corruption of the body designates vice and offers a site of pollution and purification. There is no escaping the body for the Prioress, no matter what her own efforts and elegant manners of disavowal might suggest.

Similarly, religious tales are riddled by desire at two levels: one at the level of the story's fiction, the other elaborated in its telling. Desire sets Custance in motion once the Sultan of Syria hears the stories about her; it inflames a near rapist in Northumbria; and it eventually moves King Alla

---

14. In an essay on what he calls "the poetics of virginity," R. Howard Bloch explores the paradoxes at the heart of its evisceration of human desire. The writings of the Church Fathers on virginity betray "the desire to transcend desire, to be beyond perception, [which] is indistinguishable from the desire to escape the body altogether." See Bloch, "Chaucer's Maiden's Head: 'The Physician's Tale' and the Poetics of Virginity," *Representations* 28 (1989): 113–34, at 120.

to wed her and the Man of Law to apologize for just those "manere necessaries" on their wedding night (2.711). In fact, the more spectacularly monstrous desires of two mothers-in-law set Custance adrift at sea.[15] Despite Custance's own lack of desire to part from her family and marry "unto the Barbre nacioun" (2.281), hers is a story that does nothing so much as follow desire's itinerary; it literally moves her from place to place, even if the desire propelling her is emphatically not her own. She steadfastly endures all the events to which she is subject, remaining constant against a dramatically displacing world of desire. Thus, instead of being the abjected background of the story, as the Man of Law's reticent language might suggest, desire operates more pervasively as its engine.

As its readers have long recognized, the Man of Law's Tale originates in language—it is itself a tale he learned from a merchant "goon is many a yeere" (2.132)—which coordinates elements concerning the heroine's movements and its romance plot with the invisible forces at work seeming to drive the tale's conversion narrative. Within the narrative too, desire for Custance arises when merchants relate a story about her to the Syrian sultan upon their return from Rome. Even at this early juncture, desire is located in language. Analogously, throughout the Man of Law's Tale, an unlocalized narrative desire for and interest in the beautiful and virtuous Custance, which we see mirrored in the desires various figures have for her in the tale's adventurous plot, figures a cultural desire for the constancy of Christianity she brings with her, as the tale traces a circuit of conversion and transformation in its heroine's rather unpleasant peregrinations. This is the greater good for which the marriage is arranged:

> I seye, by tretys and embassadrie,
> And by the popes mediacioun,
> And al the chirche, and al the chivalrie,
> That in destruccioun of mawmettrie,
> And in encrees of Cristes lawe deere,
> They been acorded, so as ye shal heere.
> (2.233–38)

The Sultan will be christened in exchange for Custance, literally, "and certein gold" (2.242). The tale's plot, full of undesirable events and Custance's

---

15. These "monstrous" desires are not simply wishes for "unfeminine" political power or to retain their heathen "law" but are related to the incest narratives at the source of romances like the Man of Law's Tale. See Carolyn Dinshaw, "The Law of Man and Its 'Abhomynaciouns'" in *Chaucer's Sexual Poetics* (Madison: U of Wisconsin P, 1989), esp. 100–105.

resistance to the desire of others, dis-covers another desire that we have had a harder time seeing. Like the Clerk's political figuration of marriage, the Man of Law's Tale follows a cultural itinerary of desire larger than the disavowed, personal one their analogous romance-like narratives typically track. These narrative desires might also be seen circulating in and through the more problematic hagiographies and tales of feminine virtue that offer similar kinds of resistance at their surface.

Reading disavowed and dispersed desire in these stories is helpful for reading the more difficult religious tales of Chaucer's collection in which the protagonists similarly deny desire from the start. For example, the Physician's Tale initially appears as a tale of disavowed and misdirected desires. Apius's lust is misplaced on the morally perfected Virginia, and the rest of the story follows this misdirection in its aggressively violent narrative. His desire for the girl may be clearly insupportable, but its genesis and effects are curiously manipulated and dispersed in the Physician's story, particularly by the abbreviated and dialogic form in which Chaucer renders the civic exemplum. In its brief narrative, the tale analyzes the shaping force of desire in the generation and deformations of Apius's attraction to Virginia, which thus propels the outrageous injustice he does to her father, Virginius, to procure her. But rather than stop with this local observation, which might produce yet another isolated reading of the Physician's story, we can look at the way the tale relies on the signifier, in what gets "seyd" and in the "sentence" the story proffers, and thus resonates with, and makes its claim upon, other Canterbury narratives.

The Physician's Tale, as I have just described it, has hardly appeared so focused to its critical readers. Its component parts have made little sense and provoke debate principally over source material and the tale's place in the chronology of Chaucer's works.[16] The Physician cites Livy's authority in the story's first line, but clearly another source was also used (if Livy's history was consulted at all).[17] The Physician's rendering more closely follows

---

16. C. David Benson's editorial notes betray the critical irony inherent in the matter: while the Physician's Tale is generally assumed to be derivative and is "assigned to a date before or at the beginning of the Canterbury period" (provoking "widespread agreement that it is an artistic failure"), most of the tale's "material and treatment are original" to Chaucer (427–28). Thus, what would otherwise be a sign of artistic choice and specificity winds up here relegated to some category of early experimentation.

17. Chaucer's knowledge of Livy is still an open question because we lack clear evidence of the direct influence of the Latin text. It also seems possible that Chaucer used a French translation of

Jean de Meun's in the *Romance of the Rose,* where Reason tells a similarly brief version of the tale as proof that love is stronger than justice. Like Jean, Chaucer also reframes the story in the voice of a fictional speaker, thus loosening it from its original historical context. As Jean had adapted Livy's exemplum for his erotic and pedagogic purposes for the Lover in the *Rose,* so too does Chaucer reformulate the story as a contribution to the Canterbury contest and its terms of "sentence" and "solaas."

The problem posed by the Physician's Tale in this process of narrative reframing has largely been a problem of expectations. An exemplum generally depends on a frame, which announces in advance the tale's purpose. Jean makes this clear from the inception of his story, which begins with a rhetorical question: "Wouldn't Appius have done well to hang?" (114; "Ne fist bien Appius a pendre," 5559).[18] This opening gestures toward the juridical sentence upon the false judge, death by hanging, averted only because of his suicide. Livy also provided an interpretive framework to the tale of Virginia when he analogized it to the story of Lucretia's death. Where the suicide of Lucretia brought down the Tarquin kings, the tragedy of Virginia incites a revolt against the tyrannical decemvirs. Following this tradition, John Gower's version of this story is placed within book 7 of the *Confessio Amantis* and is thus subordinated to a demonstration of the proper education of a king. The various introductory claims forecast the events of each exemplum and indicate how it should be read. Chaucer's contest, by contrast, offers no such stable framework.

Medieval English versions of the story, as Elizabeth Allen has shown, change matters considerably by removing them from their authoritative context and placing them in the discourse of partial and unreliable narrators.[19] Without a clearly articulated trajectory and no linking material connecting the story to the rest of the *Tales,* the Physician's Tale has been treated as quasi-hagiography, despite its pagan setting, with Virginia as a martyr "sowded to virginitee," much like the Prioress's clergeon (7.579).

Livy, such as Pierre Bersuire's early fourteenth-century *Tite-Live.* See William H. Brown, "Chaucer, Livy, and Bersuire: The Roman Materials in *The Physician's Tale,*" in *On Language: Rhetorica, Phonologica, Syntactica,* ed. Caroline Duncan-Rose and Theo Vennemann (New York: Routledge, 1988), 39–51. However, given the expansion Chaucer made to the story and some of his unique details, it is more likely he knew of Livy through another source, like Gower, who more closely follows the classical text. Despite what may be mediated relations between texts, a comparative reading of Livy remains valuable for reading Chaucer's version of the tale.

18. All quotations from the Old French *Roman de la Rose* are taken from Felix Lecoy's three-volume edition (Paris: Champion, 1965). English translations come from Charles Dahlberg, *The Romance of the Rose,* 3rd ed. (Princeton: Princeton UP, 1971, 1995).

19. Elizabeth Allen, *False Fables and Exemplary Truth in Later Middle English Literature* (New York: Palgrave Macmillan, 2005).

Chaucer's attention to Virginia, who is more carefully described than in any of his possible sources or analogues, is unusual and has contributed to its hagiographic effect. As readers have often noted of her opening exaltation, Chaucer includes perspectives no one was expecting (certainly no reader of Livy) and ends with a shift in focus that has been hard to reconcile with the rest of the story as he reframed it. Attention to the paternal sacrifice and to Apius in the tale's moralizing conclusion has provoked the Physician's audience. Extolling virginity at its opening, the tale ends with a warning about the trembling "worm of conscience" and the eventual exposure of sinfulness "though it so pryvee be" (6.280–82), as well as an injunction to "Forsaketh synne, er synne yow forsake" (6.286). How, exactly, does this moral apply to the story? How (or why) have we shifted our attention to the sinful perpetrators and away from Virginia when Chaucer's tale drew us to her in the first place?

That lengthy description of Virginia comes with an admonition to governesses and parents about the care of such virtuous creatures, deviating even further from its possible sources both by the terms of its description and by the admonishing voice of the narrator. These materials (6.5–104) make up about a third of the story, sharply individuating Chaucer's writing. Typically, Virginia has been little more than the beautiful daughter of the virtuous Virginius, and she is barely named as a character. Jean's introduction is instructive for the way her name and her virtue are coterminous. One nearly wipes out the other: "Virgine la pucele, / qui fu fille Virginius" (1.5562–63). "Virgine" (virgin) and "pucele" (maiden) are synonymous terms that both designate a young, unspoiled girl. This is a feature of most versions of her story in which the name "Virginia" and the word for "virgin" are nearly identical, one signifier harboring within it the other. In Livy the proper name "is rarely used: she is almost always referred to as the girl, the daughter, the fiancée, according to her relation to the men."[20] Indeed the close alignment of the declined form of "virgo" (virgin) and the "name" Virginia (the girl who belongs to Virginius) in Latin and Old French, "vergine," lies at the origin of the conflation and the disappearance of the daughter's name.

Chaucer's own tale has been accused of conflating Virginia with virginity, an equivalence he practically reads out of his sources' use of her name and the loss of the maiden's head in Jean's redaction, a dramatic change in

---

20. Rebecca Langlands, *Sexual Morality in Ancient Rome* (Cambridge: Cambridge UP, 2006), 108. Langlands's argument is that the Verginia story is really the Verginius story; the analogy between figures whose sacrifices support Roman republicanism links Lucretia and Verginius, rather than the female figures.

the manner of sacrificing Virginia in the *Romance of the Rose*, and repeated in the *Canterbury Tales*, that has yet to be explained. But it also comes from Chaucer's unique description of and attention to the girl, which usurps the place of much of Livy's historical surround. Where classical writers value Virginia's status as a chaste maiden for her representation of the precarious status of the Roman state, Chaucer's Virginia provokes a more individuated encomium on virginity itself as well as the dangerous response it provokes in this tale of misplaced desire.

As others have noted before, the Roman historical context of the story is stripped from Chaucer's version, leaving his readers to focus their attention elsewhere.[21] But that freedom has only led to Apius himself and to the genesis of his desire for Virginia, which both Chaucer and Gower spend far more time explaining. By contrast, classical scholars distinguish Virginia's story from Lucretia's in significant ways, though their tales are surely analogous sacrificial narratives upon which Roman foundations depend, which is why they are linked together in *Ab urbe condita*, when Livy explicitly recalls Lucretia's story at the beginning of Virginius's. However, the analogy between stories does not necessarily forge an analogy between women. As Rebecca Langlands argues, the center of the story of Apius's lechery is the wronged father, Virginius. He is the individual who sacrifices (as Lucretia does in the time of kings), turning his daughter's death into a rallying cry for the Roman republic. The medieval versions of the story (Jean's, Gower's, and Chaucer's) must recontextualize when they decontextualize it, removing it from the exemplary function it plays in Roman history, or in Anne Middleton's words, making "a historical example . . . [into] a moral exemplum."[22]

For Livy's medieval redactors, the analogy between fatherhood and civic virtue makes the scene of intimate violence even more troubling. According to Allen, "Virginius's mingling of murder and pity troubles most medieval authors of the tale."[23] Instead of sharply distinguishing between Apius and Virginius, the medieval versions emphasize their similarity. With neither Livy's specific historical framework, nor Gower's explicitly political one, Chaucer readers are left with hardly any explanation or context for the genesis of the intrigue, which was located in a history of Apius's larger infamy. Chaucer puts the tale back in the minimalist frame of the French

---

21. See Sheila Delany, "Politics and the Paralysis of Poetic Imagination in *The Physician's Tale*," *SAC* 3 (1981): 47–60.

22. Anne Middleton, "The *Physician's Tale* and Love's Martyrs: 'Ensamples Mo Than Ten' as a Method in the *Canterbury Tales*," *Chaucer Review* 8 (1973): 9–32, at 11.

23. Allen, *False Fables and Exemplary Truth*, 72.

Romance of the Rose, often at what seems the expense of the Physician's historical understanding, which we ought to reframe as gestures toward "sentence" and "solaas" because of the way the tale speaks with the same judgmental terms governing the whole collection. In looking at the ways the Physician's Tale deviates from its sources, we can situate the story in the *Canterbury Tales* more securely through its desiring discourse.[24]

As most readers have noted, Chaucer adds material to the tale's opening as he refocuses on Virginia herself. Coordinating this attention to the heroine with the moralizing shift of focus at the tale's end, Middleton shows the very Chaucerian nature of the Physician's (mis)understanding of his moral story and the way morals are read out of such tales. Reading the "equivocal role of Virginius," as both ethical victim and criminal actor, "reflects a fundamental literary problem of exemplary narrative. The narrator must control his 'sentence' almost to the point of falsifying the human conflicts in the event which give his message urgency or applicability" (Middleton 27), which itself makes for an interesting contribution to the self-conscious play of tales in Chaucer's collection.

In the Physician's hands, the Roman daughter's situation becomes a more individual and a more general matter—hence the introduction of Nature, a universal power over living things and a force marking Virginia's development to adulthood. Nature is a figure adapted from Jean's *Romance of the Rose,* though not the part that includes the Virginia story. And this situation has made for some of the confusion about Chaucer's source material, and it perhaps ought to change the way we too rigidly think about his use of books. He names Livy (as Jean does too) but clearly uses Jean, indicating so with this kind of interpolation. Further, such materials distance Chaucer's tale from sources like Livy's and Gower's, sources that think explicitly about the tale's political dimension. But that surface distinction, I will argue, has obfuscated important connections between Chaucer and Gower that suggest that the contemporary Gower may have been Chaucer's source for Livy. In the place of the historical information Livy elaborates or the argumentative frames that Gower and Jean provide, the Physician gives us a general description of the heroine that mimes the discourse of Nature herself.

---

24. In the most important essay on the tale to date, Middleton shows the Physician's Tale more centrally involved in Chaucer's corpus, "a point about halfway along a quite clear line of development in Chaucer's conception and use of 'exemplary' narrative, a line connecting the 'Seintes Legendes of Cupide' with those of love's martyrs in the *Canterbury Tales*" ("Love's Martyrs" 10). She thereby links the Physician's Tale to the Franklin's, Prioress's, Second Nun's, Man of Law's, and Clerk's Tales in ways few have known how to develop further.

Gower, by contrast, is much more interested in the backstory: those events that lead to the situation in Apius's courtroom. These include the plotting between men that results in the legal threat against Virginia as well as the domestic situation allowing for it: Virginius's absence has caused a delay to her wedding to the man Gower calls Ilicius.[25] Because Gower, like Livy, writes about the intrication of domestic and civic behavior, matters of state are embroiled in matters in the household and vice versa. (And, as I will discuss shortly, Livy's Virginius will make his impassioned plea for the support of the plebs as he enters Apius's court by appealing to this very connection.) Not only does Gower describe Virginia, he describes Apius's desire: "al his herte hath set afyre, / That he began the flour desire / Which longeth unto maydenhede" (7.5144–46). Where Livy and Jean are satisfied merely to mention that lechery motivates Apius, we see Gower's villain (like Chaucer's) corrupted through his senses. Both Middle English poets chart the change that comes across Apius through their concerns for the narrative features of the tale beyond the exemplary identifications Livy and Jean engineer.

No unusual circumstance occurs, nor does Virginia do anything, despite the long description of her careful and circumspect behavior. Virginia is merely seen "in the toun / [going] Toward a temple, with hire mooder deere, / As is of younge maydens the manere" (6.118–20). Like the "manere necessaries" that affect the Man of Law's Custance on her wedding night, here we see the very same necessary customs and practices of an emerging, independent adult as Virginia appears with her mother in the public sphere. No matter how protected and decorous, going "toward a temple," Virginia is subject to a public gaze that ultimately threatens her. We might expect that gaze to be demonized as the source of her corruption. Instead, it is her reticence that the Physician so carefully describes, its "fame" (6.111)

---

25. A word about spelling: my comments in this chapter adopt the spelling of names as they appear in Chaucer, my principal concern, except for when they appear in quotations from other texts. Here I would note the spellings as given in various versions as well as the Physician's Tale: Livy's Verginius, Verginia, Appius, and Icilius; Jean's Virginius, Virgine, Appius; Gower's Virginius, Appius, and Ilicius; Chaucer's Virginius, Virginia, and Apius. Gower's unusual version of the fiancé's name, though consistent within his text, looks like a simple metathesis of letters. Interestingly for a writer producing his own Latin headnotes and apparatus in the *Confessio Amantis*, Ilicius also resembles the Latin "licit." Given the near allegorical importance of names in the story, Gower's mistake is telling. The etymological play of names in the Physician's Tale also compels Bloch. Apius's "very name resonates with the deponent Latin verb *apiscor* (a rare form of the compound *adipiscor*) meaning 'to reach after,' 'to seize,' 'to get possession of,' 'to perceive,' just as Claudius' name summons *claudo*, 'to close,' 'shut,' 'hem in,' which is also his function" ("Chaucer's Maiden's Head" 118). The play of these signifiers is not unlike those in the Reeve's names Aleyn and Malyne discussed in chapter 2.

published "as in a book" (6.108), changing the judge's "herte . . . and his mood" (6.126).[26]

In the context of Apius's sensory stimulation, the Physician's extended opening description makes Virginia herself the problem: her appearance prompts Apius's desiring gaze and dastardly plan to gain possession of her, aspects of the story not examined by earlier versions.[27] Narrative focus on Virginia directly precedes Apius's view of her. Thus our attention to Virginia precedes and prefigures his own, anticipating the change in mood that comes over him once she comes into view. Narrator and character are in collusion; her beauty literally overtakes him just as its description overtakes the opening of the tale. Following the very terms of Virginia's attractive idealization, Apius's desire is thereby set in counterpoint to Virginia's lack of desire, and, as has been noted in various critical readings, her purity becomes the incitement to its own violation.[28] That desiring relationship is not one of absolute presence and absence but one of discipline, restraint, and control. Virginia's story is the story of how desire *appears*, despite all efforts at its constraint and erasure. In telling the tale this way, Chaucer emphasizes desire's genesis rather than merely assuming lechery's guilt.

A perfectly created figure without any desire of her own, Virginia wants only to avoid the desires of others:

And of her owene vertu, unconstreyned,
She hath ful ofte tyme syk hire feyned,
For that she wolde fleen the compaignye
Where likly was to treten of folye,
As is at feestes, revels, and at daunces,
That been occasions of daliaunces.
Swich thynges maken children for to be
To soone rype and boold. . . .
(6.61–68)

The valorization of this kind of retiring virtue has left readers with the impression that the Physician's Tale and its avatar of virginity are set against

---

26. In Gower too Virginia's "fame . . . cam in his ere" (7.5140–41) and sets Apius's heart "afyre, / That he began the flour desire / Which longeth unto maydenhede" (7.5143–45).

27. Critics have been hard-pressed to read it this way despite the Physician's explicit statement that "Hire beautee was hire deth" (6.297). Such a claim could produce the same kind of critical consternation as that surrounding the "monstrous" Griselda.

28. See Bloch, "Chaucer's Maiden's Head," 117–18 and, more generally, Sarah Kay, "The Sublime Body of the Martyr," in *Violence in Medieval Society,* ed. Richard Kaeuper (Cambridge: Brewer, 2000), 3–20.

the erotic and earthly desires assumed as natural in other stories. All the terms for her excellence are terms of natural restraint, control, and limitation. For instance, Virginia "ne lakked" (6.41) any praiseworthy quality, exhibiting both "discreciorun" and "abstinence," "attemperaunce" and "mesure" (6.42; 45–46). These are not superlatives or excesses, but precisely the opposite; they are curtailments of them. She does not speak unnecessarily (6.51–54), imbibe (6.58–59), or leave her home (6.63–66). Her actions, as well as her virtues, are circumscribed, restrained, and controlled, even to the point of deceit: she feigns illness in order to avoid a greater threat to her virtue. By contrast, her virtue is "unconstreyned" (6.61). Rather than implying that she herself lacks the constraint we have been noting, this term articulates her autonomous *self*-control. She has no need of external constraint or law because she so naturally constrains herself. Virginia's virtue is articulated in terms of avoidance and even negation.

Restraint does not indicate desire's absence so much as its presence, a power that must be exerted to counterbalance another force. Such restrained terms also explain the change that overtakes Apius, "*caught* with beautee of this mayde" (6.127; my emphasis). Where Virginia's virtue is figured as an unforced self-restraint, her attraction for Apius is couched as a form of constraint on him and his power. In Livy's history and Gower's adaptation, her father and her intended husband stand in the way of Apius's personal desire. This detail helps foreground the conflict's terms of political power and juridical corruption, even the domestic politics of the situation. Much of Livy's history attends to the political figuration of Apius's lust for Virginia, a figure whose proper name and social function are coterminous. The Latin "verginiem" denotes her unmarried, chaste status as well as her relationship to her father, "Verginius," who is probably named for her as this story is adapted into Livy's history out of mythology.[29] Indeed, these two aspects of her identity are intertwined, as we have seen, leaving translators to choose whether to render "verginiem" as "daughter" or as a proper name.[30] This story's embeddedness in a civic history of plebian revolt and the deposition of the decemvirate, as well as its close ties to the story of Lucretia and the expulsion of the Tarquinii, extend matters well beyond Virginia's fate, as it uses her unfortunate death as an example of the threat posed to all men's families, and their posterity, by the unjust power of men like Apius.

---

29. See R. M. Ogilvie, *A Commentary on Livy, Books 1–5* (Oxford: Clarendon, 1965), 476–78, who writes "for all its beauty the story of Verginia is entirely devoid of historical foundation" (477).

30. All quotations from Livy's *Ab urbe condita* and its translation are taken from the Loeb Classical Library edition of Livy, ed. and trans. B. O. Foster, 14 vols. (Cambridge: Harvard UP, 1967). All citations are from vol. 2, books 3–4.

By contrast, Chaucer omits Icilius entirely, making Virginia's status as a "virgin" a universal condition rather than an historical contingency. The political function of the family dynamics compelling Livy and Gower are fraught in the Physician's Tale: they are at once diminished (by removing Icilius) and exacerbated (by relocating the sacrificial drama in the home). Chaucer elides Virginia's fiancé entirely from the Physician's simplification of the story, only to imagine a future married state in his insertions to the tale's opening. At the conclusion of her description, he explains the threats to virtue that accompany the revels and dances, much like the one the Franklin's Dorigen attends, which Virginia studiously avoids: "Swich thynges [that] maken children for to be / To soone rype and boold" (6.67–68). Even then, children were growing up too fast: "For al to soone may she lerne loore / Of booldnesse, whan she woxen is a wyf" (6.70–71). The Physician may have left Icilius out of the story, but Virginia's miserably knowledgeable future as a wife appears in this disdainful aphorism. If Virginius's action saves her from Apius's designs, the Physician's Tale works just as hard to save her from the fate of such "boold" wives.[31]

These comments align the narrator with Virginius, both of whom are interested in preserving the daughter's virtue. The tale offers sentiments that would appear to follow (whether on the heels or at some distance) the tales of the marriage group, taking a different approach to the themes of marriage and womanhood at the center of those stories. At the surface, the Physician seeks to tell a tale in an entirely different register that we might little connect with the Wife's discourse or any of the various responses to it. And yet, as this aggressive insertion to the beginning of the exemplum shows, the Physician can hardly control—or maybe even know—his tale's desire, even as he openly diverges from the tales preceding his own. In the Ellesmere manuscript that has provided the order for most modern editions of the *Canterbury Tales,* the Physician follows the Franklin. In this context, his disdain for the "compaignye / Where likely was to treten of folye, / As is at feestes, revels, and at daunces, / That been occasions of daliaunces" (6.63–66) contrasts directly with the previous story, out of which some of this descriptive language would seem to originate. Circumstances in the previous tale matter because of the very situation the Physician both invokes and rebukes in this opening insertion. Dorigen's ordeal begins at just such a "feeste" where there is reveling and dancing, and readers have been at pains to decide whether her "daliaunce" with Aurelius is her own

---

31. This adjective is used to describe the Wife of Bath both in the General Prologue and repeatedly in her own Prologue, a connection discussed more fully in the pages that follow.

fault.³² This kind of dangerous environment, it would seem, is precisely what the Physician resists in his tale, recalling the Franklin's opening with the very terms he uses to describe Virginia's reticence. And yet, despite this reference, the Physician's response misreads the Franklin's Tale for his own narrative ends. He mistakes the care with which the Franklin describes events in the May garden, particularly the nature of speech. Where the Physician finds such company dangerous, we might recall the helpful "compaignye" (5.843) that Dorigen's friends urge upon her to distract her from "hir sorwe" (5.841) in Arveragus's absence.³³ These same friends remove her from the seaside, where she obsesses about the danger the rocks pose to her husband's safe return. Precisely because these companionable walks prove no diversion, they must "shopen for to pleyen somwher elles" (5.897). The Franklin carefully prepares us for the May garden dance at which Aurelius, eventually and with some resistance, makes his complaint to her in person.

The Franklin's self-styled Breton lai is a mere 890 lines long, and it spends 290 of them on Dorigen's initial situation: her sorrow following Arveragus's departure up through her notorious conversation with Aurelius (and its effects) just before her husband's return (5.1087). In other words, the Franklin, who loves a good party himself, gives a full third of his story over to the events of the garden revelry and especially what is recuperative about it.³⁴ We ought not to dismiss the care with which the Franklin foregrounds the nature of the occasion and the appropriateness of Dorigen's conversation with Aurelius, "hire neighebour / . . . a man of worshipe and honour" whom she "hadde yknowen . . . of tyme yoore" (5.961–63). Indeed, this description, with its overdetermined insistence on the appropriateness of their talk, would make any reticence toward Aurelius into a slight.³⁵ If Dorigen cannot be criticized for speaking with him, neither is she fully responsible for cultivating his declaration of love. The Franklin is supremely careful, remarking over and over again how "Unwityng of this Dorigen [was] at al" (5.936); "But nothyng wiste she of his entente" (5.959). And, for that matter, neither did he plan to say anything: "He was

---

32. Intensifying the questions of "entente" in the Franklin's Tale, Dorigen's "rash promise" also raises questions of blame and guilt. See, for instance, Anne McTaggart, *Shame and Guilt in Chaucer* (New York: Palgrave Macmillan, 2012), 74–77.

33. Both might be coordinated with the formation of the "compaignye" of pilgrims in the *Tales* more generally.

34. One might note the structural similarity in these tales in which the first third, resisting the general compression of the narrative, elaborates a point important to the rest.

35. For a discussion of the importance of this polite language in Franklin's Tale in relation to its characterization as a Breton lai, see my "Ysworn . . . Withoute Gilt: Lais of Illusion-Making Language in the *Canterbury Tales*," *Etudes Épistémè* 25 (2014): n.p. www.etudes-episteme.org.

despeyred; no thyng dorste he seye, ... Ne dorste he nat to hire his wo biwreye, / Save that . . . It may wel be he looked on hir face / In swich a wise as man that asketh grace" (5.943–58). The caution with which the Franklin describes the accidental and emphatically unintentional way these two enter into conversation is striking and extends even further to the way Dorigen comes to the dance with her friends in the first place.

The Franklin's epicurean conviviality aside, his tale's interest in social conventionality, conversation, and the effects of one's polite speech, whether courtly love-marital contract or rash promise-like refusal, makes his prolonged attention to this setting crucial. He emphasizes in some detail how Dorigen and Aurelius got themselves into the situation since they are both to be held accountable for it. But this is precisely what the Physician's Tale picks up on, misreads, refuses to read even, when it characterizes the dangerous nature of these "revels, and . . . daunces, / That been occasions of daliaunces," which, of course, does not make him wrong. Neither does it make him particularly responsive to the Franklin or his tale. The Physician is not offering a rebuttal and certainly not entering in the marriage debate. His tale is working rather hard, it would seem, to avoid the issue of marriage entirely, which explains why Chaucer removed Icilius from the story and, perhaps, places Virginia's mother squarely within it. The girl, whose age is clearly stated as "twelve yeer . . . and tweye" (6.30), is made younger: more innocent surely and perhaps more inappropriate for marriage. The Physician's Tale, I would argue, offers some of the most pointed connections to other stories in the very act of trying to say something completely different and divergent from them.

Misreading the Franklin's Tale and its care in elaborating the setting "in compaignye," the Physician removes Virginia from proximity to marriage and revelry. He offers an exemplum explicitly set against such values and for an absolute standard of virginity, in which its sacrificed heroine will declare "Blissed be God that I shal dye a mayde!" (6.248). This strategy would place his tale in a medievalized context consonant with Livy's rhetorical force. But we could also see Livy's Virginius and the Physician's working, ultimately, at cross-purposes—even when the Physician claims he is most closely following his source. Whereas Livy's Virginius protects his daughter from lust and lechery, the Physician protects his innocent from any carnal knowledge, licit or not. His narrative not only preserves her chastity, it prevents her from growing up, showing an aggression to women and to wives, in the form of knowledgeable guardians who know "the olde daunce" (6.79) or corrupted governesses, "ye maistresses, in youre olde lyf, / That lordes doghtres han in governanunce" (6.72–73). Given the stereotype of this "over-knowledgeable" femininity being invoked, a resemblance to the description of the Wife of Bath is perhaps inevitable. The stereotypic signifiers the Physician uses make such an association even more explicit. Picking up the very terms of the General Prologue description of the Wife, the Physician imagines the possibility of an un-virgin Virginia in the Wife's "boold" habit (1.458). The Wife is also expert in "the olde daunce" (1.476) and married off, at twelve, far too young. Indeed, Virginia's age, fourteen, is both a detail unique to Chaucer's version and one articulated with the same signifier, "twelve . . . and tweye" (6.30), the Wife uses.

Our reading of Chaucer's source and analogue texts, then, is more than merely identificatory and hardly direct; we are not interested in the text he followed for its own sake. The texts instead witness a set of relations in which they have read and misread each other in their various appropriations of Virginia's courtroom drama. If she herself is dragged into court and placed in a corrupt setting, so too is the exemplum about her. For a genre that always arrives in a narrative context—a history of Rome or a set of sermons, here a tale-telling competition—Chaucer threatens us with a lack of meaning without one. What would we understand of Livy's story without the explicitly political frame he places around it? A father's spontaneous murder of a child could only be seen as an assertion of freedom ("libertas") if properly couched in terms of the civic virtues Apius threatens. In Livy's history, the close relation between Virginius and his progeny, Virginia, are spoken in the very relation of those signifiers, as we have noted, where the daughter's name marks her as his possession. In taking her life, Livy's Virginius marks her freedom as well as his own free status in the status of the plebs—indeed the two are conflated.

This metonymy between father and daughter is both meaningful and disturbing, particularly to the medieval redactors of the story. His actions on her behalf are increasingly more difficult to justify beyond the historical moment Livy narrates. Virginius's act of heroism and self-sacrifice, in the era of its Christian reception, is more tenuously proffered. Gower's tale shows the desperation of the father in the tense courtroom scene as Apius awards the maiden to his brother. Because Virginius can make no "appel" (7.5233), reason gives way to animal instinct:

> Rict as a leon in his rage,
> Which of no drede set acompte
> And not what pité scholde amounte,
> A naked swerd he pulleth oute,

The which amonges al the route
He threste thurgh his dowhter side.
(7.5240–45)

The lack of pity that Virginius shows his daughter gets explained by the lion's animalistic rage that overtakes him. He protects her chastity in the only way left to him. This lack of pity is important both for the way it posits the affect we (like Gower) might expect of a father for his child, what it "sholde amounte" to, and for the way pity is allocated elsewhere in medieval versions of the classical exemplum. In the *Rose,* Virginius's pity appears when he argues for a pardon for Apius's henchman. Jean writes, "Claudius . . . would have been condemned to death as a thief, if Virginius, through his pity, had not saved him" (114; "et Claudius, chalangierres, / juigiez iert a mort conme lierres, / se ne l'en eüst respitié / Virginius par sa pitié," 5621–24). The "hireling" Apius manipulates into helping him receives the pity (lit. "respitié") we might have expected for the daughter, thus placing all the blame for this event upon Apius himself. Those terms of blame are even more heavily emphasized in Chaucer's version in which Virginia is not stabbed spontaneously in the courtroom in a scene of paternal desperation but sacrificed more ceremoniously at home.[36] When her father returns from court to relate the verdict against her, he passes his own sentence: "For love, and nat for hate, thou most be deed; / My pitous hand moot smyten of thyn heed" (6.225–26). Where Gower's Virginius's desperate act lacks pity, Chaucer's claims his action *is* a form of pity, thus linking it with the pity he shows the condemned Claudius.[37]

Chaucer's tale is swept up in a drama of the signifier, shown in the submerged desires registered in the Physician's story and its language. Each successive version of the tale, Livy's, Jean's, Gower's, Chaucer's, is determined by the signifier's location within it, here where "pity" is located in the tales but also in other terms. The names of Virginia and her father serve as a case in point; they are what get read and reread in each version of this tale of illicit desire. The roots of these clearly related names are openly meaningful in Livy's text, in which Apius's tyranny extends to a much larger historical field than this brief episode intimates on its own.

---

36. While Virginia's delayed death at home has been much discussed, her beheading has not. Clearly following Jean, the only source for this change in method, neither French nor English scholars have speculated on the nature of the shift from stabbing penetration to this more hagiographic form of sacrifice.

37. Notably, he can also direct pity toward himself (for having to kill her) too since "pitous" is ambiguously attached to its antecedent in this line. His hand is "pitous" in that it shows pity for Virginia in sacrificing her, or his hand deserves pity for having to do so.

With pride foregrounded, the decemvirs he leads rule with secret tyranny: "They concocted their judgments in private, and pronounced them in the Forum" (3.121; "Iudica domi conflabant, pronuntiabant in foro," 3.120). In this environment "the plebians felt only one concern: how were they ever going to restore the tribunician power (their bulwark of liberty) which had been suspended?" (3.123; "Id modo plebes agitabat, quonam modo tribuniciam potestatem, munimentum libertati, rem itermissam, reparaent," 3.120–22). Livy sets these questions of justice and factionalism in the context of Roman anxieties about war and the legal status of the election of the decemvirs, in which Apius's notoriety for violence and power-mongering is pre-eminent. Against this background Livy introduces Lucius Virginius, a "centurion of rank . . . a man of exemplary life at home and in the army" (3.145; "Pater virginis, L. Verginius, honestum . . . vir exempli recti domi militiaeque," 3.142–44). Already the very terms of our discussion of genre and meaning are embedded in the Latin terms naming and defining the victims of unregulated desire both political and domestic. Virginius is himself "exemplary" ("vir exempli") before the tale about his daughter becomes an exemplum of anything that can be lifted out of Livy's Roman history. His name intimates a sense of truth ("ver-") as well as purity ("virgo") and strength ("vir") in its component parts, which we can read in the relation of Virginius to his daughter, Virginia. Indeed, the Latin text introduces him "Pater virginis" (3.142; "the girl's father," 3.143), before his proper name, "L. Verginius," which is also a form of hers. Livy announces their close tie in the signifier, within her very name conflating her unmarried, chaste status with her status as Virginius's daughter. Indeed, his name likely comes from hers, "virgo," the virgin Virginia, even as the virgo is a feminized form of masculine strength ("vir").[38] She is thus an abstraction in the signifier before Livy or anyone else can take her voice or give her symbolic meaning.

That strong, chaste status is at issue everywhere in this story. Explicitly set in line with the "rape and death of Lucretia," the story of Virginia is one that leads to the end of the decemvirs just as Lucretia's "led . . . to the expulsion of the Tarquinii from the city and from their throne" (3.143; "stuprum caedemque Lucretiae urbe regnoque Tarquinios expulerat," 3.142). In this way, the "truth," "purity," and "strength" of Virginius and his daughter, which we can read out of their very names, are directly the issue of the story and its function in Livy's history. Livy makes the analogy explicit before he tells about Virginius's exemplarity: "thus not only did the same

---

38. Ogilvie, *Commentary,* 477.

end befall the decemvirs as had befallen the kings, but the same cause deprived them of their power" (3.143; "ut non finis idem decemviris qui regibus sed causa etiam eadem imperii amittendi esset," 3.142). Virginia's name is ambivalent and overdetermined, a powerful signifier that can operate in more than one way, and its English translations make those multiple senses explicit. "Virginia" operates nominally to identify Virginius's daughter, a maiden, whose as-yet-unmarried status is crucial, even definitional. She is the object of Apius's lust ("App. Claudium virginis plebeiae stuprandae libido cepit," 3.142; "Appius Claudius was seized with the desire to debauch a certain maiden belonging to the plebs," 3.143), and a woman betrothed to another man, Lucius Icilius, "an active man of proven courage in the cause of the plebeians" (3.145; "viro acriet pro causa plebis expertae virtutis," 3.144). The tale relies on the very meaning of her possession ("virginis"), even as it emplots a narrative of false legal possession in order for Apius to gain sexual possession of her. Apius's plot to "debauch" the girl centers around a false claim upon her status: "He commissioned Marcus Claudius, his client, to claim the girl as his slave, and not to yield to those who demanded her liberation, thinking the absence of the maiden's father afforded an opportunity for the wrong" (3.145; "M. Claudio clienti negotium dedit ut virginem in servitutem adsereret neque cederet secundum libertatem postulantibus vindicias, quod pater puellae abesset locum iuiuriae esse ratus," 3.144). Her name, of course, signifies her father's possession of her as well as her symbolic status as "a maiden of the plebians": "virginis plebeiae" and "pater virginis" are the terms introducing these principal figures, and her possession "by the plebs" and "of" her father are written in the genitive and accusative, the possessive and objective cases on the page, making Claudius's false charges all the more significant. Possession is no mere ruse in this story but the very matter at hand in multiple senses both within the narrative and in the signifier.

The Latin text shifts between "Vergini" and "virgini" with ease as alternate spellings for the same term—capitalized forms usually referring to the father and declined forms to the girl. The text thus encourages us to read her name not only as a feminine form of her father's but as a categorical one, such as "puella" is elsewhere. Such lexical flexibility allows us to see the daughter of the plebs and the centurion as the concurrent center of the conflict. As the story moves toward its climax in the courtroom, Livy invokes the feminine form of Virginius's name to signal precisely the problems of objecthood and possession at stake. Temporarily rescued from Claudius's plot (before her father's arrival), Virginia is finally named ("nec ultra minas tamen processum est, cum Appius non Verginiam defendi ab

Icilio," 3.150). Her name will only appear as such, definitively proper, once more. The Latin text prefers "virginis" (maiden) or "puella" (girl) and sometimes "filia" (daughter) to any properly nominated signifier. Or put another way, these other terms are her "proper" name, as they are names proper to her status and designate her relation to others and the city, the principal subjects of this tale.

The importance of names is not lost in the Roman forum, where "the names of Verginius her father and of her betrothed Icilius were known and popular" (3.145; "Vergini patris sponsique Icili populare nomen celebrabatur," 3.144), and they prevent Claudius from openly seizing the girl. Read out of the signifier, the tale of Virginia is a tale of representation, and its stakes, as Virginius goes through the marketplace on his way to the court gathering supporters

> not merely to ask for their aid as a favour, but to claim it as his due, saying that he stood daily in the battle-line in defense of their children and their wives; that there was no man of whom more strenuous and courageous deeds in war could be related—to what end, if despite the safety of the City those outrages which were dreaded as the worst that could follow a city's capture must be suffered by their children? (3.155)

> non orare solum preciariam opem, sed pro debita petere: Se pro liberis eorum ac coniugibus cottidie in acie stare, nec alium virum esse cuius strenue ac fortiter facta in bello plura memorari possent; quid prodesse si, incolumi urbe, quae capta ultima timeantur liberis suis sint patienda? (3.154)

Virginius is owed public support for the way he safeguards the city, particularly its women; he represents their freedom on the battlefield. Similarly, the assault on Virginius represents a threat to the families of everyone he fights to protect. Thus at the level of structure, the tale of Virginius works in *Ab urbe condita* by analogy as yet another representation of the political threat men such as Apius pose to the Republic. Livy tells the story for the very same reason that Virginius seeks support—to prevent the doom of Virginia from becoming the fate of the Roman state. Virginia and her father stand as representatives of the ethical virtues threatened by tyranny and its unchecked aggressive desire. The very political (and in many ways impersonal) narrative of Virginia and Virginius that has been read in the larger context of his history and the political exemplum he offers occurs *in the signifier*—in the way the maiden's name always signals beyond her identity as a mere individual that will be taken up differently in the medieval redactions of Livy's story.

Jean's use of this exemplum and his reading of the signifier appear in the more compressed poetic lines of the *Rose* and its introduction of "Virgine la pucele, / qui fu fille Virginius" (5562–63). In Old French "virgine" (virgin), "pucele" (maiden), and "fille" (daughter, girl) form a chain of signifiers leading from Virginia to Virginius in ways similar to Livy's history. Additionally, Jean is able to use his allegorical figure of Reason to clarify the relations of these terms, "virgo" to "vir," so as to play up the conflict between justice and love she wishes to illustrate. But to do so, Reason inverts the associations of love and justice seen in Livy. In *Ab urbe,* both Icilius and Virginius defend the "freedom" of the maiden; there is no mention of love for her. In fact, the love ("amor") that enflames Apius is the problem; it blocks his reason. Livy claims: "In the face of all these things Appius hardened his heart—so violent was the madness, as it may more truly be called than love, that had overthrown his reason" (155; "Adversus quae omnia obstinato animo Appius—tanta vis amentiae veruis quam amoris mentem turbaverat," 154). Yet for Jean's purposes in the *Rose,* it is love that gets idealized and thus associated with Virginius, "exchang[ing] shame for injury. . . . For, through love and without any hatred" he ends his daughter's life (114; "change honte por domage. . . . car il par amor sans haïne," 5602; 5605). In this transfer of affection, from the corrupting "amor" of the lustful judge to the pitiful father, Jean recasts Livy's story; but in the medieval versions that follow, such a shift has placed Virginius in a more vertiginous position.

With its historical context removed and the Roman political drama of the decemvirate erased, the identification between Virginia and Virginius displayed in the French names does not merely reveal the strength of the "virgine" but also suggests, reciprocally, the purity and innocence of the wronged father. Such a reading lies implicit in the medieval versions of the story, where any such sacrifice (like Lucretia's suicide) is more problematically assimilated to Christian morals and might require defense.[39] Chaucer and Gower offer two tales that read these inherited signifiers in unexpected ways. Gower opens with a rubric announcing (and likely helping to find) the "[Tale of Virginia]" (7.380). But her name never appears in the text

---

39. It is also a possible effect of the story's abbreviation. Removing Icilius, Virginia's impending marriage, and the ways in which she stands for the Roman citizenry more generally, we read a closer tie between "virgine" and "virginius," a virgin and the masculine guarantor of her status. Indeed in Jean's text Virginia's name precedes her father's. She is no nameless "filia," as is customary in Latin, until the middle of the story; her status and/as her identity is foregrounded from the start.

of the *Confessio*. Much like Livy, Gower is more likely to talk in other terms: "she," "a gentil maide" (7.5135), or the "douhter" (7.5153). Gower thus offers a more conventionally "classical" version, in which taboos on women's names kept them private in civic narratives; they are mentioned only in the most scandalous of ways.[40] Like Gower, Chaucer also suppresses her name, similarly attentive to the "mayde" (6.630).[41] These are not surprising terms to be emphasized in their stories—both terms speak the alternate significances of her name, "virgin" and "daughter," in submerged ways. Chaucer's preference for "mayde" belies an abstract reading of her name pervading the tale and responsible for its associations with hagiography. As we have seen, his narrative makes Virginia a decidedly young girl of fourteen and omits her betrothed, thus reading the signifier as "virginity" itself. Indeed, this is where her proper name lies submerged early in the story. As the Physician offers his unique discussion of her virtuous beauty, he notes her chastity: "As wel in goost as body chast was she, / For which she *floured in virginitee*, / With alle humylitee and abstinence" (6.43–45; my emphasis). Only later when Virginius delivers to her the news of the courtroom verdict do we first hear her proper name, and it emphasized as such: "'Doghter, quod he, 'Virginia, *by thy name*'" (6.213; my emphasis), in a gesture that further identifies her as virginity, the ideal for which she dies, itself.

Chaucer's (and Gower's) avoidance of Virginia's name follows classical example, and their description of the "flower" of maidenhood is also conventional. In Gower, Apius's

> ... herte hath set afyre,
> That he began the flour desire
> Which longeth unto maydenhede.
> (7.5143–45)

It is not so much the specific usage as the commonality of its collocation, "flour ... maydenhede," that I would emphasize. This very commonness underwrites what Howard Bloch has labeled the "unspoken pun" in the Physician's Tale: Apius's desire for "maydenhede" results in a literal rendering of the maiden's head he did not anticipate, lending an irony and poetic justice to the tale that its readers have found in conflict with its domestic

---

40. I am indebted to conversations with my colleague from Classics, Timothy Moore, for these observations and for his general helpfulness about Livy.
41. Chaucer uses "mayde" approximately twice as much as Gower, who calls her "douhter" just as often as maiden.

sympathies. In these intensified moral stories, desire circulates and returns as a reading of the signifier—perhaps even Chaucer's literal reading of the signifier in Gower's version of Livy's story. For as we shall see, Chaucer shares with Gower an attention to Virginia's legitimacy, suggesting that Gower may in fact be a submerged source for Chaucer.

This exchange, maiden's head for maidenhead, returns us to Chaucer's tale and the desires it tracks and condemns in new ways. It forces us to acknowledge the invention of what has seemed central to his narrative: the beheading of the virgin, maiden's head for maidenhead. In Gower's story, which follows the details of Livy's more closely, Virginia is stabbed with a knife in the forum in a symbolic assertion of freedom, a stabbing gesture that explicitly echoes the suicide of Lucretia. But not so in the *Romance of the Rose* or in Chaucer. These medieval texts associate Virginia's sacrifice with a more hagiographic martyrdom that we see in the *Canterbury Tales* itself in the Second Nun's Tale and the clergeon's near beheading in the Prioress's story. Chaucer, we assume, took this detail from Jean; the importance of "maydenhede" making the act supremely "reasonable" as the tale's end. While no such pun or play on words is available in Old French, it is certainly alive to Chaucer as a reader of this aspect unique to Jean's story. Yet we should not be so dismissive of Chaucer's possible knowledge of Livy and thus what his rejection of Livy's details, most likely via Gower, might suggest.

Despite the general consensus that Chaucer's tale shows no influence of Gower's version, the Middle English poets share at least one significant detail against other sources. Both Chaucer and Gower insist on the legitimacy of Virginia's birth, ensuring it from the very beginning of their stories. In Gower's brief description, he mentions that the maid was legally "Begeten [of Virginius] . . . upon his wif" (7.5137) before he notes her extraordinary beauty. Chaucer not only ensures her paternity, he puts her mother in the story itself.[42] Like Gower, Chaucer legitimates Virginia before he describes her: "This knyghte a doghter hadde by his wyf; / No children hadde he mo in al his lyf" (6.5–6). This identical introduction is then buttressed by the mother's appearance as Virginia "wente in the toun / Toward a temple, with hire mooder deere, / As is of yonge maydens the manere" (6.118–20). This mother makes no further appearance, and had the story unfolded in the courtroom (as in all other versions), we might not have remarked her absence later on. But the Physician dramatizes Virginia's

---

42. Corsa's *Variorum* edition notes that "Shannon . . . suggests that Livy's reference to *uxor* (3.44) 'doubtless inspired' Chaucer to speak of Virginia's mother here and in lines 118–19" (90n5). See Edgar Shannon, *Chaucer and the Roman Poets* (Cambridge: Harvard UP, 1929), 402.

sacrifice at home and at some length, intensifying the scene of domesticity without any reference to the mother he added to the story. This absence from the domestic scene prompts us to ask why she appears in the tale in the first place.

Gower and Chaucer seem anxious to respond to Livy's narrative, which raises the question of Virginia's birth as part of the perfidious plan to spoil her and to dupe her father. The plot that Apius invents preys upon Virginius as much as the daughter. The plot to secure her rests upon a claim of false paternity: "The girl had been born, said Marcus, in his house, and had thence been stealthily conveyed to the home of Verginius and palmed off upon him as his own; he had good evidence for what he said, and would prove it even though Verginius himself were judge, who was more wronged than he was" (3.147; "puellam domi suae natam furtoque inde in domum Vergini translatam suppositam ei esse; id se indicio compertum adferre probaturumque vel ipso Verginio iudice, ad quem maior par iniuriae eius pertineat," 3.146). Gower and Chaucer appear to be responding in advance to this claim by Apius's hireling ("cliens"): that Virginius himself has been duped by his wife and may be considered "more wronged" than the man who here brings the charge. Gower's version, and Chaucer's more so than his, recuperates Virginius's status at the same time that they attempt to preserve Virginia's because the means by which the classical story works itself fails in their medieval context. Neither Middle English poet entertains any such fiction that Virginius has been cuckolded and deceived from the start. Both writers exclude this lie from the courtroom accusation at the same time that they clarify Virginia's legitimacy from the start. In both Chaucer and Gower we see a fissure in the historical context out of which the moral example has been appropriated.

The medieval rehistoricization of the story has other consequences. The Physician's version (and not just his closing moral) sharpens our attention to Apius and his relation to Claudius, his own servant, in Chaucer's text. In Livy, [Marcus] Claudius is Apius's "client" and equal in riotous living, but Jean reduces him to "a hireling" in the *Rose*. Chaucer uses the same terms to designate Claudius's relation to Apius ("servant," "cherl"), terms that echo Virginia's trumped-up relation to Claudius ("servant," "thrall"), and to make an analogy among them. Since Claudius's lie intends to procure Virginia as the thrall of Apius's lust, the analogy makes perfect sense. Claudius is the mere middleman in a plot to make Virginia the servant and possession of the judge. But these relations between figures in the tale and the roles that they play are advertised even more openly by the close tie between Virginia's and Virginius's names. These designations make us more acutely aware of the way various actions are analogized and thus equated—how, in Livy's context, the crime against Virginia signifies a crime against Virginius and the entire state. Many have remarked on the suspect nature of Virginius's act, what may amount to the potentially incestuous nature of Virginius's smiting of the maiden's head that Livy and Gower initially represent as a stabbing penetration of the virgin's body to preserve her physical "purity."[43] These differing means of sacrificing Virginia produce a sexual excess of signification. Each emphasizes the latent erotics in Virginius's act because of the ways it answers, *and thus openly articulates,* the erotic desire hidden beneath Apius's verdict.

We can see that articulation in the transfer of violence among these analogous relations. The violence of Apius's desire for Virginia is directed toward the "cherl" he employs in his fraudulent scheme to obtain her. "No force ne . . . no meede" (6.133) will seduce Virginia, but these are precisely the rewards and threats Apius imposes on his conspirator. The churl works under the threat of losing his head (6.145) and is given "yiftes preciouse and deere" for his coerced assistance (6.148). There is thus an almost direct correlation between the desire and aggression working upon Apius in Chaucer's story. In seeking to claim Virginia as a stolen "servant" of Apius's "cherl" in court, the judge fashions his own servant as his conspirator in legal terms (6.199). His desire for sexual possession of Virginia is transposed into legal possession of a servant by the terms of the case. Even as Bloch has shown how maidenhead and maiden's head stand in for one another, the father's "sentence" (6.224) is called to replace the false judge's "diffynytyf sentence" in court (6.172). But these plays on words seem to be part of a more meaningful structure than mere verbal pun. Gower too is aware of the terms manipulated by Apius and, implicitly, reclaimed by Virginius. He concludes his story with just such a recognition: "And thus th'unchaste was chastised, / Whereof thei myhte ben avised / That scholden afterward governe" (7.5301–3). These terms circulate and shift positions, forging relations and transferring effects both within and between versions of the story.

We tend not to think about the speakers in the exemplum. We notice, instead, what the *exemplum* speaks: what the tale works to exemplify. But recent work on the genre reveals such speech to be central to the work the exemplum performs. Comparison of Chaucer's tale to the sources and analogues reveals the speaker's power over the abstract "sentence" an exem-

---

43. Uneasiness with Virginius's sentence is pervasive. Angus Fletcher, for example, calls it a "perversion of parental authority" in "The Sentencing of Virginia in the *Physician's Tale*," *Chaucer Review* 34 (2000): 300–8, at 305. See also Daniel Kline, "Jephthah's Daughter and Chaucer's Virginia: The Critique of Sacrifice in The Physician's Tale," *JEGP* 107 (2008): 77–103.

plum affords. If this observation only repeats the terms by which such stories have been formerly understood—that is, in terms of sources and the narrator—it does so with a self-conscious difference. These terms are meant not to isolate the Physician's Tale but to return it to the larger taletelling structure, the centrality of "sentence" to the "solaas" of the whole. Jean claims that "Livy . . . knows well how to recount the case" ("Tytus Livius, / qui bien set le cas raconter," 5564–65), but it is the Physician who makes a theatrical spectacle out of the pathetic situation of Apius's plot and Virginius's actions by dramatizing as speech and dialogue what is otherwise merely recounted in other versions. Tracing these versions from Livy's original, Allen has shown the ways Livy refuses to represent the speech of liars and deceivers directly, and thereby refuses to lend authority and credence to those speeches with quotation.[44] Alternately, Jean authoritatively narrates his exemplum through the mouth of a personified "Reason," thereby shaping it as a particular kind of discourse. The one speaker quoted in Reason's discourse, however, is "the evil traitor, the minister of the false judge" (114; "Ainsinc parloit li maus traïstres, / qui du faus juige estoit menistres," 5585–86). No one else in Jean's narrative—other than Reason herself—utters a word. This arrangement itself passes judgment on the story, framing the false claim of Claudius with Reason's interpretation of the situation: "Virginius was quite ready to repay and confound his adversaries, but, as the case went, Appius spoke before he did and made the hasty judgment" (3.114; "Virginius palast, / qui touz estoit prez de respondre / por ses aversaires confondre, / juja par hastive sentance / Appius que

---

44. Allen, *False Fables and Exemplary Truth*, 54. In this study of the exemplum form and the crisis of interpretation it provokes in vernacular use, Allen compares these versions of the Virginia story through their deployment of direct and indirect speech. According to Allen, the classical exemplum places a premium on directly reported speech, reserving it for the form's most highly endorsed articulations. In Livy's original, the perfidy of Apius was rendered indirectly so as to avoid confusing (or worse, seducing) its readers. Livy's story is part of his larger history of Rome, and this historically specific context is crucial to the reworkings of the exemplum in the various contexts provided by Jean, Gower, and Chaucer we have been attending. Allen writes, "Because Virginia's death generates republican reform, Livy's account goes to some lengths to endorse the events of the story" (53). The strategy of quotation that Livy uses "is based on an assumption that direct quotation grants moral authority to a character, while indirect discourse calls attention to the narrator's invention, as he issues a warning or attaches blame to the character in the process of paraphrasing his speech" (54). These assumptions are very different from those operating over later medieval versions, in which "quotation does not serve moral judgment; both Gower and Chaucer use unreliable narrators and complex framing devices to reveal" other aspects of the story in these alternate contexts, such as "the violence inherent in Virginius's ideal fatherhood" (54). For the medieval texts, direct discourse "serves to stage moral questions"; it does not unproblematically "shore up moral authority" (54). For an interesting account of the importance of dramatic spectacle in Livy's history, see Andrew Feldharr, *Spectacle and Society in Livy's History* (Berkeley: U of California P, 1988).

sanz atendance / fust la pucele an serf rendue," 5588–93). And, as Reason explains and, in the very act of speaking herself, *defines as reasonable,* when Virginius "couldn't defend his daughter against Appius . . . he exchanged shame for injury, *in a marvellous process of reasoning,* if Livy doesn't lie. For, through love and without any hatred, he immediately cut off the head of his beautiful daughter Virginia and then presented it to the judge before all, in open court" (114; my emphasis; "c'est a savoir Virginius, / qui bien voit que vers Appius / ne peut pas sa fille deffendre, / ainz li convient par force rendre / et son cors liverer a hontage, / Si change honte por domage / par merveilleuz apensement, / se Tytus Livius ne ment, / car il par amor sans haïne / a sa bele fille Virgine / tantost a la test coupee /et puis au juige presentee / devant touz en plein consitoire," 5597–609). Jean's allegorical narrative structure does the talking in these scenes, rendering the interpretation of the action for us. That is, Reason quotes Claudius's language, as Livy would not, precisely because it is not hers; it is the unreasonable language of another. We see here the practice Allen has marked in Livy in the reverse. Quotation does not necessarily authenticate the words quoted; it may differentiate the narrator's words from a character's, a difference important to Chaucer and Gower's framed tale collections. But even further, Reason demarcates what she describes and narrates as reasonable, by definition, when she delineates Virginius's "marvellous process of reasoning," making clear the nature of Apius's desire—the maidenhead of the virgin—latent in his judgment. The logic of Virginius's reasoning lies in this linguistic exchange, which explains how we get a beheading in the story in the first place. Livy's history, Jean's source, claims that Virginius stabs Virginia in front of the judge, rendering the defense of her virtue and assertion of her freedom in advance of its violation, and thus analogizing Virginius's action to Lucretia's similarly performed suicide. But Reason changes the means of the sacrifice from stabbing to the loss of her head "in [her] marvellous process of reasoning"—in Old French, "apensement" (from "penser," to think)—a word that makes her thinking paramount and that makes the action, beheading, an act of reasoning. Indeed, the maiden's loss of her head may be an emblem of the very unreasonableness of Apius's judgment.

Chaucer's dependence on Jean and the "discourse of Reason" as source thus explains a number of anomalies otherwise plaguing the Physician's Tale. In his more fully dialogic and thus dramatic version of the story, Virginius delays execution of his child; it is not a response enacted in the courtroom in anger or desperation; nor is it, through the words of Reason, a literal rendering of Apius's unreasonable judgment and revelation of Apius's private desire: maiden's head for maidenhead. Discussing her fate with her at home, Virginius allows her to bewail her impending death. In a statement lifted out of the *Rose,* he gives her the sentence, "For love, and nat for hate, thou most be deed; / My pitous hand moot smyten of thyn heed" (6.225–26), in advance of his action rather than as an answer to Apius in court. Chaucer follows Jean in the minor details of the story, but its new context changes everything. His reliance on Jean explains for us what otherwise appears inconsistent in the Physician's rendering: his sentence explicitly "for love," which comes from Reason's explanation of these matters. If this claim has befuddled Chaucer's readers, it makes more sense when we realize his source text locates the story within a larger debate on the relative powers of love and justice. The tale is meant to show the superiority of love in the face of the corruptibility of justice. But the Physician's Tale, like the other medieval renderings of Livy's historical example, implicates love as much as justice. In a Christian universe, there is no way to recuperate sacrificial murder (or Lucretia's suicide, for that matter), even if the alternative is also sinful.

Chaucer follows the details of Jean's version but lacks the frame Reason imposes as he enlivens it into dramatic dialogue. Thus, the Physician's Virginius is dragged into court and Apius's judgment is delayed, only to silence him at the very moment he was poised to defend himself. So too does Virginius delay his sentence upon his child by speaking to her about it outside of court. He stretches out his sentence "for love," as he claims, rather than answering the judge in the heat of anger. In the dialogic performance of its scenes, Chaucer's story emphasizes the force of speech: how and when one speaks before another can act or answer—and the effects that this situation provokes. The Physician's Tale thus becomes a tale of "sentences," a tale of judgment and judgments gone awry but also a story about where and when articulations are made and their effects. Given the generative means of responding to and rewriting other stories, either as sources or provocations on the Canterbury road, these ideas have some purchase on the tale-telling contest.

The Physician's Tale is a story in which saying something first sets other things in motion, a feature that describes the structure of the *Canterbury Tales* as a whole. Virginia, Virginius, Claudius, and Apius each work in advance of the problems they foresee, and their actions—whether it is Virginia's feigning illness to avoid the folly of dances and feasts or Claudius's urge to receive judgment before Virginius appears to answer charges—are pre-emptive. This connection between the very different actions of Virginius and his daughter and the villains in the tale makes some sense of the tale's seemingly misplaced moral at the end: "Forsake synne, *er* synne you forsake" (6.286; my emphasis). A number of readers have remarked on the inappropriateness of the tale's moral, its uncomfortable fit with the rest of the story.[45] With this ending and its central "synne," the tale's focus shifts to Apius, who slays himself in prison, or at least moves more generally to the tale's end, where Apius and Virginius have gone wrong. Where the beginning of the story centers on Virginia, the warning the Physician offers to readers makes Apius's sin the center of its moral focus:

> Heere may men seen how synne hath his merite.
> Beth war, for no man woot whom God wol smyte
> In no degree, ne in which manere wyse;
> The worm of conscience may agryse
> Of wikked lyf, though it so pryvee be
> That no man woot ther of but God and he.
> For be he lewed man, or ellis lered,
> He noot how soone that he shal been afered.
> Therfore I rede yow this conseil take:
> Forsaketh synne, er synne you forsake.
> (6.277–86)

This final section of the poem is worth quoting at length for its shift of emphasis and metaphor. Along with the other explicit references to religion in the story, it offers the tale's best effort to moralize the exemplum in specifically Christian terms. But it fails to register the tale's emotional alignments. The audience has occupied the position of "the peple" in the story, watching the courtroom drama and suspicious of Apius but powerless to do anything before the end. Yet this "conseil" to forsake sin before it forsakes them puts the audience in Apius's place, as one whose secret sin could not be hidden. This moral's most stunning image of the fearful and trembling "worm of conscience" is arresting, and perplexing. Chaucer is quoting either Innocent III, *De contemptu mundi* 1.3.2, "vermis conscientiae tripliciter lacerabit" [the worm of conscience shall tear apart with threefold force] or Jean's *Testament*, "Li vers de conscience."[46] One might

---

45. See those readings catalogued by Corsa, *Variorum Edition*, 136–37n286. Additionally, Marta Powell Harley sees it as part of the tale's general misreading of Jean's version of the story in "Last Things First in Chaucer's Physician's Tale: Final Judgment and the Worm of Conscience," *JEGP* 91 (1992): 1–16, at 9.

46. See Corsa, *Variorum*, 135n280. Corsa cites E. Koeppel for Jean's ultimate source for the phrase "the worms of conscience," Mark 9:43, 45, 47 "vermis eorum non moritur" [where the worm dieth not], but it can also be found in Isaiah 66:24. See Koeppel, "Chauceriana," *Anglia* 14 (1892): 227–67.

read the moral ending of the tale as a compulsive return of the political repressed, the Roman context excised by Jean and Chaucer, or perhaps a return of the *Rose*'s theme of justice. These gestures offer a way of universalizing the story, but the internalizations of this moral of sin and conscience carry individual rather than collective weight. While this ending seems strangely appended, it accords rather well with its earlier attention to the vigilance of guardians and governesses. Thus, against the classical operations of exempla, in which verbal articulation results in endorsement, the Physician offers a surprising story of unexpected consequences.

The moral swerve at the end of the tale ought to be calibrated against Chaucer's original opening gestures, which return us to what Elizabeth Allen has marked as "conflicted moral desire" in Chaucer's use of exemplary materials.[47] The closing moral of the story generates a crisis of knowledge in the "worm of conscience," from whose devouring motion ("agryse") nothing can remain private or hidden. Unlike any of its possible sources, the Physician's Tale is one in which knowledge and know-how are at stake. With its admonition for vigilance, the story is ultimately interested in who can see what is coming in advance. This sense of the ending returns us to the narrator's seemingly misplaced attention to criminal expertise. He seems unduly fascinated with the expert knowledge sin itself confers:

> A theef of venysoun, that hath forlaft
> His likerousnesse and al his olde crafte,
> Kan kepe a forest best of any man.
> (6.83–85)

This kind of expertise is antithetical to the innocence and inexperience elsewhere valorized as "maydenhede" (8.126). Reversals are what make logical sense to the Physician, which is perhaps why he reverses his ending, making Apius rather than Virginia its focus, and where he locates the moral of his story. This is the tale's largest statement of the pre-emptive (and chiastic) logic governing its events and is consistent with the rest of the sentiments in the story. With dramatic reversals of "sentence" and language, of servants and masters, subjects and objects, the Physician rewrites his tale, in the end, as a story of bad timing. As such, the efforts of Chaucer's Physician and his Virginia to avoid desire only drive her further toward it. Her monitory tale is disfigured by the desires put into circulation as she attempts to erase them and avoid them—and they ultimately lead to her death.

---

47. Allen, *False Fables and Exemplary Truth*, 52.

In the Second Nun's Tale, we have a story of desire's even more emphatic denial and transformation in its firmly hagiographic idealization of virginity. In fact, one of the things uniting the religious stories, even in the loose manner in which I have defined them, is the way they idealize virginity and a feminized innocent purity, or what the *Canterbury Tales* would more properly call "maydenhede." In the Man of Law's Tale and the Clerk's Tale, those ideal virgins quickly become wives and mothers, so a better term might be "wommanhede."[48] But the feminine focus of these religious stories, which could include the Prioress's Marian miracle and the Tale of Melibee, is striking.

From its very beginning, the "lyf" of St. Cecilia is rooted in her feminine sexual status. Its first stanza begins with "this mayden" and ends by describing her love for God in terms of her wish for "hym to kepe hir maydenhede" (8.127; 126). She grounds her faith, as most of the virgin martyrs in popular saint's lives, in the physical integrity of her body. This alignment makes for some spectacular "pious pornography" in many of these holy narratives, as Sarah Kay remarks. She writes: "Medieval audiences appear to have relished accounts of nubile young girls being subjected by pagan rulers to sexually charged tortures, in which . . . [they are] stripped naked, roasted alive, broken on wheels, boiled in oil, and hav[e] their breasts ripped off."[49] Chaucer's tale offers little of such pornography, but the structure of its excitement remains. Cecilia's desire to have God "kepe" her virginity is a desire to preserve it intact so as to give it up, through a spiritual union with the divine or by a more violent means at tale's end. Thus, the logic of the saint's life, whether descriptively pornographic or not, tempts violation. The saint's faith, aligned with chastity and physical integrity, is always demonstrated on the body.

Where other hagiographies depict the erotic desires of pagan tyrants for the virgin martyr as part of their scandalous plots, the Second Nun's Tale redirects erotic desire in unexpected ways. As is often remarked by Chaucer's readers, Cecilia's legend is one of the few such narratives in which marriage is not spectacularly resisted. Instead, the tale avoids such scenes of erotically charged resistance and dramatic refusal. Never protesting the union

---

48. I would thus classify the Prioress's Tale this way too. Its devotion to the Virgin Mary through its narrative of the innocent child speaks a feminine power extolled by the story. On the importance of womanhood in Chaucer, see Tara Williams, *Inventing Womanhood: Gender and Language in Later Middle English Writing* (Columbus: The Ohio State UP, 2011).

49. Kay, "Sublime Body," 4.

with Valerian that her parents have arranged, Cecilia submits, co-opting the institution of marriage for her private purposes. Chaucer's choice of the Cecilia story as the saint's life in the *Canterbury Tales* compels us in light of this feature, for it embroils hagiography in conversation with other tales the genre might seem to oppose.[50] Cecilia shapes her relation to God and her reproductive Christian power in terms of desire, making converts out of her new husband and his brother in terms of and using conventions we have seen before. But rather than refute the claims of desire completely as these strategies seem designed to do, they are part of a sophisticated deployment of erotic longing that produces connections to other tales. If Cecilia does not avoid marriage or rebel against her parents as do other virgin martyrs, neither does she merely consent to their strictures. Her resistance is built upon private meanings that underwrite her public actions.

Cecilia goes to her wedding, for example, wearing traditional raiment as if in full conformity with her parents' plans, but she secretly possesses a hair shirt beneath her dress:

> She, ful devout and humble in hir corage,
> Under her robe of gold, that sat ful faire
> Hadde next hir flessh yclad hire in an haire.
> (8.131–33)

The layers of Cecilia's clothing reveal layers of meaning to her seemingly singular action. The celebratory "robe of gold" on the surface belies "an haire" next to her skin. This means of mortifying her flesh signifies the private meaning of the occasion and inverts the terms of its public significance. But even more abstractly, she has already clothed her heart ("corage") in humility and devotion, of which the division in material finery is only an outward sign. She has similarly commended her body to Christ, equating her faith in God to her virginity itself. All the more surprising then that Cecilia does not foreswear the earthly marriage she spiritually declines. Instead, the Second Nun's Tale uses the contrast between public behavior and private thought to do its ideological work:

> And whil the organs maden melodie,
> To God allone in herte thus sang she:

---

50. Here we might take seriously Chaucer's claim in the Retractions to have written "othere bookes of legendes of seintes," from which he would have selected the life of St. Cecilia purposefully (10.1088).

> "O Lord, my soule and eek my body gye
> Unwemmed, lest that I confounded be."
> (8.134–37)

Music, once again, invokes an erotic context, here in terms of orthodox marital celebration. Cecilia must deny such power over her, singing instead "to God allone." Aligning the bodily corruption of sex with moral and spiritual "confounding"—the confusion of reason in the Garden of Eden that led to human damnation and the loss of Paradise in the first place—Cecilia makes herself a physical battleground, a stage upon which to display God's power. Her body itself is like the saint's "lyf" about her, the demonstrable text of an inviolable Christian power.

Cecilia's desire to confront and herself confound the worldly desires normally ascribed to young lovers is constrained and translated by her private song. This saint, associated with divine music, is married in customary Roman fashion but sings privately, erotically, in her heart "to God allone." Like the hair shirt under her wedding clothes, this private song makes Cecilia's wedding into something more than a civil union with Valerian, and perhaps even more than a mere opposition between the two events might suggest. Instead of excluding him from her private union with God, Cecilia hopes to make him part of it. The division between public wedding and private commitment to Christ does not divide Cecilia from her husband but connects them intimately in a different way. It is a secret she seductively shares with him. Deploying, rather than denying, the erotic desires of young spouses, the Second Nun describes the wedding night as the revelation of a feminine secret. Her attention to what "ofte is the manere" of newlyweds at night is rather different from the Man of Law's embarrassed claims:

> The nyght cam, and to bedde moste she gon
> With hire housbonde, as ofte is the manere,
> And pryvely to hym she seyde anon,
> "O sweete and wel biloved spouse deere,
> Ther is a conseil, and ye wolde it heere,
> Which that right fayn I wolde unto yow seye,
> So that ye swere ye shul it nat biwreye."
> (8.141–47)

Cecilia couches her "conseil" to her new husband in suggestive language, piquing his interest (and ours)—"and ye wolde it heere"—by including him in a private circle. The structure of secrecy itself is enticing. Whispered on their wedding night, Cecilia's "conseil" suggests a new intimacy between the couple that both titillates (she "fayn" would tell him) and threatens (he might "biwreye" her). Trusting him not to betray her, this confidence game works to co-opt his participation from the start. But what secret knowledge does Cecilia possess? Given that carnal knowledge is precisely what Cecilia is supposed *not* to have, this bridal secret she hopes to share with Valerian appears dangerously suggestive.

That danger is magnified when Valerian hears the secret: that an angel loves Cecilia and preserves her chastity by "keeping" her body for himself. This new husband is taken momentarily aback, "corrected as God wolde" (8.162), but not without skepticism about what she has revealed to him and the possible double meanings of "keep," a sense of preservation, as in the Physician's Tale, that also suggests sexual possession. Valerian answers cautiously:

> If I shal trusten thee,
> Lat me that aungel se and hym biholde;
> And if that it a verray angel bee,
> Thanne will I doon as thou hast preyed me;
> And if thou love another man, for sothe,
> Right with this swerd thanne wol I sle yow bothe.
> (8.163–68)

Valerian's extremely human response to the extraordinary situation reveals the tale's investment in and dependence on desire as it rescripts its terms and values. Valerian's suspicion of such figures that appear to supposedly innocent young women (as dramatized in songs like *Angelus ad virginem*) aligns his thought with the strategies of the clever Nicholas, who plays the visiting angel to the woman of a very different narrative genre. This brief echo of the comic turn invoked by the Miller's fabliau clarifies the erotic energy of the scene. The figures in the story become less distant to us, and the plot less stiff and formulaic precisely through such comedy and the admission of the very human desires it trades upon. Has this young husband married a spoiled virgin, duped by this "angel"—a plot sounding like something from the French fabliaux or farce—or, worse, is she complicit in this plot and thus attempting to dupe him? Forestalling Valerian's nuptial desires with talk of this angel's "greet love . . . my body for to kepe" (8.153–54), Cecilia uses the situation's eroticism to convert her husband to a different kind of passion. Pope Urban, to whom Cecilia sends Valerian, describes his transformation before God in terms that express the ardor Valerian must restrain and redirect. Urban celebrates his conversion in prayer to Christ: "For thilke spouse that she took but now / Ful lyk a fiers leoun, she sendeth heere, / As meke as evere was any lomb, to yow!" (8.197–99). The tension generated in Valerian's investigation of Cecilia's secret, acknowledging his threatening demeanor, figures Valerian as a "fiers leoun" before he is transformed to belief and gentle acceptance. Cecilia's ruse has co-opted and converted her husband's nuptial desires to more perfect Christian longing in one fell swoop. She uses, rather than resists, desire's erotic force.

The transformations of desire witnessed in these religious tales do not so much repudiate desire's power as translate it to different terms, sublimating it as Christian ideology. The desire for chastity thus operates in an analogous economy to the desire for more worldly satisfactions. In particular, the religious tales place desire "beyond the pleasure principle," making it look as if they contain little desire at all. But the legend of St. Cecilia actively translates all desires—for marriage, worldly and political power, and even bare life—into another form, making the bodily senses a battleground for the perception of Christian truth. Knowledge of Christ and ignorance of him are both represented in sensory terms. The poem indulges in bodily pleasures, a "soote savour" (8.229), for six stanzas. Understanding and belief appear, literally, in the sensuous image of heavenly flowers, the "Corones two" of roses and lilies Cecilia's angel fetches from paradise, and are thus described in miraculous terms inscribed on the body:

> Ne nevere mo shal they roten bee,
> Ne lese hir soote savour, thrusteth me;
> Ne evere wight shal seen hem with his ye,
> But he be chaast and hate vileyne.
> (8.228–31)

This "soote savour" (8.229; 247) and "sweete smel" (8.251) has extraordinary power in the story and over the body. Valerian returns from Pope Urban to find his young wife "Withinne his chambre with an angel" (8.219) bearing the two floral crowns "Fro paradys . . . broght" (8.227). The flowers are intoxicatingly sweet and invisible to others, and the tale retails their wonder, repeating again and again the transformative effects of this "soote savour." Not only is their sweet scent and sight a physical proof of Valerian's true belief, they are a reward for his speedy conversion, "for thow so soone / Assentedest to good conseil also" (8.233–34). The angel thus rewards him with a boon, and Valerian's wish also confirms his virtue: "I pray yow that my brother may han grace / To know the trouthe, as I do in this place" (8.237–38). Tiburce appears just at that moment, and "withinne his herte he gan to wonder fast" at the overwhelming odor of the flowers he cannot yet see.

When Valerian explains the matter to him, he does so through the language of vision and understanding, the doubled meaning of "seeing," that differentiates natural vision from a deeper understanding and insight. Knowledge of Christ renders those who can merely see with their eyes blind to the truth. Similarly, Cecilia argues with the Roman prefect, Almachius, in terms of the sense of sight that he both possesses and lacks:

> Ther lakketh no thyng to thyne outter yen
> That thou n'art blynd; for thyng that we seen alle
> That it is stoon—that men may wel espyen—
> That ilke stoon a god thow wolt it calle.
> I rede thee, lat thyn hand upon it falle
> And taste it wel, and stoon thou shalt it fynde,
> Syn that thou seest nat with thyne eyen blynde.
> (8.498–504)

Cecilia uses Almachius's "outter yen" and his mere physical sense of sight, "thyng that we seen alle," to prove to him he worships nothing but cold stone. She prods him—"lat thyn hand upon it falle"—as she argues for his blindness to an invisible truth. This use and inversion of the immediacy of sense perception undergirds the tale's metaphysics, in which temporal power and concerns for survival are reshaped and reinterpreted. Cecilia tells Almachius that he has no "power and auctoritee / To maken folk to dyen or to lyven" (8.471–72), as he claims, because he is but a "Ministre of deeth" (8.485), since he has no idea what life is. But Cecilia has described that "bettre lif" to Tiburce earlier in the tale:

> Men myghten dreden wel and skilfully
> This lyf to lese, myn owene deere brother,
> If this were lyvynge oonly and noon oother.
>
> But ther is bettre lif in other place,
> That nevere shal be lost, ne drede thee noght,
> Which Goddes Sone us toold thurgh his grace.
> (8.320–25)

The inversions of worldly value and perception in this story suggest an otherworldly metaphoricity upon which its signifiers trade. Like Cecilia's teaching, the Second Nun's Tale turns the language of this world—power and powerlessness; life, death, pain—against its everyday meaning in order to suggest a different order of being. One set of sense perceptions, seeing and feeling, gives way to another kind of knowledge and proof. But they are not merely oppositions in which one "scene" completely displaces the other; they are mutually independent. In denying earthly senses (sights, sounds, smells) for another order, the tale uses the very sensory excitements it repudiates: the sweet savor of floral scents, the smooth cold stone of chiseled idols. Thus Almachius's frustration at having every word of his own turned against him by Cecilia's faith in this other order and every action against her into a scene of the spiritual conversion of others. Cecilia dramatizes and produces a continual scene of misreading through desire's linguistic disfigurations.

The figure of Almachius as a mere "Ministre of deeth" is a striking one, not only for its appearance in the Second Nun's Tale but for the way it resonates for a number of religious stories in which virtuous feminine figures openly court death. Neither Constance nor Griselda blanch in the face of death (they merely weep for their children). We watch the Prioress's clergeon walk through "a Jewerye" singing his song "in . . . despit," openly (if unknowingly) inspiring his own destruction (7.489; 563). The Physician's Tale presents a story that clearly prefers, like the Franklin's Dorigen, death to dishonor and revels in it by extending its scene of sacrifice. In different ways and to different effects these stories defy the assumptions of the preservative life instincts celebrated in other tales and instead seek the destructivity they would avoid. The perversion of the life instinct in the religious tales thus exhibits the (il)logic of what Freud called the death drive and its fundamental aggressivity that seems so alien to the self-preservative and pleasure-seeking instincts we intuitively comprehend and a storytelling contest, undertaken for "confort" and "myrthe," validates.[51] Trying to understand the religious stories in the *Canterbury Tales* is thus like trying to understand the logic of the death drive in the psychic scenario. It appears at the surface illogical or at least antithetical to what has gone

---

51. R. Michael Haines argues that the theme uniting the Physician's Tale and the Pardoner's Tale is death in "Fortune, Nature, and Grace in Fragment C," *Chaucer Review* 10 (1976): 220–35. Marc Pelen argues for another relation to death in "the opposition of murder and immortality to their sacramental analogues of contrition and the Redemption [a]s the major theme" of this fragment in "Murder and Immortality in Fragment VI (C) of the *Canterbury Tales*: Chaucer's Transformation of Theme and Image from the *Roman de la Rose*," *Chaucer Review* 29 (1994): 1–25, at 16.

before, an entirely counterintuitive force that contradicts basic instincts of self-preservation and, by analogy, narrative continuation.

In Freud's writing, the death drive is what operates "beyond the pleasure principle," a point at which the religious tales appear to be located. We may intuitively think humans act to make themselves happy but experience shows that they do not: they defer present pleasure for a greater one later; they sacrifice their own pleasure for others'; they repeat traumatic events in dreams and neurotic behavior rather than letting it go. Instead of actively pursuing pleasure, they avoid displeasure by moving to decreasing states of psychic excitement. This is the logic Freud found at work beyond the principles of human happiness that could ultimately be located in the drive to the quiescence of inanimacy. Life then could be redefined as an elaborate mystification of the process of avoiding or delaying an inevitable obedience to this primal impulse.

In his return to Freud, Lacan revises and radically rereads the death drive in terms of the ego rather than the organism itself. In Richard Boothby's words, "the death drive has its origin in the tension between the imaginary ego and the real of the body that is only partly encompassed by the ego . . . for Lacan, the traumatic force of the death drive aims not at the biological organism but at the unity of the ego," or the fiction of sovereignty, as we have called it earlier. [52] The death drive stages a confrontation, then, between human psychic and emotional organization, our consciousness of ourselves, and our creaturely form. Since all desire is the desire for an impossible duality, a return to a state of things "before" (language, socialization, separation—all the forms of law we define as human and the "manere necessaries" they come with), the death drive as Lacan reads it is, in effect, "a mythical expression of pure desire," a loosening and dissolution of the constraints, identifications, and alienations the ego is predicated upon (Boothby 70). The death drive is thus the return of the Real "refused by its [the ego's] imaginary unity" (Boothby 144). As a symptom of a desire for the state of things before the advent of the cohering ego, the death drive depends on a rethinking of psychic development and its organizations implicit in these comments. In many narratives of the self, the ego, we implicitly begin *ex nihilo,* either developing existence out of nothing

---

52. Richard Boothby, *Death and Desire: Psychoanalytic Theory in Lacan's Return to Freud* (New York: Routledge, 1991), 71. Boothby explores Freud's theory of the death drive (as well as Lacan's further appropriation of it) to explain just these counterintuitivities in psychic organization, which we can here apply to narrative organization. The death drive challenges our basic assumptions, leading us to interrogate them further, and thus reads as the "unconscious" of psychoanalytic theory. It is the central negativity on which psychic organization depends.

or coming to the awareness of existence as a slow accumulation of sensory perceptions—what is, essentially, another building of something out of nothing. Lacan reformulates this model, decentering the ego (and rendering it different from the self) by beginning with the overwhelming Real: the everything of and connectivity to the whole of the world in which the infant is situated from its time in the womb. The world is not something slowly encountered, learned, and gained but an entirety *lost,* from which one has to be separated and individuated. This fundamental loss marks the subject forever and places it in various forms of alienation and imaginary being. Biology and its dependencies situate us in what becomes an imaginary set of relations as we struggle with the loss of Real.

This definition is consonant with (but not identical to) medieval conceptions of a primary human state of loss in original sin, which also accepts death as the final aim of life. In both religious and psychoanalytic frameworks, we are called upon to understand a largely counterintuitive logic that reverses the meanings of terms as they are normally given. This reversal and manipulation of terms places us firmly in Lacan's Symbolic: the realm of linguistic signification. Whether Lacanian theory or literary texts, the movement of the signifier remains our primary focus. The essence of imaginary and symbolic relations, those structures superimposed over the Real, is conflict. For Augustine, like Freud, life "must be regarded as only a circuitous route to death," an idea that installs conflict (and mostly self-conflict) at the heart of the psychic and moral process and (since the time of the Fall) tells us from where the guilt mechanism arises. Boothby writes, "Desire originates from a primordial lack, a hole or gap, a manqué-à-être (lack, or want, of being). In the captures of the imaginary, 'desire is essentially a negativity' [S.1.147]. The function of the symbolic is to give this negativity a name" (108). Thus, while Lacan's psychoanalysis figures three interconnected dimensions of Imaginary, Symbolic, and Real, they are known and expressed only through the linguistic power of the Symbolic. Language, even, and especially, when it fails, remains our central key to understanding anything of the Real and the Imaginary.[53] The death drive seems as if it would end everything, all striving, all conflict, all maintenance, so as to be overwhelmed by the Real's *jouissance*—the ecstasy of the martyr's triumphant death—and yet we are given access to this only in language: "The function of language appears in the role of a liberating influence, which opens up the possibility of testing a foreclosed and forbidden *jouissance*"

---

53. "Excluded and alienated by the imaginary, desire is retrievable in some measure through the power of language" (Boothby, *Death and Desire,* 109).

(Boothby 110). By contrast, the Symbolic's power lies in its "capacity to pass beyond the alienation of the [I]maginary and to represent the [R]eal. The [S]ymbolic functions to give desire a name in the sense of lending form to an inarticulate dimension beyond the ego" (Boothby 111). But the death drive also propels us *to* life in a fight against its principles; no one merely gives up the will to live and acquiesces to the death drive without pressure to do so (illness, neurosis, age). Similarly, for medieval Christians death may be "an ende of every worldly soore" (1.2849), but that truth does not enjoin (or even allow) believers to seek death by direct means. Suicide, as well as the despair that precedes it, is a grave mortal sin. The Pardoner's Tale dramatizes these ideas in terms of both the spiritual despair driving his compulsive story and the three blasphemous rioters in it, who venture out in absurdly literalistic fashion to seek and slay Death.

Translating its terms to narrative, the death drive sits behind the odd but compelling power of the religious tales, even our difficulties assimilating them to the collection as a whole. For they too challenge our basic assumptions about narrative, asking us to interrogate them further, and to see them as a kind of unconscious discourse to the *Canterbury Tales* and certainly of its critical tradition. But what if we continue the analogy, and see them as the central negativity on which the storytelling contest depends? Are these tales limits to the contest, threats to its continuation, as each seeks to violate the means by which we could render judgment? The unfinished nature of Chaucer's collection has long provoked us. The General Prologue promises a return journey and a scene of concluding judgment—Harry Bailly's at least. We think that we want to know which story wins the contest. But every idealization (or brilliant critique) that each tale tenders is negated and undone by another in an exchange that we can only call a scene of intelligent misreading.[54] Each tale metaphorically perpetuates life by killing (refuting, distorting, improvising upon) the last one. Exalting death, the religious tales reveal what each story has been about all along, despite whatever extravagant celebrations of living they seem to offer: the silent end of the contest we are at pains to avert.

Perhaps the most important thing about the death drive, particularly for these tales, is its location of aggression. Reorienting human aggression toward others, the death drive articulates this hostility as a manifestation of a more primal aggression toward oneself. In the religious stories, the characters' "drive" to death appears as the same kind of counterintuitive

---

54. And, in fact, the contest has already been judged. As intimated in chapter 1, we already know the Host will award the prize to the Knight.

pulsion. Whether by superior knowledge (like Cecilia's) or innocent ignorance (like the Prioress's clergeon's), the protagonists actively seek their own violent ends. In their pursuits, these stories transform punishment into reward, pain into enjoyment. As Sarah Kay notes of the martyrologies, these tales sublime the violence they describe and elicit: "the sublime results from lethal destructiveness, and yet it also blocks out the reality of death, translating its horror into" the martyr's glory.[55] They amount to a rejection of the passions and vicissitudes of the living, the untruths of the pagans, Muslims, and Jews otherwise occupying these stories. But such a move merely reinscribes desire in yet another form, as the desire to renounce desire.

This explanatory narrative too works beyond the pleasure principle, a problematic formulation for a tale in a storytelling contest founded on the relation of "sentence" to "solaas." If we are to get beyond pleasure, in fact, to indulge obscenely in unpleasure in the religious tales, then we need to learn to speak about their enjoyments in different terms. In opposition to mere pleasure Lacan posits a particular kind of enjoyment, *jouissance,* a form of supreme unpleasurable pleasure that momentarily brings the entire system to a standstill by dissolving the very structures that maintain it in the emergence of the Real, all that is unrepresentable by symbolic (i.e., linguistic) systems. Such dissolution appears to be what the religious taletellers are after: these stories and their spectacular sublimations are designed to bring the contest to some explosive, even orgasmic, end. When we talk about "transcendence" in the religious stories, we talk about the same kind of obviation of language and the obliterating return of the Real in somewhat "safer" ways, which do not have to acknowledge but clearly depend upon the pleasures of the process of transcendence—what in the *Canterbury Tales* could amount to the inability of another story to follow from the one at hand.

Recently, the concept of the death drive has been elaborated by Mark Miller to help us read the aristocratic valuations of *Sir Gawain and the Green Knight,* particularly its fascination with and investment in violence and dismemberment in its cultural rituals and pastimes. He makes a compelling point about the interpretive foreclosures of moralization that I find relevant to the works under discussion here:

> Where discussions of Gawain's sinfulness go awry, then, is not in overvaluing the religious and theological discourses of sin, but in restricting

---

55. Kay, "Sublime Body of the Martyr," 7.

the scope of an interest in the topic to questions of moral evaluation. The poet's interest in sin . . . is analytical and phenomenological rather than moralistic. He is interested in exploring, in quite different but complementary ways, the condition of a creature in love with strife and loss, a creature for whom the very condition of being animate is a stain.⁵⁶

Moralization has similarly foreclosed the religious tales and disabled them from playing the Canterbury game. Once the moral of the story is detected, all discussion of the tale stops, as if to interrogate the story is to question the validity of its moral terms, which is why labeling the religious tales as such once seemed to do all the interpretive work that was needed. And yet, the Pardoner dramatizes the question alive here in its most arresting form: "For though myself be a ful vicious man, / A moral tale yet I yow telle kan" (6.459–60). He repeats his moral often and in advance, "*Radix malorum est Cupiditas*" (6.334). It is the very logic of his story of the three rioters whose greed causes their death, as well as the subject he knows best, as he openly presents himself as its example in competition with the exemplum of the three rioters he tells. The Pardoner works for purely avaricious ends with no care as to the condition or fate of the people who buy his pardons and relics. As many readers have asked before, does the meaning of the Pardoner's story—its knowledge that such sinful avarice directly leads to the death sought all along—invalidate the "honest[y]" (6.328) of his discourse? Given all that he has admitted, can the tale "know" that Christ's pardon "is best" (6.918)? The Pardoner may thus offer the most perfect expression of the paradox of moral understanding, but Chaucer renders this difficulty of moralization throughout the collection. We have seen it before in the Clerk's anxious allegorization and de-allegorization at the close of his tale. But there are a number of other places where morals are rendered in problematic fashion, disrupting or falsifying the narrative to which they are attached. The Physician's moral about the need to forsake sin is one, but the Friar's awkwardly imposed moral, "the leoun sit in his awayt alwey / To sle the innocent, if that he may," also misunderstands its tale (3.1657–58).⁵⁷ The death drive, as a form of desire, gives a motor to what seems like the alternate aims of the religious tales: to depict the suffering endurance deprioritizing the desires of ideal individuals.

---

56. Mark Miller, "The Ends of Excitement in *Sir Gawain and the Green Knight*: Teleology, Ethics, and the Death Drive," *SAC* 32 (2010): 215–56, at 254.

57. To which we might add the proliferation of morals in the Nun's Priest's Tale, which threaten to dissolve the very possibility of taking the fruit from the chaff, as well as the Manciple's awkward rendering of the morals inside and at the end of his Ovidian fable.

The religious tales argue for transcendence, as Barbara Nolan has shown.[58] These tales illustrate the transcendence of earthly life and in many ways seem to themselves transcend the worldly interests of the storytelling contest. But responses to these tales must ultimately do so in verbal terms. Even the Parson's Tale prompts a retraction in language, and it has been by no means unambiguously understood.[59] In Chaucer's *Canterbury Tales*, this desire for transcendence, which can itself be read as an aggressive gesture toward the contest and its judgments, is often met with misrecognition and thus misreading. The ending of the Clerk's Tale offers a good case in point. We have seen how the Clerk recoils from his own desire in proffering the story of Griselda, but what about his audience, those he directs to read the story as allegory rather than instruction?

> This storie is seyd nat for that wyves sholde
> Folwen Grisilde as in humylitee,
> For it were inportable, though they wolde,
> But for that every wight, in his degree,
> Sholde be constant in adversitee
> As was Grisilde; therfore Petrak writeth
> This storie, which with heigh stile he enditeth.
> (4.1142–48)

Where the Clerk claims to translate this story from Latin and Petrarch's "heigh stile" (4.41), he must also translate it further for his audience. Griselda's patience with the impossible Walter ought to make us "Receyven al in gree that God us sent" (4.1151) precisely because he is no curious husband whose desires are inscrutable. Griselda's behavior is thus admittedly insupportable, whereas our experiences, the "sharpe scourges of adversitee," merely exercise us (4.1156–57). In many ways the Clerk obviates his tale as part of its meaning. Griselda is irrelevant to us because Walter is no model for God. This is a story in excess and in extremis, unfit to tell us anything about life in its everyday particulars. Only its shape has meaning.

And yet, this unfitting way is precisely how it is read. Whether in the potentially cancelled endlink containing Harry Bailly's response (4.1212A–D) or in the Merchant's Tale itself, the Clerk's Tale (somewhat hilariously, given the Clerk's hermeneutic care) is misread as a wife's story. As such, it

---

58. Barbara Nolan, "Chaucer's Tales of Transcendence: Rhyme Royal and Christian Prayer in the *Canterbury Tales*," in Benson and Robertson, 21–38.

59. Patricia Clare Ingham reads the Retraction in terms of disavowal in "Psychoanalytic Criticism" in *Chaucer: An Oxford Guide*, ed. Steve Ellis (Oxford: Oxford UP, 2005), 461–78.

provokes Harry to mention his own wife: "By Goddes bones, / Me were levere than a barel ale / My wyf at hoom had herd this legende ones!" (4.1212B–D). This additional stanza is marked in the standardizing *Riverside* "[The following stanza appears after the Envoy in most of the manuscripts that preserve it]," but it is difficult to know if it "belongs" here. Harry Bailly has made similar comments after the Tale of Melibee in what is now the Prologue to the Monk's Tale (7.1891–94), which he embellishes with even more domestic detail about his wife's aggressive behavior. Because the short stanza following the Clerk's Envoy sounds similar to these remarks in the Monk's Prologue, editors have conjectured that the lines following the Clerk's Tale were likely meant for cancelation.[60] Additionally, they also echo (perhaps too repetitively) the sentiments of the Merchant, who begins his own story in direct quotation of the Clerk's Envoy and its high-pitched and exasperated advice to "archewyves" like the Wife of Bath (4.1195). The textual rationale pretends to be reading what is a dramatically performed misreading.

The Clerk may be at wits' end as he enjoins wives to make such husbands as Walter "care, and wepe, and wrynge, and waille!" (4.1212). But the Merchant knows about this situation firsthand:

"Wepyng and waylyng, care and oother sorwe
I knowe ynogh, on even and a-morwe,"
Quod the Marchant, "and so doon other mo
That wedded been."
(4.1213–16)

If Chaucer intended to cancel Bailly's response, it seems he did so because the Merchant's version more effectively misreads and misapplies the lesson learned from the Clerk's Tale (and, as a bonus, insults the Wife of Bath because it misreads her Prologue and Tale as well), generating yet another story in response to the desire it betrays. Even where a narrator like the learned Clerk explicitly directs the reading of a story with a spiritual (rather than worldly) significance and clarifies its religious message, Chaucer can offer no guarantee as to how it will be taken. Provoking the Merchant's fabliau—yet another tale probing the self-duping nature of human desire in its conclusion—can hardly have been what the Clerk's meant.[61] In this

---

60. John Matthews Manly and Edith Rickert, eds., *The Text of the Canterbury Tales, Studied on the Basis of All-Known Manuscripts*, 8 vols. (Chicago: U of Chicago P, 1940), 2:422–23.

61. For a recent contribution on the ways the Merchant's Tale speaks about desire, see R. Jacob McDonie, "'Ye Gete Namoore of Me': Narrative, Textual, and Linguistic Desires in Chaucer's *Merchant's Tale*," *Exemplaria* 24 (2012): 313–41.

way the religious tales are much like Chaucer's others, a set of stories as woefully misread, and sometimes resisted, as the rest. The quiet that they sometimes generate or the break that appears after them do not signal the success of their transcendence so much as the misrecognition characterizing the interpretive process throughout the poem more generally. In their disfiguring representation of desire they participate more fully in the complex narrative of the *Canterbury Tales* and engage with, rather than turn away from, the issues and terms of the rest of Chaucer's collection.

conclusion

READING AND MISREADING CHAUCER

Calling the *Canterbury Tales* a discourse of desire is a tricky business. To label the poem this way is at once a complex formulation and something as simple as saying the tales are intensely interested in and self-conscious about language. At one point, this book was merely an essay on the Franklin's Tale as the beginning of a language or "entente" group in the *Canterbury Tales*. But as I sought to understand the relation of "entente" and words "in pleye" in fragment 6, I found the issue already active well before the Franklin got hold of it. All of Chaucer's tales are about language in different ways: the courtly prayers to the gods in the Knight's Tale, the terms of poetic justice in the Miller's and Reeve's Tales, the binding oaths and intentions of the Friar's Tale—not to mention the "principal entente" of the Pardoner's story (6.432). Chaucer was deeply concerned with the interplay of the figurative and the literal, the play of the signifier, for his entire career.

Recognizing the ways Chaucer uses language for and against a tale's purposes has forced me to rethink the introduction of the Canterbury pilgrims as narrators and how we understand their role in the tale-telling game. They are a notoriously difficult group to discuss. Whenever we begin talking about the pilgrims (indeed whenever we have to use the titles of their stories, all of which bear their names), we get caught up in the question of priority: the pilgrims or the tales? Which creates which? The tales create the pilgrims for us and give us the illusion of a speaking "voice," yet the tales bear the names of the pilgrims in advance of their telling. And while the General Prologue portraits may be creations of another order (estates satire, rogues gallery, iconography, physiognomy, observation, etc.), they tend to elicit expectations for what that name suggests. The tales, then, are situated as divided subjects burdened by the signifier in advance of what they say.

But the problem appears in what we say: it is nearly impossible to talk about the tales without also talking about the pilgrims and imputing to them intentions, if for nothing other than obedience to the game. But the minute we start talking about the Man of Law and what he does or presents in the Man of Law's Tale, we have begun thinking of the tale as the intended/presented discourse of the Man of Law and giving that agency credit for what is different from what has come before. This is partially an effect of the tales' titles and their connection to the fiction of different speakers (and thus what allows Chaucer to fake his irresponsibility for anything indecorous that they say). It is also a reflex of interpretive sophistication; we assure our audience that we are not merely imputing everything unproblematically to Chaucer's intentions. But it is also, I want to suggest, what happens when they are put into a sequence, even an incomplete and fragmented one. I have tried to work against and around the problem by alternately assigning Chaucer responsibility for whatever connections are produced in the way tales pick up the signifiers in other stories. The more general Lacanian framework for reading the tales in terms of the circulation of the signifier—and thus giving the signifier agency—also helps alleviate the problem of treating the pilgrims like they are real people.

We have long been on the lookout for the ways the tales are related to each other as variations on plots, genres, and conventions. The models used to understand those relations have produced compelling readings of the poem, especially its most well-known parts. My goal in treating desire as the subject and mobile force behind the substitutive logic of the competitive tale collection has been to find a way to talk about those well-known stories and those less easily assimilated ones—the points at which a tale would seem to take off from the rest and do something entirely unconnected and different. Chaucer was always a genre-bending writer who invoked and exploded literary convention in the process of imagining his stories. He rarely simply uses a genre; more often, he remakes it, even when introducing it to his medieval English audience. In doing so, Chaucer identifies problems in genres we did not know they had, revealing how they work and work upon us. He often makes what is familiar—romance, exemplum, satire—different from itself with its very conventionality. Trying to read the tales in order to discover a particular interpretive paradigm or set of themes has not led to entirely satisfying results. Much has been left out, which is unsurprising for a tale collection that is clearly incomplete. We have instead looked toward less restrictive models: the miscellany, the collection, figures that replicate the manuscript context in which the poem was conceived and promulgated. These are helpful models and are certainly capacious, but they locate agency outside of the poem when Chaucer has worked hard to dramatize its engine from within and to show the productivity of the failures of any "fynal answere" (5.987) on a variety of fronts. Hence my turn from models of reading to misreading as a way to talk about that productive force.

Part of the attraction of desire and misreading as a heuristic for Chaucer's poem lies with us, as well as the fictions of the poem itself. We have desires on the *Canterbury Tales*, which the poem and its stories engage, and they arise in our readings—our productive critical misreadings—of Chaucer's poem. Rather than standing above and firmly outside of Chaucer's fiction, then, we have been caught up in its productive manner of producing more stories about and from the *Canterbury Tales* for a very long time.

bibliography

Aers, David and Lynn Staley. *The Powers of the Holy: Religion, Politics, and Gender in Late Medieval English Culture.* University Park: Pennsylvania State UP, 1996.

Alford, John A. "The Wife of Bath versus the Clerk of Oxford: What Their Rivalry Means." *Chaucer Review* 21 (1986): 108–32.

Allen, Elizabeth. *False Fables and Exemplary Truth in Later Middle English Literature.* New York: Palgrave Macmillan, 2005.

Amtower, Laurel. "Mimetic Desire and the Misappropriation of the Ideal in the *Knight's Tale.*" *Exemplaria* 8 (1996): 125–44.

Axelrod, Steven. "The Wife of Bath and the Clerk." *Annuale Mediaevale* 15 (1974): 109–24.

Beidler, Peter, ed. *Masculinities in Chaucer: Approaches to Maleness in the "Canterbury Tales" and "Troilus and Criseyde."* Cambridge: Brewer, 1998.

Benson, C. David. *Chaucer's Drama of Style: Poetic Variety and Contrast in the "Canterbury Tales."* Chapel Hill: U of North Carolina P, 1986.

Benson, C. David and Elizabeth Robertson, eds. *Chaucer's Religious Tales.* Cambridge: Brewer, 1990.

Benson, Larry D., gen. ed. *The Canterbury Tales, Complete.* Based on *The Riverside Chaucer* (1987). Boston: Houghton Mifflin, 2000.

Bloch, R. Howard. "Chaucer's Maiden's Head: 'The Physician's Tale' and the Poetics of Virginity." *Representations* 28 (1989): 113–34.

———. *The Scandal of the Fabliaux.* Chicago: U of Chicago P, 1986.

Boccaccio, Giovanni. *The Book of Theseus.* Trans. Bernadette McCoy. New York: Medieval Text Association, 1974.

———. *Decameron.* Ed. Vittore Branca. 6th ed. Torino: Einaudi, 1991.

———. *The Decameron.* Trans. Mark Musa and Peter Bondanella. Harmondsworth: Penguin, 1982.

Boitani, Piero. "Style, Iconography and Narrative: The Lesson of the *Teseida*." In Boitani, 185–99.

———, ed. *Chaucer and the Italian Trecento*. Cambridge: Cambridge UP, 1983.

Boothby, Richard. *Death and Desire: Psychoanalytic Theory in Lacan's Return to Freud*. New York: Routledge, 1991.

Bowers, John. "Three Readings of *The Knight's Tale*: Sir John Clanvowe, Geoffrey Chaucer, and James I of Scotland." *Journal of Medieval and Early Modern Studies* 34 (2004): 279–307.

Brinkman, Baba. "Wrestling for the Ram: Competition and Feedback in *Sir Thopas* and *The Canterbury Tales*." *LATCH* 3 (2010): 107–33.

Brooks, Harold. *Chaucer's Pilgrims: The Artistic Order of the Portraits in the Prologue*. New York: Barnes and Noble, 1962.

Brooks, Peter. *Reading for the Plot: Design and Intention in Narrative*. New York: Vintage, 1983.

Brown, Peter. *Chaucer at Work: The Making of the "Canterbury Tales."* London and New York: Longman, 1994.

Brown, William H. "Chaucer, Livy, and Bersuire: The Roman Materials in *The Physician's Tale*." In Duncan-Rose and Vennemann, 39–51.

Bullough, Vern. "Sex in History: A Redux." In Murray and Eisenbichler, 3–22.

Burlin, Robert. *Chaucerian Fiction*. Princeton: Princeton UP, 1977.

Burrow, J. A. "The *Canterbury Tales* I: Romance." In Mann and Boitani, 143–59.

Butler, Judith. *Subjects of Desire: Hegelian Reflections in Twentieth-Century France*. New York: Columbia UP, 1987. Rpt.1999.

Carella, Bryan. "The Social Aspirations and Priestly Pretense of Chaucer's Reeve." *Neophilologus* 94 (2010): 523–29.

Carlson, David. *Chaucer's Jobs*. New York: Palgrave Macmillan, 2004.

Carruthers, Mary. "The Wife of Bath and the Painting of Lions." *PMLA* 94 (1979): 209–22.

Chaucer, Geoffrey. *The Canterbury Tales: Complete*. Ed. Larry D. Benson. Boston: Houghton Mifflin, 2000.

The Chester Mystery Cycle. Ed. R.M. Lumiansky and David Mills. 2 vols. Early English Text Society SS 3. Oxford: Oxford UP, 1974.

Chickering, Howell. "Form and Interpretation in the *Envoy* to the *Clerk's Tale*." *Chaucer Review* 29 (1995): 352–72.

Coletti, Theresa. "Purity and Danger: The Paradox of Mary's Body and the En-gendering of the Infancy Narrative in the English Mystery Cycles." In Lomperis and Stanbury, 65–95.

Cooper, Helen. *Oxford Guides to Chaucer: The Canterbury Tales*. Oxford: Oxford UP, 1986.

———. *The Structure of the "Canterbury Tales."* London: Duckworth, 1984.

Corsa, Helen Storm, ed. *A Variorum Edition to the Works of Geoffrey Chaucer. Volume II: The Canterbury Tales. Part 17: The Physician's Tale*. Norman, OK: Pilgrim, 1987.

Cowell, Andrew. *At Play in the Tavern: Signs, Coins and Bodies in the Middle Ages*. Ann Arbor: U of Michigan P, 1999.

Cowgill, Bruce Kent. "Clerkly Rivalry in the Reeve's Tale." In Fein, Raybin, and Braeger, 59–71.

Crane, Susan. *Gender and Romance in Chaucer's "Canterbury Tales."* Princeton: Princeton UP, 1994.

Cunningham, J. V. "The Literary Form of the Prologue to the *Canterbury Tales*." *Modern Philology* 49 (1952): 172–81.

Dane, Joseph. "The Wife of Bath's Shipman's Tale and the Invention of Chaucerian Fabliaux." *Modern Language Review* 99 (2004): 287–300.

David, Alfred. *The Strumpet Muse: Art and Morals in Chaucer's Poetry.* Bloomington: Indiana UP, 1976.

Dean, James. "Dismantling the Canterbury Book." *PMLA* 100 (1985): 746–62.

Delany, Sheila. "Politics and the Paralysis of Poetic Imagination in *The Physician's Tale*." *SAC* 3 (1981): 47–60.

Denny-Brown, Andrea. "*Povre* Griselda and the All-Consuming *Archewyves*." *SAC* 28 (2006): 77–115.

Derrida, Jacques. "Différance." In *The Margins of Philosophy.* Trans. Alan Bass. Chicago: U of Chicago P, 1984. 1–28.

Desmond, Marilynn. *Ovid's Art and The Wife of Bath: The Ethics of Erotic Violence.* Ithaca: Cornell UP, 2006.

DeWeever, Jacqueline, ed. *The Chaucer Name Dictionary.* New York: Garland, 1987.

Dinshaw, Carolyn. *Chaucer's Sexual Poetics.* Madison: U of Wisconsin P, 1989.

Donaldson, E. Talbot. *Chaucer's Poetry: An Anthology for the Modern Reader.* Second Edition. New York: Harper Collins, 1975.

Dubin, Nathaniel, trans. *The Fabliaux.* Introd. R. Howard Bloch. New York: Liveright, 2013.

Duncan-Rose, Caroline and Theo Vennemann, eds. *On Language: Rhetorica, Phonologica, Syntactica.* New York: Routledge, 1988.

Edmondson, George. "Naked Chaucer." In Scala and Federico, 139–60.

Edwards, Elizabeth. "The *Knight's Tale* and the Work of Mourning." *Exemplaria* 20 (2008): 361–84.

Edwards, Robert. *The Flight from Desire: Augustine and Ovid to Chaucer.* New York: Palgrave Macmillan, 2006.

Ellis, Steve, ed. *Chaucer: An Oxford Guide.* Oxford: Oxford UP, 2005.

Epstein, Robert. "'Fer in the north, I kan nat telle where': Dialect, Regionalism, and Philologism." *SAC* 30 (2008): 95–124.

Evans, Dylan. *An Introductory Dictionary of Lacanian Psychoanalysis.* London and New York: Routledge, 1996.

Evans, Ruth and Lesley Johnson, eds. *Feminist Readings in Middle English Literature: The Wife of Bath and All Her Sect.* London: Routledge, 1994.

Everest, Carol. "Sex and Old Age in Chaucer's *Reeve's Prologue*." *Chaucer Review* 31 (1996): 99–114.

Fairchild, Hoxie. "Active Arcite, Contemplative Palamon." *JEGP* 26 (1927): 285–93.

Farrell, Thomas J. "The 'Envoy de Chaucer' and the *Clerk's Tale*." *Chaucer Review* 24 (1990): 329–36.

Fein, Susanna Greer. "'Lat the Children Pleye': The Game Betwixt the Ages in The Reeve's Tale." In Fein, Raybin, and Braeger, 73–104.

Fein, Susanna Greer, David Raybin, and Peter C. Braeger, eds. *Rebels and Rivals: The Contestive Spirit in "The Canterbury Tales."* Kalamazoo: Medieval Institute, 1991.

Feldharr, Andrew. *Spectacle and Society in Livy's History.* Berkeley: U of California P, 1988

Feldstein, Richard, Bruce Fink, and Maire Jaanus, eds. *Reading Seminars I and II: Lacan's Return to Freud.* Buffalo: State U of New York P, 1996.

Ferster, Judith. *Chaucer on Interpretation.* Cambridge: Cambridge UP, 1985.

Fink, Bruce. *Lacan to the Letter: Reading "Écrits" Closely.* Minneapolis: U of Minnesota P, 2004.

Finlayson, John. "The *Knight's Tale*: The Dialogue of Romance, Epic, and Philosophy." *Chaucer Review* 27 (1992): 126–49.

Finnegan, Robert Emmett. "'She Should Have Said No to Walter': Griselda's Promise in *The Clerk's Tale*." *English Studies* 75 (1994): 303–21.

Fletcher, Alan J. "Chaucer's Norfolk Reeve." *Medium Aevum* 52 (1983): 100–103.

Fletcher, Angus. "The Sentencing of Virginia in the *Physician's Tale*." *Chaucer Review* 34 (2000): 300–308.

Fletcher, John and William Shakespeare. *The Two Noble Kinsmen.* 3rd ed. Ed. Lois Potter. Surrey: Arden Shakespeare, 1997.

Fowler, Elizabeth. "The Afterlife of the Civil Dead: Conquest in the Knight's Tale." In Stillinger, 59–81.

Fradenburg, L. O. Aranye. *City, Marriage, Tournament: Arts of Rule in Late Medieval Scotland.* Madison: U Wisconsin P, 1991.

———. *Sacrifice Your Love: Psychoanalysis, Historicism, Chaucer.* Minnesota: U Minnesota P, 2002.

———. "Sacrificial Desire in Chaucer's *Knight's Tale*." *Journal of Medieval and Early Modern Studies* 27 (1997): 47–75.

———. "Simply Marvelous." *SAC* 26 (2004): 1–27.

———. "The Wife of Bath's Passing Fancy." *SAC* 8 (1986): 31–58.

Freud, Sigmund. *The Complete Psychological Works of Sigmund Freud.* Ed. and trans. James Strachey. 24 volumes. London: Hogarth P, 1958,

Ganim, John. "Chaucerian Ritual and Patriarchal Performance." *Chaucer Yearbook* 1 (1992): 65–86.

———. *Chaucerian Theatricality.* Princeton: Princeton UP, 1990.

———. "Identity and Subjecthood." In Ellis, 194–238.

Gaunt, Simon. *Gender and Genre in Medieval French Literature.* Cambridge: Cambridge UP, 1995.

Gaunt, Simon and Sarah Kay, eds. *The Troubadours: An Introduction.* Cambridge: Cambridge UP, 1999.

Georgianna, Linda. "The Clerk's Tale and the Grammar of Assent." *Speculum* 70 (1995): 793–821.

———. "Love So Dearly Bought: The Terms of Redemption in *The Canterbury Tales*." *SAC* 12 (1990): 85–116.

Ginsberg, Warren. "The Lineaments of Desire: Wish-Fulfillment in Chaucer's Marriage Group." *Criticism* 25 (1983): 197–210.

Girard, René. *Deceit, Desire and the Novel: Self and Other in Literary Structure*. Trans. Yvonne Freccero. Baltimore: Johns Hopkins UP, 1965.

Godefroy, Frédéric, ed. *Dictionnaire de la Ancienne Langue Française*. Paris: F. Vieweg, 1883.

Gorton, Kristyn. *Theorising Desire: From Freud to Feminism to Film*. Basingstoke and New York: Palgrave Macmillan, 2008.

Gower, John. *Confessio Amantis*. Ed. Russell Peck. 3 vols. Kalamazoo: Medieval Institute, 2004.

Green, Donald C. "The Semantics of Power: *Maistrie* and *Soveraynetee* in *The Canterbury Tales*." *Modern Philology* 84 (1986): 18–23.

Green, Richard Firth. *Poets and Princepleasers: Literature and the English Court in the Late Middle Ages*. Toronto: U of Toronto P, 1980.

Greenblatt, Stephen. "The Touch of the Real." *Representations* 59 (1997): 14–29.

Guillaume de Lorris and Jean de Meun. *Le Roman de la Rose*. Ed. Felix Lecoy. 3 vols. Paris: Champion, 1965.

———. *The Romance of the Rose*. 3rd ed. Trans. Charles Dahlberg. Princeton: Princeton UP, 1971, 1995.

Gustafsson, Marita, ed. *Essayes and Explorations: A "Freundschrift" for Liisa Dahl*. Turku: Anglicana Turkuensia, 1996.

Haines, R. Michael. "Fortune, Nature, and Grace in Fragment C." *Chaucer Review* 10 (1976): 220–35.

Hammond, Eleanor Prescott. *Chaucer: A Bibliographic Manual*. New York: Macmillan, 1908.

Hanawalt, Barbara. *The Ties That Bound: Peasant Families in Medieval England*. New York: Oxford UP, 1986.

Hanning, Robert. "'The Struggle Between Noble Designs and Chaos': The Literary Tradition of Chaucer's *Knight's Tale*." *The Literary Review* 23 (1980): 519–41.

Hansen, Elaine Tuttle. *Chaucer and the Fictions of Gender*. Berkeley: U of California P, 1992.

Harder, Kelsie. "Chaucer's Use of the Mystery Plays in the *Miller's Tale*." *Modern Language Quarterly* 17 (1956): 193–98.

Harley, Marta Powell. "Last Things First in Chaucer's Physician's Tale: Final Judgment and the Worm of Conscience." *JEGP* 91 (1992): 1–16.

Heffernan, Carol Falvo. "Tyranny and *Commune Profit* in the *Clerk's Tale*." *Chaucer Review* 17 (1983): 332–40.

Heng, Geraldine. *Empire of Magic: Medieval Romance and the Politics of Cultural Fantasy*. New York: Columbia UP, 2001.

Hermann, John. "Dismemberment, Dissemination, Discourse: Sign and Symbol in the *Shipman's Tale*." *Chaucer Review* 19 (1985): 302–37.

Hinton, Norman. "Two Names in *The Reeve's Tale*." *Names* 9 (1961): 117–20.

Hirsch, John C. "Chaucer's Roman Tales." *Chaucer Review* 31 (1996): 45–57.

———. "Modern Times: The Discourse of the *Physician's Tale*." *Chaucer Review* 27 (1993): 387–95.

Hoffman, Arthur. "Chaucer's Prologue to Pilgrimage: The Two Voices." *ELH* 21 (1954): 1–16.

Homer, Sean. *Jacques Lacan*. London: Routledge, 2005.

Howard, Donald. *Chaucer: His Life, His Works, His World.* New York: Dutton, 1987.

———. *The Idea of the "Canterbury Tales."* Berkeley: U of California P, 1976.

Hudson, Anne, ed. *Selections from English Wycliffite Writings.* Oxford: Oxford UP, 1978.

Hunter, Brooke. "*Remenants* of Things Past: Memory and the *Knight's Tale*," *Exemplaria* 23 (2011): 126–46.

Huppé, Bernard. *A Reading of the Canterbury Tales.* Albany: State U of New York P, 1964.

Huth, Jennifer. "'For I have tools to truss': Women in the York Mystery Plays." MA thesis, University of Texas, 1993.

Ingham, Patricia Clare. "Homosociality and Creative Masculinity in the *Knight's Tale.*" In Beidler, 23–35.

———. "Psychoanalytic Criticism." In Ellis, 461–78.

Johnson, Barbara. "The Frame of Reference: Poe, Lacan, Derrida." *The Critical Difference.* Baltimore: Johns Hopkins UP, 1980. 110–46.

———. "Rigorous Undecidability." *A World of Difference.* Baltimore: Johns Hopkins UP, 1987. 17–24.

Johnson, Lesley. "Reincarnations of Griselda: Contexts for the *Clerk's Tale*?" In Evans and Johnson, 195–220.

Johnston, Andrew James. "Wrestling with Ganymede: Chaucer's *Knight's Tale* and the Homoerotics of Epic History." *Germanisch-Romanische Monatsschrift* 50 (2000): 21–43.

Jordan, Robert. *Chaucer's Poetics and the Modern Reader.* Berkeley: U of California P, 1987.

Justice, Steven. "Who Stole Robertson?" *PMLA* 124 (2009): 609–15.

Kaeuper, Richard. *Chivalry and Violence in Medieval Europe.* Oxford: Oxford UP, 1999.

———, ed. *Violence in Medieval Society.* Cambridge: Brewer, 2000.

Karras, Ruth Mazo. *From Boys to Men: Formations of Masculinity in Late Medieval Europe.* Philadelphia: U of Pennsylvania P, 2003.

Kaske, R. E. "An Aube in the *Reeve's Tale.*" *ELH* 26 (1959): 295–310.

———. "The *Canticum Canticorum* in the *Miller's Tale.*" *Studies in Philology* 59 (1962): 479–500.

Kay, Sarah. "Desire and Subjectivity." In Gaunt and Kay, 212–27.

———. "The Sublime Body of the Martyr." In Kaeuper, 3–20.

Kittredge, George Lyman. *Chaucer and His Poetry.* Cambridge: Harvard UP, 1915.

———. "Chaucer's Discussion of Marriage." *Modern Philology* 9 (1912): 435–67.

Kline, Daniel. "Jephthah's Daughter and Chaucer's Virginia: The Critique of Sacrifice in The Physician's Tale." *JEGP* 107 (2008): 77–103.

Knapp, Peggy. *Chaucer and the Social Contest.* New York: Routledge, 1990.

Koeppel, E. "Chauceriana." *Anglia* 14 (1892): 227–67.

Kohanski, Tamara. "In Search of Malyne." *Chaucer Review* 27 (1993): 228–38.

Kolve, V. A. *Chaucer and the Imagery of Narrative.* Stanford: Stanford UP, 1984.

Lacan, Jacques. *Écrits: The First Complete Edition in English.* Trans. Bruce Fink. New York: Norton, 2006.

———. *On Feminine Sexuality, the Limits of Love and Knowledge: The Seminar of Jacques Lacan XX, Encore.* Ed. Jacques-Alain Miller. Trans. Bruce Fink. New York: Norton, 1999.

———. *The Seminar of Jacques Lacan Book II: The Ego in Freud's Theory and in the Technique of Psychoanalysis, 1954–1955.* Ed. Jacques-Alain Miller. Trans. Sylvana Tomaselli. New York: Norton, 1991.

———. *The Seminar of Jacques Lacan Book VII: The Ethics of Psychoanalysis, 1959–60.* Ed. Jacques-Alain Miller. Trans. Dennis Porter. New York: Norton, 1992.

Ladd, Roger. *Antimercantilism in Late Medieval English Literature.* New York: Palgrave Macmillan, 2010.

Langlands, Rebecca. *Sexual Morality in Ancient Rome.* Cambridge: Cambridge UP, 2006.

Laplanche, Jean. *Life and Death in Psychoanalysis.* Trans. Jeffrey Mehlman. Baltimore: Johns Hopkins UP, 1976.

Lavezzo, Kathy. "Beyond Rome: Mapping Gender and Justice in *The Man of Law's Tale.*" *SAC* 24 (2002): 149–80.

Lawton, David. *Chaucer's Narrators.* Cambridge: Brewer, 1985.

———. "Chaucer's Two Ways: The Pilgrimage Frame of *The Canterbury Tales.*" *SAC* 9 (1987): 3–40.

Leicester, H. Marshall. *The Disenchanted Self: Representing the Subject in the "Canterbury Tales."* Berkeley: U of California P, 1991.

Livy. *Ab urbe condita.* Ed. and trans. B. O. Foster. 14 vol. Cambridge: Harvard UP, 1967.

Lochrie, Karma. "Women's 'Pryvetees' and Fabliau Politics in the Miller's Tale." *Exemplaria* 6 (1995): 287–304.

Lomperis, Linda and Sarah Stanbury, eds. *Feminist Approaches to the Body in Medieval Literature.* Philadelphia: U of Pennsylvania P, 1993.

Manly, John Matthews. *Some New Light on Chaucer.* New York: Holt, 1926.

Manly, John Matthews and Edith Rickert, eds. *The Text of the Canterbury Tales, Studied on the Basis of All Known Manuscripts.* 8 vols. Chicago: U of Chicago P, 1940.

Mann, Jill. *Chaucer and Medieval Estates Satire.* Cambridge: Cambridge UP, 1973.

———. *Feminizing Chaucer.* Rev. ed. Cambridge: D. S. Brewer, 2002.

———. *Geoffrey Chaucer.* Atlantic Highlands: Humanities, 1991.

Mann, Jill and Piero Boitani, eds. *The Cambridge Companion to Chaucer.* 2nd ed. Cambridge: Cambridge UP, 2003.

Martin, Loy. "History and Form in the General Prologue to the *Canterbury Tales.*" *ELH* 45 (1978): 1–17.

Matheson, Lister M. "Chaucer's Ancestry: Historical and Philological Re-Assessments." *Chaucer Review* 25 (1991): 171–89.

McClellan, William. "'Ful Pale Face': Agamben's Biopolitical Theory and the Sovereign Subject in Chaucer's *Clerk's Tale.*" *Exemplaria* 17 (2005): 103–34.

McDonie, R. Jacob. "'Ye Gete Namoore of Me': Narrative, Textual, and Linguistic Desires in Chaucer's *Merchant's Tale.*" *Exemplaria* 24 (2012): 313–41.

McTaggart, Anne. *Shame and Guilt in Chaucer.* New York: Palgrave Macmillan, 2012.

Middleton, Anne. "The *Physician's Tale* and Love's Martyrs: 'Ensamples Mo Than Ten' as a Method in the *Canterbury Tales*." *Chaucer Review* 8 (1973): 9–32.

———. "War By Other Means: Marriage and Chivalry in Chaucer." *SAC Proceedings* 2 (1984): 119–33.

Miller, Jacques-Alain. "Introduction to Seminar I and II: Lacan's Orientation Prior to 1953 (I–III)." In Feldstein, Fink, and Jaanus, 3–35.

Miller, Mark. "The Ends of Excitement in *Sir Gawain and the Green Knight:* Teleology, Ethics, and the Death Drive." *SAC* 32 (2010): 215–56.

———. *Philosophical Chaucer: Love, Sex, and Agency in the "Canterbury Tales."* Cambridge: Cambridge UP, 2004.

Minnis, Alastair. *Fallible Authors: Chaucer's Pardoner and the Wife of Bath*. Philadelphia: U of Pennsylvania P, 2008.

Mitchell, J. Allen. "Chaucer's *Clerk's Tale* and the Question of Ethical Monstrosity." *Studies in Philology* 102 (2005): 1–26.

Morse, Charlotte. "The Exemplary Griselda." *SAC* 7 (1985): 51–86.

Murray, Jacqueline and Konrad Eisenbichler, eds. *Desire and Discipline: Sex and Sexuality in the Premodern West*. Toronto: U of Toronto P, 1996.

Muscatine, Charles. "Form, Texture, and Meaning in Chaucer's *Knight's Tale*." *PMLA* 65 (1950): 911–29.

Nolan, Barbara. "Chaucer's Tales of Transcendence: Rhyme Royal and Christian Prayer in the *Canterbury Tales*." In Benson and Robertson, 21–38.

Ogilvie, R. M. *A Commentary on Livy, Books 1–5*. Oxford: Clarendon, 1965.

O'Keefe, Timothy. "Meanings of 'Malyne' in *The Reeve's Tale*." *American Notes & Queries* 12 (1973): 5–7.

Owen, Charles. *Pilgrimage and Storytelling: The Dialectic of "Earnest" and "Game."* Norman, OK: Pilgrim, 1977.

Page, Barbara. "Concerning the Host." *Chaucer Review* 4 (1970): 1–13.

Parker, Patricia. *Inescapable Romance*. Princeton: Princeton UP, 1979.

Parkin-Gounelas, Ruth. *Literature and Psychoanalysis: Intertextual Readings*. New York: Palgrave, 2001.

Patterson, Lee. *Chaucer and the Subject of History*. Madison: U of Wisconsin P, 1991.

Payer, Pierre J. *The Bridling of Desire: Views of Sex in the Later Middle Ages*. Toronto: U of Toronto P, 1993.

Pearsall, Derek. *The Canterbury Tales*. New York: Routledge, 1985, 1993.

———. "The *Canterbury Tales* II: Comedy." In Mann and Boitani, 160–77.

———. "Chaucer's Religious Tales: A Question of Genre." In Benson and Robertson, 11–20.

———. *The Life of Geoffrey Chaucer*. Oxford: Blackwell, 1992.

Peikola, Matti. "'Whom clepist þou trewe pilgrimes?': Lollard Discourse on Pilgrimages in *The Testimony of William Thorpe*." In Gustafsson, 73–84.

Pelen, Marc. "Murder and Immortality in Fragment VI (C) of the *Canterbury Tales*: Chaucer's Transformation of Theme and Image from the *Romance de la Rose*." *Chaucer Review* 29 (1994): 1–25.

Perryman, Judith. "The 'False Arcite' of Chaucer's *Knight's Tale*." *Neophilologus* 68 (1984): 121–33.

Price, Merrall Llewelyn. "Sadism and Sentimentality: Absorbing Antisemitism in the Prioress." *Chaucer Review* 43 (2008): 197–214.

Prior, Sandra Pierson. "Parodying Typology and the Mystery Plays in the *Miller's Tale*." *Journal of Medieval and Renaissance Studies* 16 (1981): 57–73.

Raybin, David. "Chaucer's Creation and Recreation of the *Lyf of Seynt Cecile*." *Chaucer Review* 32 (1997): 196–212.

Rea, John A. "An Old French Analogue to General Prologue 1–18." *Philological Quarterly* 46 (1967): 128–30.

Reaney, P. H. *A Dictionary of British Surnames*. London: Routledge, Kegan & Paul, 1958.

Richardson, Cynthia. "The Function of the Host in *The Canterbury Tales*." *Texas Studies in Literature and Language* 12 (1970): 325–44.

Rimmon-Kenan, Shlomith. "The Paradoxical Status of Repetition." *Poetics Today* 1.4 (1980): 151–59.

Robertson, D. W. *A Preface to Chaucer: Studies in Medieval Perspectives*. Princeton: Princeton UP, 1962.

Rock, Catherine. "Forsworn and Fordone: Arcite as Oath-Breaker in the *Knight's Tale*." *Chaucer Review* 40 (2006): 416–32.

Rosenkrantz, Linda and Pamela Redmond Satran. *Beyond Jennifer and Jason: The New Enlightened Guide to Naming Your Baby*. 2nd rev. ed. New York: St. Martin's, 1994.

Rowland, Beryl. "The Play of the *Miller's Tale*: A Game Within a Game." *Chaucer Review* 5 (1970): 140–46.

Ruggiers, Paul. *Art of the "Canterbury Tales."* Madison: U of Wisconsin P, 1967.

Salter, Elizabeth. *Chaucer: The Knight's Tale and The Clerk's Tale*. London: Edward Arnold, 1962.

Scala, Elizabeth. *Absent Narratives, Manuscript Textuality, and Literary Structure in Late Medieval England*. New York: Palgrave Macmillan, 2002.

———. "The Deconstructure of the *Canterbury Tales*." *Journal x* 4 (2000): 171–90.

———. "Desire." In Turner, 49–62.

———. "Historicists and Their Discontents: Reading Psychoanalytically in Medieval Studies." *Texas Studies in Literature and Language* 44 (2002): 102–31.

———. "The Texture of *Emaré*." *Philological Quarterly* 86 (2006): 224–46.

———. "The Women in Chaucer's Marriage Group." *Medieval Feminist Forum* 45 (2009): 50–56.

———. "Yeoman Services: Chaucer's Knight, His Yeoman, and the Pleasures of Historicism." *Chaucer Review* 45 (2010): 194–221.

———. "Ysworn . . . Withoute Gilt: Lais of Illusion-Making Language in the *Canterbury Tales*." *Etudes Epistémè* 25 (2014): n.p. www.etudes-episteme.org

Scala, Elizabeth and Sylvia Federico, eds. *The Post-Historical Middle Ages*. New York: Palgrave Macmillan, 2009.

Shannon, Edgar. *Chaucer and the Roman Poets*. Cambridge: Harvard UP, 1929.

Sherman, Mark. "The Politics of Discourse in Chaucer's Knight's Tale." *Exemplaria* 6 (1994): 87–114.

Sidhu, Nicole Nolan. "'To Late for to Crie': Female Desire, Fabliau Politics, and Classical Legend in Chaucer's *Reeve's Tale*." *Exemplaria* 21 (2009): 3–23.

Skeat, W. W., ed. *Piers Plowman*. 2 vols. Oxford: Clarendon, 1886. Rpt. 1961.

———. *The Works of Geoffrey Chaucer*. 7 vols. Oxford: Clarendon, 1900.

Sledd, James. "The *Clerk's Tale*: The Monsters and Critics." *Modern Philology* 51 (1953): 73–82.

Smith, Nicole. "The Parson's Predilection for Pleasure." *SAC* 28 (2006): 117–40.

Spearing, A. C. *Medieval to Renaissance in English Poetry*. Cambridge: Cambridge UP, 1985.

Staley, Lynn. "Chaucer and the Postures of Sanctity." In Aers and Staley, 179–259.

Stillinger, Thomas, ed. *Critical Essays on Geoffrey Chaucer*. New York: Twayne, 1998.

Strohm, Paul. *Social Chaucer*. Cambridge: Harvard UP, 1989.

———. *Theory and the Premodern Text*. Minneapolis: U of Minnesota P, 2000.

Szittya, Penn R. "The Green Yeoman as Loathly Lady: The Friar's Parody of the Wife of Bath's Tale." *PMLA* 90 (1975): 386–94.

Taylor, Joseph. "Chaucer's Uncanny Regionalism: Rereading the North in The Reeve's Tale." *JEGP* 109 (2010): 468–89.

Taylor, Paul. B. "The Alchemy of Spring in Chaucer's *General Prologue*." *Chaucer Review* 17 (1982): 1–4.

Thomas, Susanne Sara. "The Problem of Defining *Sovereynetee* in the *Wife of Bath's Tale*." *Chaucer Review* 41 (2006): 87–97.

Thompson, N. S. *Chaucer, Boccaccio, and the Debate of Love*. Oxford: Clarendon, 1996.

Tkacz, Catherine Brown. "Chaucer's Beard-Making." *Chaucer Review* 18 (1983): 127–36.

Tolkien, J. R. R. "Chaucer as a Philologist: The Reeve's Tale." *Transactions of the Philological Society* 33 (1934): 1–70.

Trigg, Stephanie. *Congenial Souls: Reading Chaucer Medieval to Postmodern*. Minneapolis: U of Minnesota P, 2002.

Trigg, Stephanie and Thomas Prendergast. "The Negative Erotics of Medievalism." In Scala and Federico, 117–37.

Tupper, Frederick. "The Quarrels of the Canterbury Pilgrims." *JEGP* 14 (1915): 256–70.

Turner, Marion, ed. *A Handbook of Middle English Studies*. Malden and Oxford: Wiley-Blackwell, 2013.

Tuve, Rosemund. *Seasons and Months: Studies in a Tradition of Middle English Poetry*. Paris: Librarie Universitaire, 1933.

Vasta, Edward. "How Chaucer's Reeve Succeeds." *Criticism* 25 (1983): 1–12.

Wallace, David. *Chaucerian Polity: Absolutist Lineages and Associational Forms in England and Italy*. Stanford: Stanford UP, 1997.

Wetherbee, Winthrop. "Romance and Epic in the Knight's Tale." *Exemplaria* 2 (1990): 303–28.

Wilcockson, Colin. "The Opening of Chaucer's General Prologue to *The Canterbury Tales*: A Diptych." *Review of English Studies* 50 (1999): 345–50.

Williams, Tara. *Inventing Womanhood: Gender and Language in Later Middle English Writing*. Columbus: The Ohio State UP, 2011.

Woods, William. *Chaucerian Spaces: Spatial Poetics in Chaucer's Opening Tales*. Albany: State U of New York P, 2008.

Yager, Susan. "'A Whit Thyng In Hir Ye': Perception and Error in the *Reeve's Tale*." *Chaucer Review* 28 (1994): 393–404.

The York Plays: A Critical Edition of the York Corpus Christi Play. Ed. Richard Beadle. 2 vols. Early English Text Society, SS 23. Oxford: Oxford UP, 2009.

Žižek, Slavoj. "From Courtly Love to *The Crying Game*." *New Left Review* 202 (1993): 1–9.

———. *How to Read Lacan*. New York: Norton, 2006.

index

aggression, 25–26, 29–30, 39, 65–66, 67–72, 88, 121–22
aggressivity (aggressiveness), 24, 25, 29, 52, 65–70, 86, 92, 114, 120–21, 125–26, 128, 155, 194
Alford, John, 128n6
Allen, Elizabeth, 163, 165, 176, 183, 184, 187
Amtower, Laurel, 52n19
Augustine, 17–18, 196
Axelrod, Steven 136n17

belated(ness), 3, 12, 21, 81, 87, 93–94
Benson, C. David, 92n11, 153n1, 158n10, 162n16
Bloch, R. Howard, 85n2, 86n5, 105n33, 160n14, 167n25, 168n28, 179, 182
Boccaccio, Giovanni: *Decameron*, 33–36; *Filostrato*, 22, 54, 55n25; *Teseida*, 22, 44–47, 49, 82, 83, 84
Boitani, Piero, 47n12
Boothby, Richard, 205–7
Bowers, John, 61n36, 72, 83n63
Brinkman, Baba, 39n65

Brooks, Harold, 36n56
Brooks, Peter, 46n8
Brown, Peter 9
Brown, William, 163n17
Bruster, Madeleine, 14
Bullough, Vern, 17n27
Burlin, Robert, 154n3
Burrow, J. A., 44n4
Butler, Judith, 26n40, 49n15, 136n15

Carella, Bryan, 92n13
Carlson, David 38n64
Carruthers, Mary, 40n68
Chaucer, Geoffrey:
  Canterbury Tales: **General Prologue**, 32, 43–44, 48, 49, 56, 76, 85, 91, 93, 94–95, 101–2; competition in 2, 5–11, 34–40, 42, 158n9; pilgrim descriptions, 27 36, 87, 93, 94–95, 100, 101–2, 107, 120n49, 122, 124, 128, 155, 170n31, 173, 204; **Knight's Tale**, 3, 10–11, 39, 43–84, 85, 86, 88, 90–91, 100, 109, 114, 115, 116–19, 121, 147, 158n10, 203; conflation of

219

Palamon and Arcite in 54–55, 59–64; and courtly desire 52–55; and death 55–56; and leveling of heros 48–52; and Miller's Tale 85–86; and Reeve's Tale 90, 116–19, 122; and substitution 72–72; and *Teseida* 44–47; and *Thebiad* 82–84; Theseus as hero, 56–58, 78n53; victory in 74–79 and violence 65–71; **Miller's Tale,** 10–11, 21, 38n62, 76–77, 79, 84, 85–89, 91, 92–102, 108, 109, 112–14, 116–19, 121–24, 126, 131,191, 203; and clerks 123–24; and Noah Plays 96–100; **Reeve's Tale,** 11, 21, 42, 76, 84, 86–122, 123, 167n25, 203; aggression and violence of 119–22; and age 119–20; as attack on Miller 87–92; clerks in 123–24; and Knight's Tale 90, 116–19, 122; Malyne in, 90, 104–9; Place(ment) of 110–12; and proverbs 110–12; Prologue 87, 91–92, 107; **Cook's Tale,** 86; **Man of Law's Tale,** 3, 114n32, 154–56, 158n11, 159–62, 166n24, 167, 188, 190, 204; **Wife of Bath's Prologue and Tale,** 3, 17, 31, 22, 32–33, 40, 46, 113, 121n50, 124, 126–36, 138, 139–40, 141, 143, 147, 149–52; and defense of women 126–27; closing aggression of 130, 132–22; opposition to clerks 127–28; rhetoric of mastery 130; resolution of tale 134–36; **Friar's Tale,** 33nn48, 41, 199, 203: **Summoner's Tale,** 4, 33, 103, 124; **Clerk's Tale,** 5, 30, 33, 42, 127–52, 153, 154, 157, 162, 166n24, 188, 199, 200–1; allegorization of 148–49; Envoy of 136–39; and mastery 139–42; restoration of Griselda 131–32; **Merchant's Tale,** 74, 137, 200–201; **Franklin's Tale,** 12–13, 80n56, 130, 132, 166n24, 170–72, 194; **Physician's Tale,** 13, 41, 52, 154, 155–58, 160n14, 162–87, 191, 194n51, 199: and Franklin's Tale 170–72; and Gower 163–67, 170, 173–74 178–82; and Livy 162–67, 169–70, 172–85; **Pardoner's Tale,** 4, 194n51, 197, 199, 203; **Shipman's Tale,** 32, 103, 124–26; **Prioress's Tale,** 154, 155, 159, 160, 163, 166n24, 180, 188, 194, 198; **Tale of Sir Thopas,** 118n48; **Tale of Melibee,** 154, 188, 201;

Monk's Tale, 104, 154, 155, 157n6, 201; **Nun's Priest's Tale,** 19, 41, 103, 104n32, 199n57; **Second Nun's Tale,** 3,42, 154–55, 156, 157–59, 166n24, 180, 188–98; **Canon's Yeoman's Tale,** 154n3; **Manciple's Tale,** 41, 199n57; **Parson's Tale,** 9n14, 44, 200; **Retraction,** 154n3, 189n50, 200

Legend of Good Women, 50n16, 83, 84, 158

Troilus and Criseyde, 45

Chester Mystery Cycle, 97

Chickering, Howell, 136n18

Clerks 103, 106, 109–11, 114n44, 117, 119; and cleverness, 86–90, 97, 99; and competitiveness, 111, 114–15, 181; in fabliau, 89–90; and wives, 28, 33, 123–28

Coletti, Theresa 99n25

competition: 2–4, 31, 33–39, 53, 85–86, 87–88, 90–92, 115, 123–24, 133, 150, 173, 199; in *Decameron,* 34–35; 138; in fabliaux, 124, 126; in General Prologue, 38–39, 150; in Knight's Tale, 56, 58, 75–76, 115–16, 121–22; in psychoanalysis, 51–52; in Reeve's Tale, 56, 87–88, 90, 114–16; of social classes, 92; of wives and clerks, 123–34, 126–28. *See also* contest; rivalry

compensation, 11, 55, 73, 80–81, 113, 121

conflict: between narrators 3, 15, 22, 43–44, 85–87, 128, 138; between tales, 2, 10, 15, 39, 73, 102, 154; inner, 22, 25, 45, 66, 119, 196; legal 169, 176; marital, 71, 127; of morals, 41, 187; with others, 67, 86, 166; within plots, 53, 57–59, 66, 71, 72–73, 79, 85, 115, 121, 169, 178, 179; social, 36–37, 45, 68, 83, 85, 176. *See also* contest; rivalry

contest: as fiction, 31, 38, 39, 42, 43, 83, 198; as principle, 11, 44, 84, 85–87, 163, 185, 194, 197, 200; in romance, 53, 57–59; of stories, 2, 10, 15, 39, 73, 102, 154. *See also* conflict, competition

Cooper, Helen, 44n2, 85n2, 87n7, 94–95, 152n40

Corsa, Helen Storm, 180n42, 186n45, 186n46

Cowell, Andrew, 11n19, 33n50

Cowgill, Bruce, 86n4

Crane, Susan, 13n21, 140n26

Cunningham, J. V., 31

Dane, Joseph, 124n2

David, Alfred, 154n3

Dean, James, 9n14

death, 23, 36, 56, 60n35, 61, 69, 72, 75n50, 77, 81–82, 116, 118, 125, 133, 135, 145n33, 148, 155, 160, 163, 165, 169, 174, 175, 185, 187, 194–99

death drive, 155–58, 194–97

debate: critical, 3, 7, 13, 45n6, 131, 136, 154, 162; fictional, 33, 59, 85, 130, 138, 172; intellectual, 17, 19, 91, 127, 185; marital, 139, 154, 172; moral, 185; pilgrim, 33, 85–86, 131, 139, 172

Delany, Sheila, 165n21

Denny-Brown, Andrea, 129n7

Derrida, Jacques, 36, 40, 113

desire: and aggression, 24–26, 51–52, 65–71; and death, 56–57, 195–99; and identification, 50–52; as lack, 42, 50–53, 131; as lack of sexual relation, 53–55; in General Prologue, 5–6; in history, 16–20; in language, 11–15, 64–65; and misreading, 83–84, 91–96, 99–103, 203–5; and mobility, 27–29, 117; of the Other, 25–26, 51–53, 62–63, 150–51; in signifier, 12–14, 44, 112–13

Desmond, Marilynn, 41n70

DeWeever, Jacqueline, 104n32

Dinshaw, Carolyn, 20n32, 45n6, 127n5, 136n17, 161n15

disruption, 3, 6–7, 10, 14–15, 29, 34n53, 50, 56–57, 84, 86–87, 101, 103, 108, 109, 113–14, 130, 131, 137, 158, 199

Donaldson, E. Talbot, 6n6, 43n1, 45n6

dramatic principle, 2–3, 3n3, 32, 87–89, 92–93, 102, 126, 128, 136, 138, 156, 201

Edmondson, George, 20n32, 39n66

Edwards, Elizabeth, 48n13

Edwards, Robert, 16

enjoyment, 28, 42, 56, 68, 79–81, 141, 198

Epstein, Robert, 90n8

Evans, Dylan, 30n44, 65n37, 100, 101n27

Everest, Carol, 120n49

fabliau, 36n54, 45, 85n2, 86–87, 90–96, 101, 104–5, 114, 121–22, 124–36, 191, 201

Fairchild, Hoxie, 49n14

Farrell, Thomas, 136n18, 137n19, 137n22

Fein, Susana Greer, 120n49

Feldharr, Andrew, 183n44

Fink, Bruce, 21, 24, 26, 27n40, 65n37

Finlayson, John, 45n5, 47n11

Finnegan, Robert, 144n33

Fletcher, Alan, 114n44

Fletcher, Angus, 182n43

Fletcher, John, 54n23

Fowler, Elizabeth, 82n60

Fradenburg, L. O. Aranye, 16n25, 20n32, 41n70, 53n21, 55n26, 57, 58n32, 59n34, 68n39, 69, 78n53, 81, 135n14, 141n29

frame narrative: 1–5, 11, 31, 38–42, 83, 87, 126, 136, 139, 155–58, 184; compared with *Decameron,* 33–40; Host (Harry Bailly) in, 3, 15, 31–32, 43, 103, 155–56

Freud, Sigmund, 79–80, 194–95, 196

Ganim, John, 20n31, 22, 46n9, 137n19, 137n21, 138

Gaunt, Simon, 20n32, 86n5

Georgianna, Linda, 8n12, 145n34, 147

Ginsberg, Warren, 127n5, 135n14

Girard, René, 52n19, 130

Godefroy, Frédéric, 105

Gorton, Kristyn, 131n10

Gower, John, 37, 158n10, 163–70, 173–74, 178–84

Green, Donald, 139n25
Green, Richard Firth, 39n65
Greenblatt, Stephen, 38

Haines, R. Michael, 194n51
Hammond, Eleanor Prescott, 126n4, 144n32
Hanawalt, Barbara, 71n44
Hanning, Robert, 56, 59n34
Hansen, Elaine Tuttle, 46n9, 61n36, 69, 86n3
Harder, Kelsie, 96n20, 97
Harley, Marta Powell, 186n45
Heffernan, Carol Falvo, 140n27
Hegel Georg W. F., 26, 26n40, 49n15, 140n8
Heng, Geraldine, 98n22
Hermann, John, 125
Hinton, Norman, 105–6
Hirsch John, 157n7, 157n8
Hoffman, Arthur, 6n6
Homer, Sean, 27n40
Howard, Donald, 6–7, 9, 10n18, 38n64, 109n38
Hunter, Brooke, 83n61
Huppé, Bernard, 154n3
Huth, Jennifer, 98n22

Imaginary, the, 23–25, 30, 50–51, 53n20, 64–66, 88, 93, 100–2, 107, 127, 130, 195–96
Ingham, Patricia Clare, 20n32, 58n32, 60n35, 69, 73n48, 200n59

Johnson, Barbara, 53n20, 79n54, 113, 114n46
Johnson, Lesley, 136n16
Johnston, Andrew, 72n46
Jordan, Robert, 5n5, 38n64

jouissance, 30n44, 55, 80–82, 130, 196, 198
Justice, Steven, 19

Kaeuper, Richard, 70
Karras, Ruth Mazo, 59n33
Kaske, R. E., 99n26, 117n47
Kay, Sarah, 20n32, 112n41, 168n28, 188
Kittredge, George Lyman, 92n11, 126n4
Kline, Daniel, 182n43
Knapp, Peggy, 8n13
Koeppel, E., 186n46
Kohanski, Tamara, 106n35
Kolve, V. A., 112n40, 118n48

Lacan, Jacques, 11–14, 17–18, 20–31, 49–54, 56, 64–67, 74, 79, 88, 103n30, 107, 112n41, 113, 130n8, 131n10, 145n33, 195–98, 204
Ladd, Roger, 34n50
Langland, William, 37
Langlands, Rebecca 164n20, 165
Laplanche, Jean, 81
Lavezzo, Kathy, 157n7
Lawton, David, 6n8, 9n14
Leicester, H. Marshall, 3, 14, 20n32, 39n66, 67–69, 135n14
Livy, 162–67, 169–70, 172–85
Lochrie, Karma, 86n3
Lucretia, 163–65, 169, 175, 178, 180, 184, 185

Manly, John Matthews, 31n46, 102n28, 108, 137n19, 137n20
Mann, Jill, 10, 28, 31n46, 37, 38n60, 94–95, 144n32
Martin, Loy, 7n10
Matheson, Lister, 109n38
marriage: in Bible, 18, 133–34; and Clerk's Tale, 140–46, 148, 153, 162; language of, 68n39, 71–72, 80, 133–41, 141–43; and

Man of Law's Tale, 161–62; and Second Nun's Tale, 188–90, 192; in stories, 52, 68n39, 81, 90, 101, 105–6, 131, 134–35, 139; and Virginia, 172, 178; and Wife of Bath, 29, 139–40

Marriage Group, the, 2, 80n56, 126, 126n4, 127n5, 131, 138, 139n53, 154, 170, 172

mastery, 4–5, 24, 57n30, 68, 74, 129–30, 133–41, 146, 148, 150–51; interpretive, 4–5, 24, 129–30, 150–51

McClellan, William, 132n12, 142, 144n33

McDonie, R. Jacob, 201n61

McTaggart, Anne, 171n32

Middleton, Anne, 68n39, 165–66

Miller, Jacques-Alain, 27n40, 49n15

Miller, Mark, 20n32, 46n10, 53, 133n1, 198, 199n56

Minnis, Alastair, 40n68

Mirror Stage, the, 20–21, 24–26, 50, 53n21, 88. *See also* Other; rivalry

misreading, 4–6, 9, 11, 40–41, 64, 74–79, 83–84, 86, 88–100, 102, 150, 156, 171–73, 186n45, 194, 197, 200–2

misrecognition, 4–5, 11, 25 31, 40–41, 50–51, 65–66, 84, 88, 90–96,100–2, 108, 112, 122, 139–42, 151–52, 156, 200, 202

Mitchell, J. Allen, 144n33

Morse, Charlotte, 132n12

Muscatine, Charles, 56n27, 59n34, 60n35, 69

names, 3, 21–23, 46, 62, 102–9, 93, 111–12, 121, 128, 135–37, 155n5, 159, 164, 169–70, 173–79, 181, 203–4. *See also* signifier

Nolan, Barbara, 200

Ogilvie, R. M., 159n29, 175n38

O'Keefe, Timothy, 104n32

Order: in *Decameron,* 34–36; of General Prologue Portraits, 3, 27, 36n56; of tales, 3, 14, 32–33, 40, 170; thematic and social, 51, 56, 58, 69n42, 82,106, 119, 121, 157n7, 204

Other, the, 4, 8, 15, 20, 23–26, 28–31, 50–53, 62–63, 88, 95, 114, 116–17, 131, 151. *See also* Mirror Stage; rivalry

Owen, Charles, 9n14

Page, Barbara, 38n63

Parker, Patricia, 46

Parkin-Gounelas, Ruth, 45

Patterson, Lee, 14n24, 20n32, 33–34n50, 37n59, 57n30, 69, 87n6, 88n7, 92n14

Payer, Pierre, 17–18

Pearsall, Derek, 4n4, 9n14, 85n1, 93n15, 114n43, 122n51, 154n2

Peikola, Matti, 8n12

Pelen, Marc, 194n51

Perryman, Judith, 75n50

pilgrimage, 1–3, 7–9, 28–31, 37–38, 42, 82, 83n62, 84n64, 128, 158n9

pilgrims: Carpenter, 93–95; Clerk, 127–31; Friar, 4; Guildsmen, 93–94; Host (Harry Bailly), 3, 7, 15, 24, 31–32, 38, 43, 87, 95, 103, 117, 136, 138, 155–56, 197, 200–201; Knight, 3, 101; Manciple, 101, 199n57; Merchant, 30, 137, 201; Miller, 7, 10–11, 21, 85, 87, 101–2, 107; Monk, 15, 22, 93, 104, 154; Nun's Priest, 103–4; Pardoner, 4, 29, 50, 132, 199, 203; Parson, 9, 44, 101, 103n31; Prioress, 15, 31, 101, 103, 154n3, 155, 159, 160; Reeve, 21, 30, 85–89, 93; Squire, 101; Summoner, 4, 124, 132; Wife, 3, 27–30, 101, 127–30; Yeoman, 101

pleasure, 8, 10, 18, 34–35, 44, 79–81, 89, 115, 123, 130, 133, 141–43, 148, 160, 198

Pleasure Principle, 79–81, 192, 194–95, 198

Price, Merrall Llewelyn, 169n12

Prior, Sandra Pierson, 96

quiting, 79, 86–89, 123

Raybin, David, 158n9

Rea, John, 6n7

Real, the, 23, 30, 54n24, 55, 74, 79n55, 195–98

Reaney, P. H., 104n32

recognition, 4, 10–11, 15, 23, 25–31, 51, 62, 63, 67, 116–19, 120, 130, 149

religious tales, 3: avoidance of, 153–56; definition of, 153–60; denial of desire in, 160; death drive of, 194–99; feminine focus of, 188; transcendence in, 200; violence in, 155–56, 165, 175–76, 182, 184, 197–98

renunciation, 56, 116, 156. *See also* sacrifice

Richardson, Cynthia, 38n63

Rimmon-Kenan, Shlomith, 148n37

rivalry, 36–38, 86n4, 95–96: between professions, 14, 92, 126–29, 152; inner, 4 (*see also* Mirror Stage; Other); within fictions, 45n5, 62, 68, 86n4, 90, 114, 124, 126; in speech, 15; as structure, 4, 14, 31, 50–52, 68, 73, 87n7, 115. *See also* conflict

Roadside drama. *See* Dramatic Principle

Robertson, D. W., 19, 39n67, 40n68, 45n6

Rock, Catherine, 49n14

romance (genre), 11, 22, 29, 36n54, 44–47, 49, 52–60, 64, 67–73, 80, 83–84, 117–19, 121, 135, 139, 143, 149, 152, 154, 156, 159–62: and violence, 70–73, 198–99

Romance of the Rose (Jean de Meun), 50, 158n10, 163–66, 174–80, 183–87

Rowland, Beryl, 98n24

Ruggiers, Paul, 154n3

sacrifice, 55, 57, 69, 164, 165, 172, 173–74, 178, 180–81, 184, 194, 195. *See also* renunciation

Salter, Elizabeth, 138–39

satisfaction, 4, 34, 26, 45–46, 55, 56, 64, 68, 73, 78–82, 116, 131, 133, 144–45, 192, 205

Scala, Elizabeth, 9n14, 20n32, 41n69, 46n9, 56n9, 73n47, 75n49, 76n51, 102n29, 122n51, 126n4, 159n13, 171n35

Shakespeare, William, 54

Shannon, Edgar, 180n42

Sherman, Mark, 46n9

signifier, 12–16, 20–31, 48–51, 74–79, 111–13. *See also* names

Sidhu, Nicole Nolan, 106n35

Sledd, James, 145n33

Smith, Nicole, 44n3

sovereignty, 58, 130, 133–35, 139–41, 146, 150–52

Spearing, A. C., 59n34

Staley, Lynn, 130n9, 140n27, 145n34, 148

Statius, 82–83

Strohm, Paul, 20n32, 34, 39n66

substitution, 26, 30–33, 39–40, 55, 58, 58–59, 65, 70, 72–73, 77–78, 81, 84, 121, 124, 142, 204

Symbolic, the, 11–15, 21–23, 29–31, 52, 54n24, 61, 91–3, 95, 100–102, 107, 112, 117, 118, 119, 122, 127, 147n35, 150, 196–97

Szittya, Penn, 33n48

Taylor, Joseph, 114n44

Taylor, Paul, 7n11

Thomas, Susanne Sara, 139n25

Thompson, N. S., 34n5

Tkacz, Catherine Brown, 111n39

Tolkien, J. R. R., 90n8, 114n44

Trigg, Stephanie, 37n59, 41n71

Tupper, Frederick, 14n23, 92n12

Tuve, Rosemund, 6n7

Two Noble Kinsmen (Fletcher and Shakespeare), 54

Vasta, Edward, 86n4

violence, 22, 65–71, 100, 119–22: erotics of, 6, 70–72, 174n36, 182; in religious tales, 155–56, 198; in romance, 70–71, 198–99; in fabliaux, 90, 124–26; toward the other, 25, 51–52; toward the self,

195–97, in Clerk's Tale, 132n12, 134; in Knight's Tale, 29, 50, 52–53, 64–90; in the Virginia story, 162, 165–66, 173–76, 178, 188, 182, 183n44; in Prioress's Tale, 160, 180, 194; in Reeve's Tale, 88–89, 114–16, 119–22, 132; in Second Nun's Tale, 194, 197; in Wife of Bath's Tale, 130–31. *See also* conflict; rivalry

Wallace, David, 33, 36, 140n27
Wetherbee, Winthrop, 82n59

Wilcockson, Colin, 7n11
Williams, Tara, 188n48
Woods, William, 114n45

Yager, Susan, 91n9
York Mystery Plays, 97n21

Žižek, Slavoj, 14, 23–24, 26n39, 29, 52, 53n22, 68n40

INTERVENTIONS: NEW STUDIES IN MEDIEVAL CULTURE
Ethan Knapp, Series Editor

Interventions: New Studies in Medieval Culture publishes theoretically informed work in medieval literary and cultural studies. We are interested both in studies of medieval culture and in work on the continuing importance of medieval tropes and topics in contemporary intellectual life.

Desire in the Canterbury Tales
ELIZABETH SCALA

Imagining the Parish in Late Medieval England
ELLEN K. RENTZ

Truth and Tales: Cultural Mobility and Medieval Media
EDITED BY FIONA SOMERSET AND NICHOLAS WATSON

Eschatological Subjects: Divine and Literary Judgment in Fourteenth-Century French Poetry
J. M. MOREAU

Chaucer's (Anti-)Eroticisms and the Queer Middle Ages
TISON PUGH

Trading Tongues: Merchants, Multilingualism, and Medieval Literature
JONATHAN HSY

Translating Troy: Provincial Politics in Alliterative Romance
ALEX MUELLER

Fictions of Evidence: Witnessing, Literature, and Community in the Late Middle Ages
JAMIE K. TAYLOR

Answerable Style: The Idea of the Literary in Medieval England
EDITED BY FRANK GRADY AND ANDREW GALLOWAY

Scribal Authorship and the Writing of History in Medieval England
MATTHEW FISHER

Fashioning Change: The Trope of Clothing in High- and Late-Medieval England
ANDREA DENNY-BROWN

Form and Reform: Reading across the Fifteenth Century
EDITED BY SHANNON GAYK AND KATHLEEN TONRY

How to Make a Human: Animals and Violence in the Middle Ages
KARL STEEL

Revivalist Fantasy: Alliterative Verse and Nationalist Literary History
RANDY P. SCHIFF

Inventing Womanhood: Gender and Language in Later Middle English Writing
TARA WILLIAMS

Body Against Soul: Gender and Sowlehele *in Middle English Allegory*
MASHA RASKOLNIKOV

www.ingramcontent.com/pod-product-compliance
Lightning Source LLC
Chambersburg PA
CBHW020123240426
43673CB00038B/577